Rural Women in South Asia

Rural Women in South Asia

Edited by
Jaya Arunachalam
U. Kalpagam

RAWAT PUBLICATIONS
Jaipur • New Delhi • Bangalore • Mumbai • Hyderabad • Guwahati

ISBN 81-316-0095-5

Published by
Prem Rawat for **Rawat Publications**
Satyam Apts., Sector 3, Jawahar Nagar, Jaipur 302 004 (India)
Phone: 0141 265 1748 / 7006 Fax: 0141 265 1748
E-mail: info@rawatbooks.com
Website: www.rawatbooks.com

New Delhi Office
4858/24, Ansari Road, Daryaganj, New Delhi 110 002
Phone: 011-23263290

Also at Bangalore, Mumbai, Hyderabad and Guwahati

Typeset by Rawat Computers, Jaipur
Printed at Chaman Enterprises, New Delhi

Contents

Preface vii

1 Rural Women in South Asia 1
• U. KALPAGAM

2 Rural Women, Work and Empowerment 41
• PREET RUSTAGI

3 Gender Discrimination in South Asia 71
• SEEMA JOSHI

4 Rural Women and Empowerment: An Economic Perspective from Pakistan 93
• HINA NAZLI

5 Micro-Credit Programmes and Rural Women: A Case Study of Lalitpur District of Nepal 121
• PUSPA GHIMERE NIRAULA

6 Rural Women of Bangladesh: From Home to Market 141
• NAZNEEN AHMED

7 Poverty and Women in Rural Labour Markets of North-Eastern Bangladesh 159
• FAZILA BANU LILY

8 Women in Non-Farm Activities in Sri Lanka: Are Women Empowered or Not? 177
• RAMANIE JAYATILAKA

9 Single Women and Motherhood in Sri Lanka: The Consequences of War 203
• SELVY THIRUCHANDRAN

10 Bodies Without Rights: Violence in the Age of Globalization 231
• SUBHADRA MITRA CHANNA

11 Emerging Women Leadership in Panchayati Raj Institutions: The Punjab Experience 245
• PRABHJOT KAUR KAHLON

12 Towards an Engendered Poverty Paradigm in SAARC 265
• NANDINI AZAD

Notes on Editors and Contributors 286

Index 289

Preface

The book is the outcome of the joint silver jubilee seminar held at the G.B. Pant Social Science Institute in Allahabad in October, 2004. A happy coincidence brought both Working Women's Forum (India) and the Institute together when we realized that we were each in our silver jubilee year. Both the organizations have an enduring commitment to rural development in activism, outreach, teaching and research. While the Working Women's Forum (India) has been involved in the mobilization and empowerment of poor rural and urban women with micro-credit as a point of entry in the southern states, the G.B. Pant Social Science Institute has pioneered numerous research studies on issues of rural development in Uttar Pradesh. Therefore, we thought it befitting to focus on this important theme of "Rural Women and Empowerment in South Asia" for the seminar, which would bring together activists and scholars from all the countries of South Asia. Such a dialogue was intended to share our knowledge and experiences and clarify issues that need foregrounding at the regional level.

Rural women in South Asia have much in common even if countries and communities have their own specific problems. They in general face stark poverty and deprivation, have limited access to resources, assets and income, suffer from illiteracy, poor health and malnutrition, experience various forms of social exclusion, live and work under patriarchal structures of household and society, and cope with recurrent violence in their everyday lives.

Rural women's work in the region is marked by invisibility both on account of cognitive blinkers and enumerative deficiencies. But, they are in fact much overworked both in housework and care of children, homestead work like tending to livestock, post-harvest work like processing and storage in their homes that are in general unremunerated. Many work in the fields on family farms and wage-work on other's fields and some are engaged in non-farm activities. These women are also in general responsible for fuel, fodder and water collection and collection of forest produce, wild fruits and other edibles for household food security in times of scarcity. While they do much work, they in general do not possess entitlements to property and resources. In much of South Asia, women have no land rights and they work on land owned by male members of the family or on other's lands for wages. Initiatives for rural women's empowerment need to address issues such as entitlements to property and resources like land and water, wages and the division of labour, caste and class exclusion to resources, decision-making in households and communities, participatory development approaches that is inclusive of poor and marginalized women, promotion of non-farm activities through micro-enterprises, access to credit and micro-finance initiatives for women among others. They as well need to address issues of human development and the constraints women face in accessing better nutrition and health care in household and society. It must also recognize the link between empowerment and literacy and arrest the constraints in the form of social norms and taboos that keep rural women voiceless and powerless. Many of the problems that rural women in South Asia face are intricately interwoven with the politico-economic dimensions of rural social structure—who possesses power and how power is exercised. The state's effort to alleviate poverty and promote participatory development has not altered the rural power structures to any significant extent. At best, it has only lead to accretion of bureaucratic power making the rural poor more helpless and dependent.

Much optimism and enthusiasm has been generated in South Asia towards women's empowerment in the last two decades, largely arising out of the numerous social movements in the region and the growth of the NGO sector. Commendable initiatives with lasting effects have been undertaken by NGOs like Working Women's Forum (India) [WWF(I)] and Self Employed Women's Association (SEWA) in India, and Grameen Bank and Bangladesh Rural Advancement Committee (BRAC) in Bangladesh, towards enhancing the economic status of rural women through micro-credit and other inputs like training so as to serve as role models for other NGOs in other regions. Yet for all their grassroot efforts at capacity building of poor women and the gains achieved in policy advocacy by the NGOs, these have not brought about the economic empowerment of rural women on the scale and dimensions in which it is needed. Moreover, patriarchal and inequitable social structures have proved to be very resilient; such that the social empowerment of rural women has indeed lagged behind.

The seminar was intended to take stock of the contemporary challenges in rural women's empowerment in South Asia and work towards viable solutions through a process of networking and dialogue to evolve a coherent perspective for the region as a whole. It is towards this end that the papers collected here would serve as a launching pad for further discussions. Each of the country papers outlines different challenges that confront rural women and also provides the needed background for understanding the commonalties and differences in the region.

The editors would like to take this opportunity to thank all those who enthusiastically participated in the seminar and extended their cooperation through the process of revising their papers. We would like to thank the members of Working Women's Forum (India) who readily agreed to holding the seminar in Allahabad, who in their eagerness for bonding and sisterhood did not perceive it as an anomaly for a south-based organization to go to Northern India to hold the seminar. Paul ter-Weel, Rural Development Advisor of the Netherlands Embassy took a deep interest in this seminar and we thank him for all his cooperation. We would also like to thank the Chairman (K.C. Pant), the Director (R.C. Tripathi), the faculty, staff and students of the G.B. Pant Social Science Institute for their cooperation. This volume was put together with the editorial assistance of Stuti Saxena, which we are happy to acknowledge.

This seminar would not have been possible without the generous assistance of a seminar grant to Working Women's Forum (India) by the Netherlands Embassy. The Working Women's Forum (India) is very grateful and happy to acknowledge their support. The G.B. Pant Social Science Institute has indeed been lucky to be a beneficiary of double generosity—that of the Working Women's Forum (India) and the Netherlands Embassy.

Jaya Arunachalam
U. Kalpagam

Chapter 1

Rural Women in South Asia

U. Kalpagam

Rural women in South Asia have much in common despite variations in social stratification across countries and communities. There exists mass poverty and massive deprivation in rural South Asia. Of the world's 1,100 million people living on less than US $ 1 a day as of 2000, South Asia has 432 million or 39.2 per cent and mostly in the rural areas (UNDP, 2004). Living under poverty implies poor nutrition, high illiteracy, children not enrolled in schools, high infant and maternal mortality, inadequate health care, no access to good drinking water, poor sanitation, lack of proper shelter and extreme vulnerability to shocks associated with natural and human events resulting in debt bondage and further deprivation. Further, it is marked by a condition of both assetlessness and powerlessness. These impinge on rural women more severely given their lower social status in the patriarchal systems of rural South Asia.

But South Asian countries are making rapid progress towards the Millennium Development Goals (MDGs). Between 1990 and 2002, both Bhutan and Bangladesh have decreased child mortality by a commendable 72 and 67 points per 1,000 live births respectively. Yet, there are some countries that reveal setbacks on certain indicators of MDGs. Income poverty in Pakistan increased from 28.6 per cent (people living below the national poverty line) in 1993 to 32.6 per cent in 1998-99. Although income poverty decreased in India and Bangladesh by 7.4 percentage points between 1993-94 and 1999-2000 and 1.2 percentage points between 1995-96 and 2000 respectively, the problem of massive poverty still looms large on both. In Bangladesh nearly half the country's population is below the national poverty line and India is home to the largest absolute numbers of poor in the world. In primary education, Nepal suffered a setback as the net primary enrolment ratio decreased from 85 per cent in 1990-91 to 70 per cent in 2001-02 (UNDP, 2004).

Trends in Human Development Index (HDI) of the various South Asian countries since 1975 clearly show that without exception all the countries have recorded an increase in their HDIs indicating improvement in per capita income, life expectancy and literacy. Yet between them, there are quite significant differences. In 2002, Maldives topped with HDI value of 0.752 followed by Sri Lanka with 0.740 as its HDI value. At the bottom was Pakistan with an HDI value of 0.497. The Gender-Related Development Index (GDI) measure, which accounts for the inequalities in male and female achievements in the component indices of income, education and health, shows that in all the South Asian countries the GDI value is lower than the HDI value in 2002 (UNDP, 2004). This indicates that gender inequalities in attainments are widely prevalent in South Asia, though they may have reduced over the years.

How do these gender inequalities manifest in the rural areas of South Asia and are these inequalities reducing or exacerbating under globalization? Why are patriarchal structures so resilient in South Asia? How have state policies in these countries been reoriented to address gender inequalities in rural areas and to enhance women's capabilities and entitlements? How has the NGO sector facilitated rural women to sharpen their awareness and articulate their perspectives and problems and how successful have they been in both policy advocacy and capacity building among poor rural women? No doubt, the countries of South Asia opened up their economies at different points in time and under different compulsions. But, today, they share a common global situation of an ascendant neo-liberal ideology forcing them to discard their earlier protectionist policies and state-led development via the planning process for a liberalized regime of trade and exchange under market-led growth.

Some of these questions are addressed in this introductory chapter with a view to provide a background to the issues raised in the various chapters that follow. But it is necessary to first understand the dynamics of rural change in these countries. Descriptive accounts of the noteworthy changes in the rural life of the six South Asian countries of Bangladesh, Bhutan, India, Nepal, Pakistan and Sri Lanka and the ways in which they have impacted on women's lives provide an overall view to understand some of the contemporary challenges.

Thus, what follows is an account of women's role in the rural economic sectors of each of the South Asian countries excepting Maldives followed by some of the efforts at rural development. It also examines the challenges of human development and efforts at women's empowerment. The chapter concludes by introducing the various issues covered in the rest of the book.

Bangladesh

Around 76.1 per cent of the estimated population of 143.8 million persons in 2002 in the country lived in rural areas (UNDP, 2004). Women constituted 48.6 per cent of the total population. The adult literacy rate is far lower for women (31.4%) than for men (50.3%) (UNDP, 2004) and female illiteracy is higher in rural than in urban areas where only 20.2 per cent of women are literate (ESCAP, 1995).

Female Workforce Participation Rate (FWPR) of those 15 years and above was 66.4 per cent and FWPR as percentage of male WPR was 76 per cent in 2002. A total of 77 per cent of all female workers were employed in agriculture in 2002 and female workers in agriculture as a proportion of male workers was 144 per cent indicating predominance of women in agriculture. Of all family workers, women accounted for 81 per cent and of whom the majority was in agriculture.

Women in rural Bangladesh are in general responsible for most of the agricultural work in the homestead. A study on women's role in homestead activities among hundred small farmer households in Abhoynagar *upazila* of Jessore district found women to be responsible for washing utensils and cleaning house compound in 75 per cent of the households, releasing poultry and feeding in 69 per cent of the households, post-harvest activities in 50 per cent of the households, crops preservation in 90 per cent of the households, cooking in 97 per cent of the households and fuel collection within house in 91 per cent of the households (Paul and Saadullah, 1991). Owing to their crucial role in livestock care, women are generally consulted while buying and selling the livestock (Abdullah and Zeidenstein, 1982).

Despite women's important role in agriculture, the traditional social norms and customary laws combined with the *purdah* system deprive rural women of equitable economic opportunities and access to resources. Many rural women observe *purdah* as it seems to confer status on the family but economic necessity is also forcing many to abandon it as they become agricultural wage labourers. Thus, the traditional social division of labour that restricted women from working in the fields or in the market is giving way under economic pressures. About 60-70 per cent of women from landless and near-landless households work as agricultural wage labourers, whereas women from larger farms do not participate in field activities. Paddy is the major crop in Bangladesh and is grown in nearly 80 per cent of the cultivated land. In some areas in North-West Bangladesh, women equally share all tasks in rice production, even the presumably male task of irrigation (Jordans and Zwatreveen, 1997).

But occupational *purdah* in terms of work considered 'appropriate' and respectable for women does exist which severely restricts women who seek wage labour. Often home-based production in some kind of micro-enterprise activity is the only available option for rural women and here too they are unable to transact in the market because of social norms and restrictions. They are often dependent on male family members and male middlemen and male wholesalers for procurement and marketing.

In rural non-agricultural production like weaving, pottery, jute processing, sericulture, production of oil and syrup, etc., women have certain fixed responsibilities based on traditional division of labour.

While crop production is the major agricultural activity, other activities like forestry, livestock and fisheries also engage women. Forest cover in Bangladesh was only 1.89 million hectares or 14 per cent of the total land area in 1992-93. Forest cover has been rapidly dwindling in Bangladesh much like the other South Asian countries both on account of conversion to agricultural land and due to rapid urbanization. Timber, firewood, golpata, bamboo, sungrass, honey, wax and cane are some of the forest products that women use for food, fuel as well as for making handicrafts.

Much like in India and Nepal, women in rural Bangladesh are responsible for obtaining the household fuel supply. A traditional role of rural women is collecting dung for fuel from the forests where cattle grazes as cow dung is the largest source (26% in 1992-93) of traditional fuels in the unorganized sector. But collecting dung has become increasingly impossible as the number of cattle decreased due to the decline in fodder availability. Women also have a major role in homestead forestry. However, rapid forest degradation has forced women and girls to go further afield to collect fuelwood, which along with the other tasks has adverse impact on girls' opportunities to attend school. Women and girls spend on an average three hours everyday to collect water and fuel in many parts of rural Bangladesh. Moreover, mangrove destruction for shrimp cultivation has resulted in the saline inundation of the fields surrounding the homesteads along the coastline, impeding women's contribution through kitchen gardening, livestock and poultry rearing.

The innumerable rivers, canals, tanks and paddy fields and other low-lying areas provide varieties of fish. Although fishing is predominantly artisanal, there is an industrialized processing sector geared to export. Women's participation in small-scale fisheries is substantial. They are predominantly involved in net-making as family labour, the main income generating occupation in many families, freshwater fish farming and in fish processing (FAO, 1980). In some NGO and government programmes, women from landless households cultivate fish individually or jointly in leased ponds, either within or near the homestead (Jahan, 1990).

Shrimp culture that had occupied 20,000 hectares of land in 1979-80 expanded to 410,000 hectares in 1996-97. It has deprived the marginal people of their livelihood by displacing them from their ancestral homesteads, especially in the southwest region where the *gher* owners have been influential. Landless people have also lost their right to *khas* land (Halim, 2001). Women are involved in various processes of shrimp cultivation such as building the embankments around prawn ponds, maintaining service roads, weeding in the shrimp fields, collecting shrimp fry which at certain times includes even night time work, preparing *gher* as day labourers, clearing the *shaowla* and working in processing plants. But they in general work for low and discriminating wages, often under exploitative conditions of work (Halim, 2001).

Food insecurity is a critical concern with widespread child and maternal malnutrition. According to the Working Group on Targeted Food Intervention (1993), half the country's population cannot afford an adequate diet. Over 95 per cent of women-headed households, which account for about 8 per cent of rural households, fall below the poverty line (UNDP, 1997). The seasonal variations in food availability and uneven access also create household food insecurity.

Life in rural Bangladesh as in much of South Asia is one of drudgery with poor housing, lack of sanitation and electricity. The rural majority use traditional bio-mass energy predominantly. Although grid-based electrification is reaching rural areas, only 15 per cent of rural households are able to receive it. Electrification does not reach riverines, hilly areas and coastal islands called *chars*. For lighting, people in rural areas use kerosene lamps with open flame that often cause accidents as only slightly better-off households are able to afford hurricane lamps that enclose the flame in a glass case. Rural businesses operate diesel generators for evening lighting in market places. As rural women are culturally barred from the public markets, they are often left to spend the evening hours around kerosene lamps or in partial darkness. Community participation in off-grid electrification projects using renewable energy sources is becoming popular.

Char Montaz—a joint project of the World Bank and the UNDP—has trained rural women to produce and market DC lamps in a micro-enterprise manufacturing unit. For recharging the battery the project set up a women's cooperative to assemble home solar kits. Women's involvement in lamp production and solar panel construction not only provided a new opportunity for women to earn a living in which their labour is highly valued, it also changed community's perceptions of women's capabilities, breaking down the rigidly defined gender division of labour. With such lighting, women could work longer hours at home on income earning activities and their children could also study at home (www.UNDP.ESMAP).

Yusuf and Kumar (1996) note that as the sectoral sources of growth are limited, an improvement in Bangladesh's economic performance must come from an increase in agricultural productivity and the spread of rural industry. But not only are employment opportunities for rural women scarce, they are also bound by cultural restrictions to stay in their homes. Rural women have only limited access to development personnel, as they are usually not permitted to interact with men other than their direct close family members. Paul and Saadullah (1991) found that only 38 per cent of rural women were familiar with crops extension personnel, 19 per cent with livestock extension personnel and 6 per cent with fisheries extension personnel but 87 per cent of adult women were familiar with the family planning personnel.

In this context, micro-credit for income-generating activities has proved to be remarkably successful, as is well known from the success stories of Grameen Bank (Jain, 1996; Hashemi, Schuler and Riley, 1996). Apart from the Grameen Bank, BRAC (Bangladesh Rural Advancement Committee) and ASA are well known NGOs involved in providing micro-credit to women (Khandker and Khalily, 1996). More than a 1,000 other NGOs and the government departments also extend micro-credit to more than 7 million persons. Numerous studies on the empowerment and other effects of micro-credit for rural women in Bangladesh have been conducted so far. For example, Banu et al. (1998) found positive effects on women in their assessment of BRAC's programme, such effects being positively correlated with the individual's period of association with BRAC. Yet, by their own admission they did not find the women fully empowered in terms of their definition of empowerment even after 48 months of association which includes women's independent control over their income and assets on which they seemed to fall short of. They felt that BRAC needed to address the problem of changing the mindset of society as well. Goetz and Sengupta (1996) also observe that women do not always develop meaningful control over their investment activities. Some observe that micro-credit while it may produce some additional income does not change significantly a family's environment and that importantly it needs to be complemented by providing poor women access to land, water and day care for children (Crossette, 2003).

But credit from these organizations has been found to have a positive impact on women's demand for formal health care. Pitt and Khandker (1996) provide separate estimates of the influence of borrowing by both men and women for each of three credit programme: the Grameen Bank, the Bangladesh Rural Advancement Committee (BRAC), and the Bangladesh Rural Development Board's RD-12 programme (BRDB) on a variety of household and individual outcomes such as school enrolment of boys and girls, the labour supply of women and men, the asset holdings of women, fertility and contraceptive use, consumption, and the anthropometric status of children. It is found that credit is a significant determinant of many of these outcomes, especially when provided to women. Micro-credit thus has a significant effect on the well-being of poor households in Bangladesh. In order to overcome the doubts of micro-credit schemes not reaching the poorest of the poor, BRAC has launched a programme of identifying the ultra-poor for a special grant since 2001. As the targeted ultra-poor women start earning from the enterprises provided as grants, they are gradually included within BRAC's mainstream development programmes, such as micro-finance

Poverty is associated with the relatively poor treatment of women and girls in Bangladesh, and this is exacerbated by high population growth. First, levels of maternal mortality are high, so the risk of death during childbirth is high. On an average, between two and three women out of every 100 die in the process of childbirth. Second, son preference in fertility patterns is pronounced.

Third, rates of excess female mortality are high (as many as 8% of women are 'missing'), and the rates appear to be positively associated with high overall fertility rates. Thus, Anand and Morduch (1996) conclude that high fertility is both a product and a source of gender inequality.

Household survey data from 87 rural villages in Bangladesh suggests that government family planning programmes as well as other health care interventions have contributed towards the recent reduction in fertility by increasing contraceptive use and reducing infant mortality. Khandker and Latif (1996) note that increasing employment and income-earning opportunities, especially for women, and supplying family planning and health services are only short-run measures for curtailing both infant mortality and fertility. The long-run policy option should be to promote the education levels of both men and women to raise productivity, which, in turn, will increase contraceptive use and reduce infant mortality.

Public expenditure on education was only 2.3 per cent of its GDP in 1999-2001 (an increase from 1.5% in 1990), compared to 3.2 per cent in an average low-income country and 6 per cent in an average high-income country (UNDP, 2004). In recent years it has invested substantially in the education sector, with the help of World Bank and other donor agencies. These efforts have been able to promote literacy and improve school participation and school attainment rates. The effects of these interventions are more pronounced for girls than for boys, which suggest that girls would benefit more than boys from such education projects (Khandker, 1996)

Gender violence is present in all societies; it is a structural phenomenon embedded in the context of cultural, socio-economic and political power relations. The battering of women within the household appears to be widespread throughout Bangladesh. A study carried out by the Bangladesh Rural Advancement Committee (BRAC) in Jamalpur observed that most women who are beaten, suffer from beatings every week which are severe enough to leave marks on the body and cause pain for several days. Numerous commentators have remarked on beating as a punishment for failing to do the husband's bidding. Kabeer (1991) citing from other studies suggests that many men vent their own frustration at their poverty and inability to fulfil their role as the male provider, according to gender based norms, by battering their wives. Kabeer notes the seasonality of such beatings—they increased during *kartik*, the hungry season in August-October, and before the main harvest in November-December.

White (1992) notes from a study of a village in Faridpur district that the escalation of dowry demands over the last 40 years has contributed to violence against women. Dowry demands in Bangladesh is a relatively new phenomenon and the scale of demands may not have reached that of India. Parveen and Leonhauser (2004) found in their study that 92 per cent of the women in their sample of 156 women from three villages of Mymensingh district had paid dowry during their marriage or have continuous dowry pressure after marriage—either for themselves or in the case of older women for their daughters— and 69 per cent are victims of domestic violence.

The murder of women by their husbands and in-laws is associated with both the escalation of dowry demands, and with the more general harassment and severe beating of women. Many women are in fact driven to suicide by constant beating, harassment and the feeling that there is no escape (Hartmann and Boyce, 1983).

Bhutan

Bhutan had a population of approximately 2.2 million inhabitants in 2002, of whom 91.8 per cent live in rural areas (UNDP, 2004). Only 8 per cent of the land is cultivated, the rest being of rugged terrain. About 41.8 per cent of the population is under 15 years of age. With this age structure and given the high growth rate of 2.5 per cent in 2002, the population is expected to double in about two decades, resulting in a tremendous pressure on the scarce arable land.

Rural women's literacy rate is reported to be as low as around 10 per cent (Rosenegger, 1998). The government is addressing the problem through non-formal education schemes, where 70 per cent of participants are reported to be women. Enrolment rate in primary schools is 72 per cent (1995) with a boy/girl ratio of 57 to 43. The difference between enrolment by gender is decreasing rapidly. Bhutan's public expenditure on education was 5.2 per cent of its GDP in 1999-2001 (UNDP, 2004).

There are three main ethnic groups: Ngalops in the west comprise 35 per cent of the population; Sharchopas in the east comprise 50 per cent of the population; and Lotshampas (of Nepali origin) in the south account for 15 per cent of the population. The Ngalops and most of the Sharchopas follow matrilineal inheritance lines, while the Lotshampas observe patrilineal inheritance.

FWPR is 57.1 per cent and it is 65 per cent of the male rate in 2002. About 85 per cent of the population derive a living from agriculture and other traditional activities in the rural sector. Employment in the modern sectors of the economy is limited as there is little industrial development. Subsistence agriculture is still the predominant mode. In the Bhutanese farming community the system of exchange labour is widely practised. Both men and women work on another's farm as part of the labour-for-labour exchange. In this system men's and women's work are accounted as equal. Crop production, livestock and forestry activities are closely interrelated and interdependent.

Bhutanese women are usually engaged in firewood collection, crop cultivation, vegetable gardening, yak herding, traditional weaving, using vegetable dyes and other handicraft making. Men, by tradition, are engaged in ploughing, construction, trading and other business or manual activity (Gurung, 1997). Men and women can to a large extent take over tasks from each other. The division of labour by gender differs between ethnic groups, so that it is most pronounced among Lotshampas, and least among Sharchopas. But in all ethnic groups it is men's task to plough the fields with oxen. There is a traditional belief that if men carry manure to fertilize their fields, it will bring them great misfortune. Consequently, women are required to carry all the manure. Some women are questioning these kinds of beliefs and changes are being effected slowly.

Bhutan may be part of South Asia, but attitudes towards women are completely different from other countries in the region as its traditional values support equality between men and women. Unlike other countries, Bhutanese society is mainly matriarchal and women have equal status to men not only in the eyes of the law but also in the home. Historically, men moved into their wife's house when they got married and became part of the wife's family. Property is very often registered in the name of the woman, because women are the ones who look after the parents in their old age. Women own 70 per cent of the land. This pattern holds true in the ownership of the livestock as well.

Around 70 per cent of the country is covered by forests. Although state owned, rural people have traditional user rights for grazing, collection of fuelwood and non-wood forest products, and thus the forest is an important resource base for the rural communities. Forests provide over 90 per cent of the domestic fuel in the rural areas as well as timber for rural housing (Rosenegger, 1998). It also plays an important role in food security in Bhutan. Food from the forests becomes critical to the rural areas when transporting food to these areas is difficult, when people do not have money to buy food and when there is crop failure.

Fuelwood and water collection is often undertaken by women. The emerging environmental problems like degradation of forests close to settlements cause longer working hours for the rural people, as elsewhere in the region. Mushroom collection provides a sizeable income to many women and their families. About 45 per cent of the medicinal plants collectors are women. Some have even traditionally been involved in cultivating and harvesting medicinal plants (Gurung, 1997). For the various ethnic groups livelihood strategies in the mountains depend largely on their knowledge and management of its diverse genetic resources.

Livestock is an integral part of farming systems in Bhutan. Almost every household maintains at least a few cattle for draft power, animal products and for manure. Though men contribute their labour in caring for the livestock like grazing the cattle, it is women who share more responsibility by collecting fodder and water, cleaning stalls, feeding and milking (Gurung, 1997).

Off-farm activities are undertaken by both men and women. Women are traditionally engaged in weaving and petty trade. Cloth weaving is an important economic activity in the central and eastern regions. Women weave clothes for the whole family and they often do not like it as it is a painful job. In particular, they do not like the job of refining the wool before making it into thread. The weavers work at traditional looms which require them to sit with their legs straight out for hours on end. This type of loom is blamed for increasing the risks of childbirth. Women weavers lack market access and information regarding design and colour combinations in demand, and find it difficult to acquire quality raw materials, such as naturally-dyed yarn. The National Women's Association of Bhutan (NWAB) is organizing training in product development, design and quality control, and business planning through e-business which can help to reduce exploitation of rural women artisans by bringing them in touch with agents and customers.

NWAB was established in 1981 with the objective of "encouraging women to take an active part in the implementation of socio-economic development programmes and in all other nation-building activities" and "improving the socio-economic status of women, especially rural women". It carries out social work in a number of areas and provides handicraft training for women and credit to assist women in setting up their own businesses.

In much of the country subsistence agriculture is still sufficient to provide for household food security, although nine Dzongkhags (districts) are identified as food-insecure. The traditional extended family system provides security for the most vulnerable groups, and a system of lending/borrowing food among rural households during the lean season helps the poorer families. The forest also provides a buffer for food security during the lean season. For the past six years Bhutan has been losing about 1,000 acres of paddy growing land annually to development activities, natural disasters and regeneration of forests. Environmental hazards are also posed by the emerging industrial sector.

One of the biggest economic challenges facing the country is finding employment for 40 per cent of the population aged under 20 years. In the past, when people left school, they went to work on the land, but today they are eager to go to Thimpu and other towns to find more lucrative employment. Many young Bhutanese consider themselves too well-educated to do menial work, and the country has employed thousands of Indian expatriates to do blue-collar, building and road construction work.

For the rural people, life is a constant struggle for survival and it is even harder for the women. Being hundreds of miles from a doctor and with poor transportation, many women die in childbirth. As for the working lives of Bhutan's rural poor, the daily physical grind takes a heavy toll on health and happiness.

With four out of every ten children malnourished or stunted, Bhutan is trying to counter malnutrition. Six out of ten children in rural areas suffer from diarrhoea, worms, and skin and eye infections largely due to a lack of safe drinking water and poor environmental sanitation.

Three out of every 10 children of school-going age do not have the opportunity to go to school, especially in the remote areas. The majority of children in rural primary schools are the first generation in their families to have access to education and there is a general shortage of trained teachers.

About half the adults in rural areas—most of them women—do not know how to read and write. Programmes have been introduced to increase adult literacy, especially among rural women, through non-formal learning.

Bhutan is wary of indiscriminate modernization and its development policy is cautious. But it has followed planned economic development. Its current Ninth Five-Year Plan, although cash strapped, is different from earlier plans laying stress on decentralization and participatory development. In 1998, the King relinquished his role as Head of Government and granted the National Assembly the authority to elect the council of ministers, which now has full executive powers to elect the Chairman who acts as Head of Government. The people have begun electing women representatives to the National Assembly.

Nepal

Nepal has a population of about 24.6 million in which the rural population accounts for 85.4 per cent (UNDP, 2004). A total of 40.2 per cent of the population is under 15 years of age. There are 60 different ethnic/caste groups in the country. About 13.2 per cent of the households are female-headed.

The literacy rate for the population of 15 years and above is 44 per cent. However, the adult literacy rate for women is only 26.4 per cent, which is less than half the literacy rate for men (61.6%). Nepal has increased its public expenditure proportion on education from 2 per cent of its GDP in 1990 to 3.4 per cent in 1999-2001 (UNDP, 2004).

A little less than 60 per cent of women over the age of 15 are considered economically active and it is 67 per cent of the male rate in 2002. This indicates a lower economic participation by women as compared to men. This is due to the fact that many activities, which are almost exclusively performed by women, are not considered economic activities.

The vast majority of the economically active population (81.2%) in rural Nepal is engaged in agriculture and allied industries, the proportion being higher among women (90.5%) than among men (74.9%). Research has shown that women do more work in agriculture than men in the high mountain areas, equal to or more than men in the middle hills and slightly less than men in the terai (Sontheimer, Basnyat and Maharjan, 1997).

Farming systems and crops vary widely depending upon altitude and climatic conditions. Only 21 per cent of the total land under cultivation is irrigated and agriculture is still largely determined by weather conditions. Rice-based cropping systems, with wheat or maize as a secondary crop, are predominant in the terai and middle hills, whereas in the high mountains maize, millet, barley and buckwheat are cultivated. Tea, cardamom, ginger and coffee are the important cash crops of the middle hills. Vegetable growing in kitchen gardens is practised at all elevations.

Women share the responsibility of planting, transplanting, weeding, harvesting, carrying grains to the mill for grinding, including collecting wood, water and fodder. Ploughing is considered a man's job, whereas all other work, though shared by men, is mostly undertaken by women. Collecting and carrying compost to the field is normally performed by women. Women's involvement is more in producing major crops such as rice, maize, wheat, etc. In both rainfed and irrigated agriculture, time spent by women is higher relative to that of men. However, women's participation differs in the hills and the terai region. It further varies tremendously across the social groups. Despite women's important role in agriculture, traditional social norms and customary laws, which generally are biased in favour of men, are a barrier to women's equitable access to productive resources (Kumar and Hotchkiss, 1988).

Women are also involved in the care and management of livestock and poultry, and kitchen gardening. Dairy production is a major source of income for women. Trading in livestock, especially sheep and goats, and wool and woollen products, is the major livelihood strategy of hill and mountain people in Nepal as food grain production in these regions is inadequate. Women do have the right to own livestock.

The forests supply about 90 per cent of the total fuel and more than 50 per cent of the fodder. Timber and herbs are other important forest products. Women use forest products for creating saleable commodities. Collecting fodder and other forest products is most tedious and tiring, which has traditionally and primarily been performed by women. More than three-fourths of household time spent on collecting forest products is done by women (Kumar and Hotchkiss, 1988). Continuing deforestation and degrading land fertility further jeopardize the livelihood of households in the community as it increases the daily tasks of women (Bhatt et al., 1994). Where deforestation is high, time needed to collect one load of fuelwood increases by 75 per cent (Kumar and Hotchkiss, 1988).

Weaving is a part of daily life in the hills and mountains. People in these regions still produce their own version of rugs known as *radi*, *pakhi*, and clothing material known as *lukuni*. Women have a central role in such production. Women are also extensively involved in informal trade like selling food, vegetables and snacks in roadside stalls and local market. Production credit for rural women has supported women's handicrafts such as rice straw paper making and agro-products. Food security is increasingly associated with off-farm employment rather than with ownership of land as such activities like shop-keeping and retailing yield relatively stable streams of income.

Semi-feudal relations of production are still prevalent in the agrarian economy that in part explains the growth of the Maoist movement. Since 1992, Nepal has been implementing the Kamaiya (agricultural labourers bonded by an annual fixed wage) abolition programme The programme includes skills development and training for Kamaiya women. But it has not been fully successful in the abolition of the system (Regmi, 2002). Many women enter into sharecropping arrangements that sees 50 per cent of their output paid to landowners, or lead a life of constant struggle to repay money-lenders or lose what little they own. In the poorest villages seasonal migration is the main livelihood source for the poor households. Daily wage rates are very variable, but are generally in the US$ 1.50–3 range. Wage rates in India are significantly higher than in Nepal and non-agricultural wages are higher than those in agriculture.

Although there has been much discussion about the empowerment of women, in practice, it is not really visible among the vast majority. Poor rural women are inadequately served by financial, technical and social services. As elsewhere in South Asia, there are both government and non-governmental agencies delivering micro-credit to rural women, many funded by international donors and banks such as the Asian Development Bank. As the cost of administering the loans is high, the interest rate is also high but certainly less than the money-lenders or landlords extortionate rate.

The National Planning Commission estimates that 49 per cent of the population is living in absolute poverty (EIU, 1997). Income poverty in Nepal has increased since the late 1970s, mostly in rural areas. Nutritional deficiency affects 40 per cent or more of the population and women are more vulnerable than men.

Nepal's health conditions and health services remain poor. Total per capita health expenditure is about US$ 7. Many rural areas are served only by traditional healers. Maternal mortality and fertility rates are high, and the fertility rate in rural areas is almost double that in urban areas. Life expectancy across Nepal is only 55.9 years. Infectious diseases, maternal, peri-natal, and nutritional problems cause almost half of all deaths. Health facilities in rural Nepal have been contracting due to the Maoists struggles. Most government-employed health workers and an estimated 48,000 female health care volunteers (FHCVs), who play a key role in reaching out to people in the rural areas, are afraid to make field visits to regions controlled by the rebels. The health sector has been affected along with education, road building and other development activities.

In Nepal, the process of planned economic development began in 1956. Poverty has been an underlying theme of all the development plans since the 1950s. The Eighth Five-Year Plan (1992-1997) envisaged a new dimension in development approach as it was directed towards the alleviation of massive poverty at the rural level. The Ninth Plan, for 1997-2002, singled out poverty as the sole development objective. Nepal's anti-poverty effort is linked with a programme of decentralization and local empowerment.

Pakistan

Pakistan's population was officially estimated at 149.9 million in 2002, comprising 47.5 per cent women and 52.5 per cent men. A total of 41.5 per cent of the population is under 15 years of age and 3.7 per cent over 65. Likewise, 66.3 per cent of the population live in rural areas (UNDP, 2004).

The educational status of Pakistani women is quite low. Women had a literacy rate of 28.5 per cent, as against 53.4 per cent for men in 2002 but the rate for rural women is reported to be only 7.3 per cent (ESCAP, 1997). Pakistan has reduced its public expenditure proportion on education from 2.6 per cent of GDP in 1990 to 1.8 in 1999-2001 (UNDP, 2004).

Although women play an active role in the economy, their contribution has been grossly under-reported in various censuses and surveys. For example, the 1991-92 Labour Force Survey revealed that only about 16 per cent of women aged 10 years and over were in the labour force and in comparison, the men's participation rate was 84 per cent. But, the 1990-91 Pakistan Integrated Household Survey indicated that the female labour force participation rate was 45 per cent in rural areas and 17 per cent in urban areas. If women's contribution is assessed accurately, a conservative estimate of women's labour force participation would be between 30 per cent and 40 per cent (ESCAP, 1997). Overall, 36.3 per cent of women were reported to be economically active in 2002 and the female rate as proportion of male rate was 44 per cent (UNDP, 2004).

According to the 1991-92 Labour Force Survey, agricultural and allied industries absorb the largest proportion of employed persons, both women and men, particularly in the rural areas. However, the proportion of the women engaged in the agricultural sector is higher in rural areas (73%), and female rate as percentage of male rate in agriculture was 164 per cent in 2002.

Pakistan is faced with a difficult task in human resource development. The Human Development Index (HDI) rank of Pakistan was 142 of 177 countries in 2002, indicating low life expectancy at birth, low educational attainment and low income (UNDP, 2004).

The human development gap is further aggravated by substantial gender disparities.

Agriculture supports three-quarters of the population, employs half the labour force and accounts for one-quarter of Gross Domestic Product (EIU, 1997). The Punjab Province accounts for the bulk of agricultural output in the country. Baluchistan and North-West Frontier Province are poor and backward. Endowed with fertile lands, Sindh Province produces 30 per cent of the rice, 25 per cent of the cotton, 23 per cent of the sugar cane and 18 per cent of the wheat in the country.

Women play a major role in agricultural production, livestock raising and cottage industries. They participate in all operations related to crop production as well as in post-harvest operations. A woman works 12 to 15 hours a day on various economic activities and household chores (ESCAP, 1997). In some ethnic groups, especially in the southern regions, a husband may marry more than one woman to supply additional farm labour (PARC, 1988). In regions of rainfed agriculture, where crop production is not sufficient to meet subsistence needs of the households, men have traditionally sought employment in the non-farm sector. As a result, women have to take over a substantial burden of the work in agricultural production.

Moreover, increased growth rates in cotton production have generated demand for female labour. Such production-labour interactions have led to the increasing feminization of agriculture (GoP, 1995). Though to a lesser extent, rural women also work on others' holdings outside their homes. They account for 16.1 per cent of the total agricultural labour and 10.2 per cent of non-agricultural labour. Nonetheless, there is significant variation by agro-ecological zones in opportunities for wage employment. The demand for female labour, which is seasonal and limited to specific tasks, is mainly concentrated in the southern cotton belt and irrigated regions (GoP, 1995). Picking cotton is exclusively women's task.

Women's participation in agriculture labour is particularly high in cotton, rice, pulses and vegetables. Hand-threshing is a women's task. Invisible activities like carrying meals, drinks, etc. from the house to men working in the field, kitchen gardening (in cotton areas), cleaning and drying farm produce for storage, and making clay storage bins take up considerable time of women.

Women work on land which they do not own. The harvest is sold by and through men, and men control the income. Due to various social beliefs and cultural bias, women's access to property, education, employment, etc., remain considerably lower compared to men's. *Purdah* norms are followed in most communities (ESCAP, 1997).

Livestock is an important component of farming systems. Women make a considerable contribution to livestock production and this contribution is more visible than their work in crop production. Grazing animals is an important component of the daily life of rural women (PARC, 1988). Dairy production is important for women in most provinces except Baluchistan where the climate is unfavourable to dairy cattle raising. Women also generate cash income through the sale of livestock products. They also play a crucial role in poultry farming. Over 90 per cent of the rural families keep an average of 12 adult birds per family. Poor households receive almost 25 per cent of their total per capita income from livestock.

Land, forests and pastures have been degraded by prolonged misuse. The Indus basin is experiencing waterlogging and salinity, wind and water erosion and rapidly spreading desertification. Such ecological resource depletion has profound impact on women's basic roles of obtaining fuel, fodder and water. Growing desertification has made women walk for miles in search of water. Women in Sindh walk up to 10 miles to fetch water. With land degradation, food and income decline and women are further marginalized.

Women generate income through various non-farm activities. Cottage industry is one of the major areas of involvement of rural Pakistani women. Weaving clothes and rugs, and sewing constitute important components of rural women's non-routine tasks. Women's participation in the fish, spices, sweets and confectionery, fruit and vegetable industries is 10-30 per cent. The market share of the traditional foods produced by the rural-based industries is however shrinking.

In rural Pakistan, the lack of land forces the poor to earn the bulk of their livelihood from those sources of income that are not connected with land, such as non-farm employment and livestock. Depending on the year, non-farm income accounts for between 30 and 34 per cent of total per capita household income. Agricultural income is the second most important source, accounting between 23 and 27 per cent of total per capita household income. Moreover, non-farm income is the leading source of income for poor households. When the households are ranked by income, poor households receive almost 50 per cent of their total per capita income from non-farm sources—more than twice that received by poor households from any other income source, and more than seven times that received from agriculture. The incomes of poor households also fluctuate considerably. For a variety of reasons, poor households tend to move in and out of poverty (Adams, Jr. and He, 1995).

To promote agriculture and hence economic growth, Pakistan must make more credit available to agricultural small holders, the rural non-farm sector, and women. Less than a third of rural households get loans, only 10 per cent of which are from institutional sources (Qureshi, Nabi and Faruqee, 1996). The micro-finance sector is not as yet well developed as in Bangladesh or India and is currently being restructured. Non-governmental organizations (NGOs) should be encouraged to participate in micro-finance delivery for poor women, which is as yet very limited.

Nearly 34 per cent of the population lives below the poverty line in Pakistan (UNDP, 1997). The incidence of food poverty (less than 2,550 calories per adult equivalent per day in rural areas and less than 2,295 in urban areas) increased from 17.8 per cent in 1987-88 to 22.4 per cent in 1992-93 and to 32.6 per cent in the current survey. The incidence of food poverty was higher in rural areas (35%) than in urban areas (26%); the incidence of rural poverty was higher among non-farm than among farm households (MIMAP - Pakistan, Phase I). Women disproportionately share the burden of poverty, which has a two-fold impact. On one hand, the women's workload for family survival increases and on the other, their share in food and nutrition intake decreases further. About 70 per cent of rural women do not have adequate calorie intake in their diet, and 90 per cent of pregnant women suffer from anaemia.

In addition to being poor and malnourished, rural women in Pakistan suffer from too many pregnancies. The severe challenges the country faces are high birth and illiteracy rates (only 40% of girls go to school) combined with low access rates to clean drinking water and sanitation.

Historically, Pakistan has under-invested in public secular schooling, even at the primary level, particularly for girls. Girls' enrolment in the rural communities in Pakistan depends on whether or not there is a public primary school in the village and whether or not the teacher resides in the village. The schooling environment is no doubt changing in rural Pakistan. While the number of schools has increased in rural areas, many are however private schools, indicating that the government is not keeping up with the demand for schooling (Population Council, 2004).

Pakistan is a country with persistently high population growth rates and serious reproductive health concerns. Although fertility is declining, there is a huge unmet need for family planning (in the range of 37%), and maternal mortality is more than 300 per 100,000 live births. Less than 30 per cent of births in rural areas are attended by trained health care providers, which is lower even than Sub-Saharan Africa where the percentage is 42 (Terzieff, 2004). Traditional belief holds that birthing is best done at home. The belief, which is particularly strong in rural areas, contributes to the country's high rate of maternal mortality and is a reflection both of the lack of hospitals throughout the country and the low status of women.

Women in rural areas are often either housebound by the dictates of their families or reluctant to buy contraceptives from the few local pharmacies that stock the items lest someone sees them. Eight babies are delivered every minute. Many couples have as many children as possible. The average family size is 7.3. An estimated 200 non-governmental organizations are working on the issue of reproductive health in Pakistan.

Rural women in Pakistan as in the rest of South Asia are subjected to much violence. Women are treated like property by men. Woman-bashing is quite common in Pakistan. About 77 per cent of married women have to suffer beating carried out routinely by their husbands. 'Talaq' or divorce is common. Since the exodus of job-seekers to the Gulf countries, the number of talaqs has registered an increase. In Pakistan, this epidemic of talaq is attributed to what is called the 'Dubai disease'. Often men are reluctant to grant talaq when it involves a high 'Mehr' payment and prefer to murder their wife instead. Sometimes women's family writes a high 'Mehr' payment in the marriage contract to discourage frivolous divorce. Barren women are killed by setting them ablaze rather than releasing them by divorce. Village women are made to strip off their clothes and walk through a crowded bazaar, or killed on mere suspicions of her being a 'bad' girl and consequently a disgrace to the whole clan.

Not even 10 per cent of the incidents of rape that take place in Pakistan are registered with the police. As many raped women have been convicted under the *zina* ordinance, many women do not report rape for fear being charged for *zina*. Poor men who are ashamed of their daughters being raped by the landlord's son even kill their daughters and confess to the crime. Traditionally, in cases of suspected adultery, relatives are entitled to disfigure the woman by cutting off her hair or nose, as a punishment (Iqbal, 1990). In Sindh, under the notion of *kerakari*, a couple who elope may be hunted down and killed. Sindhiani Tehrik—a grassroots rural women's movement in Sindh—is active against *kerakari* (Marcus, 1993).

Sri Lanka

In 2002, Sri Lanka's population was estimated at 18.9 million, of whom 25 per cent were below 15 years of age and 6.9 per cent above 65 years. About 70 per cent of the people live in the south-western area (wet zone) which accounts for about three-quarters of all cultivated land. In 2002, 79.7 per cent of the population lived in rural areas (UNDP, 2004). The Demographic Survey of 1994 revealed that there existed a significant proportion (18.6%) of female-headed households in Sri Lanka (ESCAP, 1997).

Among all the South Asian countries Sri Lanka does well on the literacy front. The adult literacy rate for women is 89.6 per cent compared to 94.7 per cent for men in 2002. The sex difference in literacy is minimal. Moreover, the rural/urban differential in the female literacy rate is non-existent. However, the literacy rate for women in estate communities is only 52.8 per cent. Sri Lanka's public expenditure on education has decreased from 2.6 per cent of its GDP in 1990 to 1.3 per cent in 1999-2001 (UNDP, 2004). It ranked 96th out of 177 countries in the HDI ranking in 2002 (UNDP, 2004). The country performs relatively better on gender equality than on average achievements alone with respect to the HDI and GDI values.

The 1996 Labour Force Survey of Sri Lanka records an overall labour force participation rate of 49.1 per cent for the population aged 10 years and above. However, the female participation rate of 43.3 per cent is only 56 per cent of the rate for men in 2002 (UNDP, 2004). The largest proportion among employed women (49%) are engaged in agriculture and allied sectors and female rate as percentage of male rate in agriculture was 129 per cent in 2002. Around 56 per cent of women work as family labour. In the recent decades, migration of middle-level skilled and unskilled labourers to the Middle East, predominantly of women, is on a dramatic increase.

Area under agriculture represents nearly 30 per cent of the total land surface (ESCAP, 1997). The country has two major agro-ecological zones—a wet zone and a dry zone. Cultivation is carried on both in plantations and non-plantations. Spices, tea, rubber, coconut, vegetables and potatoes are grown in the wet zone, whereas rice and other field crops are grown in the dry zone under irrigation. The non-plantation sector is dominated by small farmers with holdings up to two hectares.

Despite their routine domestic work, women are actively involved in agricultural production with 56 per cent of them working as unpaid family workers (UNDP, 1997). They perform various tasks such as harvesting, cleaning, drying, grain storage, parboiling of paddy, post-harvest operations in maize and pulses, etc. In general, men assume responsibility for more strenuous types of tasks such as ploughing, hoeing and preparing the land for cultivation, while women do weeding, transplanting, harvesting, food processing and meal preparation. Women also earn cash income as agricultural wage labourers.

Women constitute the major labour force in plantations. Nearly 68 per cent of the women in agriculture are involved in plantations and more than 70 per cent of rural women in subsistence production (Wickramasinghe, 1994). After the repatriation of Indian workers, the entire increase in the Sinhalese tea estate workforce was made up of women. As many as 350,000 of them work in plantations. They represent 42 per cent of the total female workforce in the country forming the largest single labour group.

With the expansion of tea plantations, men's traditional roles related to paddy cultivation and dryland farming on the hill slopes have changed. Presently, they are involved in cash crop production on their own farm if they have adequate land. Alternatively, they opt for wage labour. Subsequently, women's responsibilities for home maintenance and household crop production have increased (Wickramasinghe, 1994). Women have the major responsibility for raising livestock and poultry.

Sri Lanka is endowed with forests and other natural resources. However, forest resources in the country are deteriorating with the reduction of the tree cover from an estimated 24 per cent of the total land area in 1989 to 20 per cent in 1992 (EIU, 1997). Rural women are heavily dependent on forests for the subsistence, consumption and maintenance of their family. Food, fuelwood and fodder constitute women's priority targets as gatherers. Food from the forest is important to the family's food basket. Women also collect various non-wood forest products that apart from household consumption, they also sell in the market to earn cash income (Kumar, 1998).

Environmental degradation has a severe impact on rural livelihoods and on women's lives. Due to fuelwood scarcity, women now avoid the parboiling of rice. In the intermediate zone of the Central Highland seasonal scarcities in food, fodder and fuelwood are acute because of the non-availability of substitutes for forest products. Most of the barren slopes are now free of perennial crops. Women are heavily dependent on riverine vegetation, hedges and isolated forests for fuelwood, fodder and some food products (Wickramasinghe, 1994).

Women actively participate in the small-scale fishery industry. About 75 per cent of women in the fishing communities of Mannar (North-West), Trincomalee and Batticoloa (East), and 25 per cent of all women in Negombo, Chilaw and Kalpitiya on the West Coast are estimated to be engaged in fishing-related activities.

Women are also engaged in non-farm income-generating activities to supplement farm income. They mostly enter home-based cottage industries using the local materials collected from the forests. Though the male member in the family does the marketing of home garden produce, the selling of surplus (over household consumption) of various items such as coconut, papaya, banana, cashew nut, etc., in roadside stalls and weekly markets is mainly done by women. These stalls are also used to sell other products made by women at home (Kumar, 1998).

Rural women make a significant contribution to the household food security. They play a key role in determining seed combinations for the short duration and of drought-resistant crops in the highlands for *chena* (shifting) cultivation. In order to minimize food shortages, women take complete charge of cultivating coarse grains, especially *kurakkan*. In the tribal society, women are in charge of *chena* cultivation (Kumar, 1998).

Non-farm rural employment is important as agriculture alone is not sufficient to raise incomes in the rural areas. Poor rural families receive close to half of all income from non-farm employment and such families are able to work their way out of poverty. Micro-credit is important to promote income-generating activities for poor women. Much like the rest of South Asia there is multiplicity of micro-credit operations functioning independently as non-governmental organizations (NGOs), government or semi-government agencies and cooperative societies. Sarvodaya—an NGO, which has been operational for almost 50 years—is Sri Lanka's largest people's organization, with a network covering 15,000 villages, and the country's largest micro-credit organization with a cumulative loan portfolio of over one billion Sri Lankan rupees. The Janashakthi Bank Society is a self-help micro-credit union with members from all communities and all cultural backgrounds formed after the fierce civil war in Sri Lanka in the 1980s that left many people destitute. The Janashakthi movement is flourishing and poor people are continuing to join. In some areas the micro-credit unions have been re-organized as *Samurdhi,* and they receive some government support. The Women's Credit Union (WCU) of Sri Lanka was formed in 1989 and in 1992 it became an independent cooperative organization managed by low-income women. Over the last thirteen years its membership has grown to 23,000 members (Albee and Gamage, 1999). The government is also taking the initiative for the creation of national and regional autonomous micro-credit funds. There are also many organizations involved in rural development and some with a long track record such as the Lanka Mahila Samithiya.

Despite these efforts, there is crushing rural poverty in Sri Lanka made worse by continuing ethnic conflict and scarce employment opportunities. In regions of severe impoverishment, men and women commit suicide being unable to cope with poverty and lack of employment. Gunathileke (2001) notes that Sri Lanka has the world's highest suicide rate, over 55 per 100,000 people—well above the average, which ranges between 10 and 25 per 100,000. This rate, he observes, has jumped dramatically over the past half century—from 6.5 in 1950 to 9.9 in 1960; 19.1 in 1970; 35.1 in 1980; 43.3 in 1993 and to the current estimate of more than 55. There has also been a significant change in the age of those committing suicide. In the 1980s, suicides among even younger children have started to increase. This is attributed to the widespread poverty.

Because of rural poverty and lack of employment opportunities, many rural women have migrated to the Middle East as domestic servants or to the Free Trade Zones (FTZs) in Colombo and elsewhere to work in garment factories. These developments have increased the levels of violence on rural women. Research in rural Anuradhapura, Nuwara Eliya, Matara and Kandy illustrates the widespread manifestations of domestic violence against women and rape in Sri Lanka (Hussein, n.d.). Rural Women's Front (RWF)—an NGO—is active in discouraging women from leaving their villages for jobs abroad. In any village, in the south of the island, there are at least 10 to 15 mothers who have left behind their families and gone overseas to work, according to the RWF. This has created a huge social upheaval in rural Sri Lanka. When the mother leaves, the father sometimes finds another companion and neglects the children (Seneviratne, n.d.).

Recently, there has been a dramatic increase in the reported cases of incest. This has mainly happened in homes where the wife is out in the Middle East and the man is left alone with the children. In many cases these men have justified saying that since their wives are away, they need to be satisfied sexually and this they get from their daughter. Women who migrate as domestic workers to the Middle East are often subjected to abusive treatment. Women working in the FTZs face sexual harassment and exploitation. FTZs have become the preying grounds for pimps from brothels in Colombo and the tourist centres on the coast, where they befriend unsuspecting village girls and gradually transform them to sex workers (Seneviratne, n.d.).

Rural women in Sri Lanka as in much of South Asia face severe physical, economic and social isolation. Common problems faced by rural women include inability to own transport, even basic ones like bicycles, and lack of appropriate intervention (Samath, n.d.).

India

India's estimated population in 2002 was 1049.5 million. Rural population accounted for 71.9 per cent (UNDP, 2004). Women constitute 48.1 per cent of the population. In 1992-93 only 9.2 per cent of the households were female-headed (ESCAP, 1997).

The adult illiteracy rate in India was 61.3 per cent in 2002. Women had 46.4 per cent literacy, whereas men had 69 per cent (UNDP, 2004). Both male and female literacy rates are substantially lower in rural areas than in urban areas. This rural-urban difference is more pronounced in the case of women. Among the rural female population in the age group of 7 years and over, the literacy rate is 30.4 per cent. The literacy rates vary considerably across the states.

The Human Development Index (HDI) rank of India in 2002 was 127 out of 177 countries, indicating low life expectancy at birth, low educational attainment and low income. The Gender-Related Development Index (GDI) rank of India in the same year was 103 out of 177 countries (UNDP, 2004).

The Indian workforce participation rate is 39.1 per cent (2001 census). The WPR of those 15 years and above for women is 42.4 per cent, which is half the rate of 84.8 per cent for men (UNDP, 2004). The rural female participation rate is much higher than the urban female participation rate. The majority of the workers (58.2%) are employed in agricultural and allied industrial sectors (2001 census). A greater proportion of women is employed in this sector as compared to men. In rural areas 89.5 per cent of the total female employment is in the agricultural and allied industrial sector.

Characteristics and potentials of agriculture strongly vary across the different agro-climatic regions. A variety of crops are grown in irrigated and rainfed areas. Rice, wheat, jowar, maize and bajra are the major food grains. Oilseed, sugar cane, cotton and jute are the important cash crops.

In the highly diversified agrarian context, no simple gender division of labour exists with regard to crop production. However, rural women are extensively involved in agricultural activities. The nature and extent of their involvement differs with the variations in agro-production systems, the landowning status of farm households and caste. Their roles range from managers to landless labourers. In overall farm production, women's average contribution is estimated at 55 to 66 per cent of the total labour with some regional variations.

Rural women in India feel the weight of poverty the most. They rarely have legal rights to land, despite the fact that they are often more engaged in agriculture than men. The oppressive practice of dowry is linked with women's inferior access and rights to land; and providing women with legal rights to land will increase their status and social and economic security. Enhancing women's access and rights to land necessitates changing state legislation to require government-distributed land to be granted jointly to husbands and wives or independently to women. Traditionally, women had usufruct rights to the community land (Agarwal, 1994). But, after the land reforms, land titles were given to men, denying women's access to land. New measures to provide land access and improved land rights to the rural poor, women and other marginalized groups are gaining ground. It is recommended that state governments allocate small house-and-garden plots to the rural landless, revise tenancy laws to increase the rural poor's access to land, provide joint titling and other protections for women, turn informal 'possessors' into formal owners, and make land markets work better for the poor.

In animal husbandry women have a multiple role. With regional differences, their activities include care of animals, grazing, fodder collection, cleaning of animal sheds to processing milk and livestock products. Women accounted for 93 per cent of total employment in dairy production (World Bank, 1991). Depending upon the economic status, women perform the tasks of collecting fodder, and collecting and processing dung. Though women play a significant role in livestock care, their control over livestock and its products is negligible. The vast majority of the dairy cooperative membership is male, leaving only 14 per cent to women.

The rural population is highly dependent upon forests. Fuelwood contributes 84 per cent of the total household energy consumption (UNDP, 1997). There are 66.5 million tribals in India and with few exceptions, the majority of them are forest dwellers (FAO, 1997). Unfortunately, forests are deteriorating and the country has been loosing 1.5 million hectares of forest cover annually. In India, about 16 per cent of the total geographical area is covered by forests.

Sharp decline in common property resources in land on one hand and the deterioration of the remaining land have jointly contributed to hardship for the rural community, particularly for women of the poor households. It has increased time and distance involved in grazing and collection of fuel and food. Moreover, it has also threatened income-generating opportunities for women by affecting livestock rearing and collection of non-timber forest products. Such reduced availability of forest products has shifted women from self-employment to wage employment. Women-headed movements for forest protection such as Chipko and Appiko have brought about environmental awareness at the grassroot in certain regions. Women have also been the source of knowledge relating to conserving and maintaining the quality of water. Depleting water resources have also impacted women severely in terms of longer walk and more work, as they are the principal collectors of water.

Women in rural India generate income in various ways. They are highly involved in small-scale enterprises like making basket, broom, rope, tasar silk cocoon rearing, lac cultivation, oil extraction, bamboo works, etc. Women constitute 51 per cent of the total employed in forest-based small-scale enterprises.

With the Green Revolution, India achieved self-sufficiency in food grains. However, it had a share of 40 per cent of the world's poor in 1990. Rural poverty was 39 per cent whereas urban poverty was 30 per cent in 1994 (UNDP, 1997). The proportion of pregnant women (age 15-49) with anaemia is as high as 88 per cent (UNDP, 1997). Despite women's key role in food production and in ensuring food and nutrition in the household as meal makers, they are much discriminated in food intake on account of social norms such that in poor households the intra-household distribution of hunger and food is unfavourable to women.

Recent years have witnessed far-reaching changes in rural India. In some regions there is an increase in women agricultural labourers suggesting feminization of agriculture. This has happened either on account of male migration to urban areas with women left behind to work on lands or has come about on account of men moving into non-farm employment being more lucrative and forcing women into agriculture. For the most part, the decade of the nineties saw real wages in agriculture either a decelerating growth or stagnation making it difficult to reconcile it with the marked decline in rural poverty revealed by official statistics (Unni, 1997). Globalization has brought changes in agriculture such as contract farming, greater commercialization and the accompanying market induced risks that in certain regions have led to losses and a spate of farmers' suicides. There is little evidence to suggest that for the mass of rural women engaged in field labour, life is any better.

Undoubtedly, education, skill formation and absorption in the rural industrial sector would be most desirable for many rural women, but the development of small and medium rural industries with backward linkages to agriculture and forward linkages to the urban areas have not been very encouraging. Many traditional household industries that had employed women as unpaid family labour like handloom weaving and other household manufacturing have had to face increased competition in recent years on account of liberalization of imports and cheaper products from China flooding the markets.

Some boost has been given to non-farm enterprises through micro-credit and self-help groups (SHGs). What had earlier remained an experimental effort of pioneer NGOs like WWF(I) and SEWA has now spread significantly. The revamping of poverty alleviation programmes by the central and state governments into the SHG mould of saving and thrift societies with a grant component and loan assistance from the banks has resulted in the enthusiastic spread of the SHGs among rural women. While it raises some optimism, there are still many problems that are inadequately dealt with (Kalpagam, 2004). The identification of viable ventures, marketing problems and the fact that it is in many instances exclusive of the poorest segments of rural society suggests that its potential as a poverty alleviation strategy may have been exaggerated. On the issue of women's empowerment it is felt that SHG encouragement by the state has led to a subtle shift in emphasis from other development programmes that are equally relevant such as adult education. Moreover, there is much doubt over the empowering capacity of bureaucratic interventions in contrast to social action by NGOs.

What has indeed been remarkable of the nineties rural scenario is the involvement of women in grassroots governance through their participation as representatives in the decentralized democratic framework of Panchayati Raj. Village level democratically elected governing body called 'Gram Panchayat' is an important component of the three-tier Panchayati Raj system. With the 73rd constitutional amendment in 1994, one-third of the seats in all Gram Panchayats are reserved for women. Now, nearly a million women function as elected representatives in these bodies. Although in many instances they face opposition and patriarchal, caste and class dominance and act as proxy candidates of husbands or male members of their family, it is still a significant initiative that in the long run would pave the way for a substantial empowerment of rural women. Already, with the support of NGOs, many of these women now have greater awareness of their rights and are raising issues of relevance such as transparency in governance, accountability and right to information. These women representatives will be far more effective with a more meaningful devolution of power and finances to the Gram Panchayats.

There are serious challenges on the human development front that require priority attention. Public expenditure on education as per cent of GDP increased from 3.9 per cent in 1990 to 4.1 per cent in 1999-2001, which is only a marginal increase. However, public expenditure on health as per cent of GDP remained at a constant low of 0.9 per cent in the period 1990 and 1999-2001. Even Pakistan, where income poverty has increased, has a marginally higher public expenditure on health at 1 per cent of GDP in 1999-2001. Bangladesh increased both its education and public health expenditure. Its health expenditure increased from 0.7 per cent in 1990 to 1.5 per cent of GDP in 1999-2001. Bhutan increased its health public expenditure from 1.7 per cent in 1990 to 3.6 per cent in 1999-2001. Sri Lanka too spends a higher percentage of 1.8 per cent of GDP on health as public expenditure (UNDP, 2004). India's lowest public expenditure on health needs to be increased, especially given the challenges like reducing maternal mortality or countering AIDS.

While India's infant mortality rate may be low and has definitely decreased over the years, its maternal mortality rate still remains high at 540 per 100,000 live births. It is higher than even Pakistan's rate of 500 in 2000 and only lower than Nepal's rate of 740. On the contrary, Sri Lanka's maternal mortality rate is only 92 per 100,000 live births (UNDP, 2004). Most of these maternal deaths are in rural areas that are reached poorly by hospitals and doctors coupled with the traditional practice of home birthing which has jeopardized the lives of rural women in certain regions. Maternal mortality is an indicator of women's low status and a low priority accorded to their health needs.

Rural women in India suffer much patriarchal and social violence, somewhat similar to what goes on in Bangladesh and Pakistan. Starting from foeticide and infanticide of girl children in a society with strong son preference, women are subjected to rape by landlords, police, criminals, etc. Dowry deaths are on the increase, and in some regions honour killings are prevalent as women are not free to choose their husbands in the society that discourages love and inter-caste marriages. Domestic violence is rampant across caste and class. Moreover, caste and communal violence that erupt ever so often in the hierarchically stratified and unequal rural communities draws women into its fold as easy targets of male violence. Dalit and tribal women bear a disproportionate burden of the rural violence on account of their powerlessness.

As in Bangladesh, social activism in rural India has become more widespread. Numerous empowerment initiatives of rural women have been taken up by the NGO sector. Some of the empowerment initiatives are the release of bonded labour, making access to common property resources like forests and ponds, irrigation and watershed management, micro-credit, micro-enterprise management, technology adoption and extension services, awareness of reproductive rights and health of women, countering domestic violence, literacy and education for empowerment, and training of panchayat members and SHGs (Murthy, 2001). Sustained policy advocacy by the NGOs has led to the recognition of the need for empowerment in the policy agenda of the state as articulated in the recent *National Policy for the Empowerment of Women* (2001).

This Volume

The various chapters in this book deal with different facets of rural women's lives and work in the South Asian context, some in a comparative perspective. They highlight issues as varied as rural women's poverty and work, invisibility of women's work and the gender ideologies that promote such invisibility, human capital and labour market discrimination in the South Asian region, and the poverty paradigm and NGO empowerment strategies in the SAARC countries. Individual country studies deal with issues such as women's labour force participation and their autonomy and decision-making power in Pakistan, state initiatives in micro-credit for women in Nepal and its effects, new employment opportunities for young rural women in Bangladesh, the empowering potential of non-farm employment for Sri Lankan women and grassroot participatory democracy in rural India to mention a few. The papers employ diverse methodologies such as statistical analysis of labour force and human capital development data and historical-anthropological analysis of the modes of violence inflicted on rural women in Haryana and North India in general.

The methodology employed reflects in part the researcher's role as social activist. Thiruchandran's analysis of women's narratives in the context of post-trauma counselling of women affected by the loss of their husbands and how they coped with their roles as mothers in war affected Sri Lanka is an instance of the activist doubling as a researcher in advocacy. The results of 'action research' in the context of poverty-stricken women in precarious livelihoods in Bangladesh similarly reflect the activist's understanding of the social dynamics of the region. And so is Azad's exemplar of Working Women's Forum (India) as a viable and successful empowerment experiment transforming itself into a social movement.

The strength of the book is that it acknowledges and highlights the differences between countries and communities and yet recognizes the commonalties of the South Asian experience. It convincingly argues that rural women's experience need to be understood in the context of the structural conditions of poverty and inequality in the region, the social and cultural shaping of gender ideologies, and the multiple patriarchies and caste and class dominance through which poor women experience power relations. A sense of optimism pervades as country experiences reflect the renewed concerns and commitments about rural women's empowerment in both state policy and the significant snowballing of social activism in the region in the last decade and more. The book reiterates yet again the importance of poverty alleviation, providing decent work opportunities, investing in education and health, involving women in decision-making and governance such that their substantive empowerment could be fostered by enhancing their capabilities, entitlements and choices. Only such an approach can in the long run whittle down the power of structured patriarchies and ensure gender equality in society.

■ References

Bangladesh

Abdullah, T.A. and Zeidenstein, S.A. (1982) *Village Women of Bangladesh: Prospects for Change,* Pergamon Press, Oxford.

Anand, Sudhir and Jonathan Morduch (November 1996). "Poverty and the Population Problem: Evidence from Bangladesh", Harvard Institute for International Development (HIID), Development Discussion Paper No. 559.

Banu, D. et al. (1998) "Empowering Women in Rural Bangladesh: Impact of Bangladesh Rural Advancement Committee's (BRAC's) Programme", Research and Evaluation Division, BRAC Centre, Dhaka.

Crossette, B. (2003) "Experts Question Wisdom of Micro-Credit for Women", Wenews, Run Date: 03/02/03.

ESCAP (1995) *Women of Bangladesh: A Country Profile,* United Nations, New York.

FAO (1980) *Role of Women in Small-Scale Fisheries of the Bay of Bengal,* FAO, Madras.

Goetz, Anne Marie and Rina Sen Gupta (1996) "Who Takes the Credit? Gender, Power, and Control Over Loan Use in Rural Credit Programs in Bangladesh", *World Development*, Vol. 24, No. 1, January, pp. 45-63.

Halim, S. et al. (2001) "Women and Children Study: Feasibility Study for the Shrimp Component of the Fourth Fisheries Project (FFP)", The Department of Fisheries and DFID, submitted by Bangladesh Centre for Advanced Studies (BCAS), Dhaka.

Hartmann and Boyce (1983) *A Quiet Violence,* Zed Press, London.

Hashemi, Syed M., Sidney Ruth Schuler, and Ann P. Riley (1996) "Rural Credit Programs and Women's Empowerment in Bangladesh", *World Development*, Vol. 24, No. 4, April, pp. 635-653.

Jahan, I. (1990) "Country Paper – Bangladesh" in *Gender Issues in Agriculture: Papers and Proceedings of the Regional Conference on Gender Issues in Agriculture* (Manila, 5-6 December) ADB and UNIFEM.

Jain, Pankaj S. (1996) "Managing Credit for the Rural Poor: Lessons from the Grameen Bank", *World Development,* Vol. 24, No. 1, January, pp. 79-89.

Jordans, E. and Zwarteveen, M. (1997) *A Well of One's Own: Gender Analysis of Irrigation Program in Bangladesh,* International Irrigation Management Institute, Colombo.

Kabeer, Naila (1991) "Gender Dimensions of Rural Poverty: Analysis from Bangladesh", *The Journal of Peasant Studies*, Vol. 18, No.2.

Khandker, Shahidur R. and Baqui Khalily (1996) "The Bangladesh Rural Advancement Committee's Credit Programs: Performance and Sustainability", World Bank Discussion Paper No. 324.

Khandker, Shahidur R. and M. Abdul Latif (1996) "The Role of Family Planning and Targeted Credit Programs in Demographic Change in Bangladesh", World Bank Discussion Paper No. 337.

Khandker, Shahidur (1996) "Education Achievements and School Efficiency in Rural Bangladesh", World Bank Discussion Paper No. 319.

Marcus, Rachel (1993) *Violence Against Women in Bangladesh, Pakistan, Egypt, Sudan, Senegal and Yemen*. Report prepared for special programme WID, Netherlands Ministry of Foreign Affairs (DGIS), Report No. 10.

Parveen, S. and Leonhauser, I.U. (2004) "Empowerment of Rural Women in Bangladesh: A Household Level Analysis", paper presented at the Conference on Rural Poverty Reduction through Research for Development and Transformation, Deutscher Tropentag, Berlin.

Paul, D.C. and Saadullah, M. (1991) "Role of Women in Homestead of Small Farm Category in an Area of Jessore, Bangladesh", *Livestock Research for Rural Development*, Vol. 3, No. 2, June.

Pitt, Mark M. and Shahidur R. Khandker (1996) "Household and Intrahousehold Impact of the Grameen Bank and Similar Targeted Credit Programs in Bangladesh", World Bank Discussion Paper No. 320.

UNDP (1997) *Human Development Report,* Oxford University Press, New York.

— (2004) *Human Development Report,* Oxford University Press, New York.

White (1992) *Arguing with the Crocodile: Gender and Class in Bangladesh,* The University Press Limited, Dhaka.

www.FAO-SD, *Asia's Women in Agriculture, Environment and Rural Production* (Available on the website)

www.UNDP.ESMAP, "Switched on Women-Bangladesh" February 2005.

Yusuf, Shahid and Praveen Kumar (1996) "Developing the Non-farm Sector in Bangladesh: Lessons for Other Asian Countries", World Bank Discussion Paper No. 340.

Bhutan

Gurung, J. (1997) "Gender Dimensions in Biodiversity Management: Bhutan and Nepal" (unpublished).

Rosenegger, P., 1998. 'Annual Report: Bhutan' (unpublished) FAO/RAP Non-Wood Forest Products of Bhutan, RAP Publication, 1996.

UNDP (2004) *Human Development Report,* Oxford University Press, New York.

www. FAO-SD *Asia's Women in Agriculture, Environment and Rural Production* (available on the website).

Nepal

Bhatt, N., Shrestha, L., Thomas-Slayter, B. and Koirala, I. (1994) *Managing Resources in Nepalese Village: Changing Dynamics of Gender, Caste and Ethnicity,* Clark University, Massachusetts.

EIU (1997) *India and Nepal: Country Profile,* The Economist Intelligence Unit, London.

ESCAP (1995) *Women of Nepal: A Country Profile,* United Nations, New York.

— (1996) *Rural Poverty Alleviation and Sustainable Development in Asia and the Pacific,* United Nations, New York.

FAO (1987) *Restoring the Balance: Women and Forest Resources,* FAO and Swedish International Development Agency.

Kumar, S.K. and Hotchkiss, D. (1988) *Consequences of Deforestation for Women's Time Allocation, Agricultural Production and Nutrition in Hill Areas of Nepal.* Research Report No. 69. International Food Policy Research Institute, Washington D.C.

Regmi, Shree Kant (2002) *Nepal: Rural Poverty Alleviation under Changing Economic Conditions,* National Planning Commission, Kathmandu.

Sontheimer, S., Basnyat, B.B. and Maharjan, K. (1997) *Gender and Participation in Agricultural Development Planning: Lessons from Nepal,* FAO, Kathmandu and Rome.

UNDP (2004) *Human Development Report,* Oxford University Press, New York.

— (1997) *Human Development Report*, Oxford University Press, New York.
www. FAO-SD *Asia's Women in Agriculture, Environment and Rural Production* (available on the website).

Pakistan

Adams, Jr., R.H. and He, Jane J. (1995) "Sources of Income Inequality and Poverty in Rural Pakistan", *IFPRI Research Report* 102.
EIU (1997) *Pakistan and Afghanistan: Country Profile*, The Economist Intelligence Unit, London.
ESCAP (1996) *Rural Poverty Alleviation and Sustainable Development in Asia and the Pacific*, United Nations, New York.
— (1997) *Women in Pakistan: A Country Profile*. United Nations, New York.
FAO (1995) *Gender Issues in Agricultural and Rural Development Policy in Asia and the Pacific*, FAO Regional Office for Asia and the Pacific, Bangkok.
GOP (1995) *Fourth World Conference on Women, Beijing, September, 1995: Pakistan, National Report*, Ministry of Women Development and Youth Affairs, Government of Pakistan, Pakistan.
Iqbal, J. (1990) "Crimes Against Women in Pakistan", *Journal of South Asian and Middle Eastern Studies*, Vol. 13, No 3.
PARC, 1988. *Rural Women in Pakistan Farming Systems Research*. Proceedings of the Workshop on 'Role of Rural Women in Farming Systems Research', Pakistan Agricultural Research Council, Islamabad.
Population Council (2004) *Transitions to Adulthood-Schooling: Educational Opportunities in Rural Areas in Pakistan* (on website).
Qureshi, Saeed, Nabi, Ijaz and Faruqee, Rashid (1996) "Rural Finance for Growth and Poverty Alleviation in Pakistan", Policy Research Working Papers, World Bank, Washington.
Terzieff, J. (2004) *Pakistan Launches Effort to Lower Maternal Deaths* WEnews Run Date: 08/22/04.
UNDP (2004) *Human Development Report*, Oxford University Press, New York.
— (1997) *Human Development Report*, Oxford University Press, New York.
www. FAO-SD *Asia's Women in Agriculture, Environment and Rural Production* (available on the website).
www. IDRC.MIMAP - Pakistan, Phase (I).

Sri Lanka

Albee, A. and Gamage, N. (1999) "Gender and Micro-finance in Sri Lanka: The Experience of the Women's Credit Union", in Datta, K. and Jones, A.J (eds.), *Housing and Finance in Developing Countries*, Routledge, London.

EIU (1997) *Sri Lanka: Country Profile,* The Economist Intelligence Unit, London.

ESCAP (1997) *Women in Sri Lanka: A Country Profile,* United Nations, New York.

Gunathileke, R.M. (2001) "Grinding Rural Poverty Leads to Suicide in Sri Lanka", 28 December, *World Socialist Website.*

Hussein, Ameena (n.d.) *Sometimes There is No Blood: Domestic Violence and Rape in Rural Sri Lanka,* International Centre for Ethnic Studies, Colombo.

Kumar, V. (1998) "Gender Dimensions in Agro-Biodiversity Management: Country Report", Sri Lanka (unpublished).

Samath, Feizal (n.d.) "Sri Lanka: Asian Rural Women Deprived of Transport", South-North Development Monitor (SUNS).

Seneviratne, Kalinga (n.d.) "Violence Against Women in Sri Lanka", *Third World Resurgence* No. (65/66).

UNDP (2004) *Human Development Report,* Oxford University Press, New York.

— (1997) *Human Development Report,* Oxford University Press, New York.

Wickramasinghe, A. (1994) *Deforestation, Women and Forestry: The Case of Sri Lanka,* International Books, Utrecht.

www. FAO-SD *Asia's Women in Agriculture, Environment and Rural Production* (available on the website).

India

Agarwal, B. (1994) *A Field of One's Own: Gender and Land Rights in South Asia,* Cambridge University Press, Cambridge.

EIU (1997) *India and Nepal: Country Profile,* The Economist Intelligence Unit, London.

ESCAP (1997) *Women in India: A Country Profile,* United Nations, New York.

FAO (1991) *Women's Role in Dynamic Forest-based Small Scale Enterprises: Case Studies on Uppage and Lacquerware from India,* Food and Agriculture Organization of the United Nations, Bangkok.

— (1997) *Forest Dependent Survival Strategies of Tribal Women: Implications for Joint Forest Management in Andhra Pradesh, India.* RAP Publication: 1997/24. Food and Agriculture Organization of the United Nations, Bangkok.

Government of India (2001) *National Policy for the Empowerment of Women,* Department of Women and Child Development.

Kalpagam, U. (2004) 'Micro-credit, Livelihood Re-integration and Empowerment in Uttar Pradesh' in U. Kalpagam et al. (eds.), *Labour and Poverty,* Segment Books, New Delhi.

Murthy, Ranjani K. (ed.) (2001) *Building Women's Capacities: Interventions in Gender Transformation,* Sage Publications, New Delhi.

UNDP (2004) *Human Development Report*, Oxford University Press, New York.

— (1997) *Human Development Report*, Oxford University Press, New York.

Unni, J. (1997) "Employment and Wages among Rural Labourers: Some Recent Trends", *Indian Journal of Agricultural Economics*, Vol. 52, No. 1, January-March.

World Bank (1991) *A World Bank Country Report: Gender and Poverty in India*, World Bank, Washington D.C.

— (1997) *India: Achievements and Challenges in Reducing Poverty*, World Bank, Washington D.C.

www.FAO-SD *Asia's Women in Agriculture, Environment and Rural Production* (available on the website).

Chapter 2

Rural Women, Work and Empowerment

Preet Rustagi

The significance of economic empowerment for rural women in South Asia poses multi-dimensional challenges while considering its potential as a transformative mechanism to achieve a gender balance in society. Can economic empowerment be viewed as employment generation and women's access to paid jobs in the context of this region where women's contribution to the economy is concentrated in unpaid work spheres? The domination and pervasive prevalence of gender ideologies that subjugate women within families, and assign lower social status to them irrespective of their roles and responsibilities, and consider them as requiring male protection and guardianship militates against any autonomy enhancing processes that women may be involved in (Mathema, 1998; Mukhopadhyay and Sudarshan, 2003; MHHDC, 2000). While patriarchy influences women and men so as to legitimize and institutionalize women's subordination and subjugation to men, not only in the private domains, but also within the public spheres, the interweaving of patriarchal systems with other institutions—social, legal, political and economic—generates multiplex structures specific to the region (for instance, brideprice and dowry practices, matriliny and male control over property affairs, the complex institutions to control and manage female sexuality and so on).

The distinctiveness of gender ideologies prevalent in the region stems from the pluralities that influence patriarchy, thereby entangling with and producing complex diversities that generate differences and overlaps among relationships between men and women across caste, class, region and religion. The principle of hierarchy derived from caste and social inequalities, that is, the socio-cultural context of power and authority structures, their non-linearity, absence of bi-polarity and constantly changing nature defines the uniqueness of gender relationships in the South Asian region (Sangari, 1995; Kalpagam, 2000; Ganesh and Risseeuw, 1998). The resilience to change noted in the prevalence of gender ideologies lies in the hierarchization and power equations that define gender relations and persist in retention of women's relatively lower position, especially in certain domains that are generally prevented from being challenged (marriage, inheritance, divorce, control over women's bodies and sexuality) even while there may be alterations in other arenas that are being accepted relatively more easily (as in the case of women's education, employment, expansion of responsibility within the domestic spheres).

The economic participation of women and their contribution is very often poverty-induced and hence assigned lower value rather than being viewed as a process towards alleviating poverty and thereby providing the opportunity for women to be considered as equal partners in improving well-being. The internalization of these perceptions of gender inequalities through socialization processes prevents even women themselves from becoming agents of change, unless they are assisted for collective awareness and organization to do so (Antony, 2001; Banerjee, 2004).

South Asia, which consists of seven independent nation-states[1], is predominantly rural (70%), populous (one-fifth of all humanity), poor (40% of world's poor), marked for its inequalities (especially gender-based; complicated further by caste, religion, ethnicities) and human deprivations. The inequalities prevalent in the South Asian region provide an interesting kaleidoscope that simultaneously poses multi-dimensional challenges for development—human and gender. The recent economic policy changes induced phenomena present conflicting and contradictory scenarios, displaying progressive and retrogressive forces, in women's development, adding to the complexities of understanding the dynamic changes being witnessed in all the seven nation-states. The situation is further complicated by the fact that these countries are located at different junctures of their social and economic development. However, the similarities, despite such heterogeneity, in the levels of gender gaps and, discrimination against women across these countries of South Asia re-emphasize and highlight the influence of gender ideologies biased against women so as to make feasible the consideration of issues relating to women's status for the region as a whole.

Efforts to generate better understanding on these gender imbalances and inequalities have intensified in the last quarter of the twentieth century. The use of quantification and measurement via media indicators formulated to focus upon gender gaps and differences have had positive impacts as well as generated criticisms. Some of these international, regional and national efforts in the context of South Asia are discussed in the first section of the essay.

The appropriateness of these measures to reflect what they purport to do and the methodologies have come under immense scrutiny and criticism. However, the significance of the conceptual framework, the ability of such endeavours in drawing attention to matters of gender concern and the awareness generated regarding the essentiality of women's equality and empowerment have been listed among the positive outcomes. These efforts have also highlighted the need for better and comparable data systems across countries that provide information and fill gaps, which aid the process of monitoring and evaluation.[2]

The second section focuses on rural women's work in the context of discussing issues relevant for economic empowerment of women. As a hold all term—empowerment—has evolved into a concept that can be invoked in virtually any context, be it human rights, basic or strategic needs, capacity building skill formation or overall economic security (Beteille, 1999; Karlekar, 2004). However, this paper considers only economic empowerment in its limited frame to evaluate whether work participation of women in South Asian labour markets is reflective of changing gender inequalities and improving the socio-economic balances. There are very progressive and exhilarating changes witnessed in certain spheres that portray the development of women in the region. While these beneficial alterations are changing the lives of few women, the mass of them remain subjugated and subordinated even when their economic participation enhances.

These divergent elements in rural women's lives in South Asia can be explained by the changes in diverse social, political, legal and economic spheres that are not in conformity with each other. The contradictions stem from women's location within the social hierarchical order and the politically derived identity of citizenship, for instance. Women are governed by social values, customs and norms, subjugated to the power of the male heads of households that impose restrictions on their mobility, autonomy in terms of decision-making, sexuality, health, reproduction and so on. Even, the universality of marriage (with the absence of the right to choose one's own partner), along with the poor access to property (since inheritance in most cases follows patrimonial, patriarchal systems)[3] constitutes segments of their lives wherein women are made to feel disempowered and dependent.

Cultural pluralism in South Asia, which is home to several major religious groups, including Hindus, Muslims, Sikhs, Buddhists, Jains, Parsis and Christians as well as many smaller, more localized traditions followed among the multi-ethnic populations of the region, defines the customary values and forms the basis very often for the legal systems followed in most countries of the region. The manner in which universal legal systems function and the simultaneous operation of community, religion based and personal laws that are followed for marriage, divorce, guardianship, inheritance and so on, introduce conflicting situations that contest gender equalities despite the constitutional provisions for it (UNIFEM, 2003; MHHDC, 2000).

Legal universalism or standardization is clearly not the desired solution, since implementing equality—a central objective to concerns of human development—is not the same as implementing uniformity. As upheld in the HDR 2004, which focuses on the theme of cultural liberty, there is a need for "internal reform of all customary laws, upholding gender equality rather than imposing identical gender-biased, prejudicial laws across all communities" (UNDP, 2004: 57).

The resilience to change and persistence of gender ideologies over generations witnessed in the region can be understood in the context of these divergences across institutional structures. Under these socio-cultural and patriarchal structures, even where women are economically active, the manner in which their contribution is treated by the various agents—within family, labour markets, the state as well as the women themselves—crucially impacts upon the extent of economic empowerment that is feasible. This chapter discusses the varied experiences in rural South Asia, to highlight the similarities shared by women across the seven countries in terms of their vulnerabilities and survival based livelihood strategies that continue to be under deep influence of the prevalent gender ideologies even in the context of structural economic reforms and modernization. The positive outcomes of the changes witnessed for women still remain minuscule, while they portend the power to bring about the desired transformation, the need to change resilient mindsets and people's perceptions towards women and their contribution to society, polity and economy remains a critical dimension to pursue for effective empowerment of women.

Gender Equality and Women's Empowerment: International, Regional and National Efforts

All over the world, historically, processes and paths of development have created imbalances and challenges that generate new understandings and evolve creative ways to address and redress them. Among the multiple approaches towards the eternal goals of equity, peace and justice are included alterations in the language of the discourses, terminologies as well as frameworks adopted. In the sphere of gender-based development, equality and empowerment are the twin terms, which have occupied pre-eminent position to encompass all earlier efforts towards bridging inequalities and social imbalances.

The last quarter of the previous century had been associated with the resurgence of women's movements internationally as well as nationally across the South Asian countries. The transition from questioning the gender neutrality assumptions of development to emphasizing the treatment of women as active agents contributing to development and therefore due for benefits of such development as their own individual right, occurred during this period (Kabeer, 1994). From the women in development (WID)—women and development (WAD) to gender and development (GAD) debates within women's studies; the changes in nomenclatures traces the path from mere tokenism to serious contemplation on matters concerning women's development and gender-based inequalities over the years.

Some of the prominent international efforts began in 1975 with the first world conference in Mexico, with United Nations (UN) and its agencies playing a key role in fostering women's equality. The fourth world conference in Beijing held in 1995 was a hallmark, when the international communities accepted the need for a strong gender perspective in all areas of development planning and implementation. The following years have seen the five yearly monitoring and evaluation processes as stipulated by the Beijing Platform for Action that have been undertaken by most of the South Asian countries.

The growing discontent in using income-based measure as an indicator of well-being occupied development theorists and researchers over a major portion of the twentieth century ever since the world wars. The nineties, with the publication of Human Development Report (HDR) by the United Nations Development Programme (UNDP), define a marked shift in conceptual framework from income to enlarging choices for enhancement of human capabilities as key to development of any country. Its flagship, the introduction of human development index (HDI) as a measure based on composite indexation used to rank countries across the globe, initiated an unparalleled process of competition. The HDI was based on three dimensions of a long and healthy life, knowledge and a decent standard of living depicted by life expectancy at birth, educational indicators and a measure of per capita incomes (UNDP, 1990).

In 1995, the global HDR focused on gender and human development. Highlighting the presence of gender-based discrimination and inequalities all over the world in varying degrees, the report introduced a set of new indices—gender-related development index (GDI)[4] and gender empowerment measure (GEM).[5] In the South Asian context, the founder of HDRs Mahbub-ul-Haq prepared the first regional report in 1997 titled "Human Development for South Asia" (HDSA).

The composite indices—HDI, GDI, GEM—calculated by UNDP HDRs, reveal an improvement in values for all South Asian countries over 1993 to 1997 (see Table 2.1). Sri Lanka and Maldives portray medium levels of human development, while all other countries fall in the low development category of nations. The gender development levels in South Asia are second lowest in the world, being just better than the Arab countries, whereas the GEM values are the lowest in the region (MHHDC, 2000).

Table 2.1

Trends in Human and Gender Development Indices for South Asia

Country/Region	*HDI*			*GDI*			*GEM*		
	1993	*1997*	*2003*	*1993*	*1997*	*2003*	*1993*	*1997*	*2003*
India	0.436	0.545	0.590	0.410	0.525	0.574	0.235	0.240	NA
Pakistan	0.442	0.508	0.499	0.383	0.472	0.469	0.165	0.176	0.414
Bangladesh	0.365	0.440	0.502	0.336	0.428	0.495	0.291	0.304	0.218
Nepal	0.332	0.463	0.499	0.308	0.441	0.479	NA	NA	NA
Sri Lanka	0.698	0.721	0.730	0.699	0.712	0.726	0.306	0.321	0.272
Bhutan	0.307	0.459	0.511	NA	0.444	NA	NA	NA	NA
Maldives	0.610	0.716	0.751	0.599	0.711	NA	0.324	0.342	NA
South Asia weighted average	0.432	0.532	0.582	0.402	0.511	NA	0.233	0.236	NA
Developing countries	0.563	0.637	0.655	0.530	0.630	NA	0.351	—	NA

Source: MHHDC, 1997 and 2000; UNDP, HDR 2003.

Although conceptually well developed, the human development and gender empowerment measures are hugely delimited since they are based on a select set of limited variables. Critiques have pointed out the problems with composition, the assigned weights and the assumed uniform/linear path of growth especially in the context of gender development, which calls for a complex, non-linear and multi-dimensional framework (Krishnaji, 1997; Hirway and Mahadevia, 1996). This is only heightened in a socio-culturally diverse region as South Asia where conventional indicators reveal little and the need for developing non-conventional approaches have been emphasized (Mukhopadhyay and Sudarshan, 2003; Sonpar and Kanbur, 2003).

The most crucial positive contributions made by these international, regional and national efforts on preparation of HDRs, apart from enhancing awareness and consciousness among the countries by drawing attention to various issues concerning gender equality and women's empowerment, have been the collation and collection of data and increasing acceptance of the dire need for filling data gaps. This is indeed a very critical requirement to make available reliable and comparable data across the different countries. For, without this basic information, analysis, evaluation and monitoring, the progress in women's status remains delimited. National level statistics on women's work participation across South Asia by rural-urban locations are difficult to come by for all seven countries, hence even in this paper the discussion on economic empowerment can not only aggregate for a South Asian perspective, but even undertake a thorough quantitative examination of rural women's work participation in each country.

At the turn of the century, 191 nations adopted the United Nations Millennium Declaration, which supports the development of 48 indicators to help track progress from 1990 through 2015 (UNIFEM, 2003). The eight millennium development goals (MDGs) are: eradicate extreme poverty and hunger; achieve universal primary education; promote gender equality and empower women; reduce child mortality; improve maternal health; combat HIV/AIDS, malaria and other diseases; ensure environmental sustainability; and develop a global partnership for development. In this global initiative too, the centrality of gender equality and empowerment for achieving all the other seven MDGs is recognized.

Thus, global, regional and national efforts to improve the status of women have come to be linked to the twin concepts of equality and empowerment. These are broad terms that have links with almost every initiative for improving women's status. What do these terms mean? Equality refers to equal opportunities in terms of access to sources of livelihood, health, and education, as well as to social, economic and political participation without discrimination. Gender inequalities stem from relations of power and authority, class-caste hierarchies and socio-cultural traditions, customs and norms (Kabeer, 1994; Carr, et al., 1996).

Empowerment is the process of transforming these structures and institutions, thereby ensuring equality. The term 'empowerment' so defined has multi-dimensional connotations which range from "development of personal instrumental competencies and skills, to the process of challenging existing power relations, to household decision-making, to gaining access and control over resources like credit, income, land, knowledge, etc., as well as to subjective variables like the sense of personal power of self-efficacy" (Mukhopadhyay and Sudarshan, 2003: 4).

The efforts towards women's equality and empowerment face certain structural and institutional constraints in the context of South Asian countries stemming from the prevailing gender ideologies in the region. It is noteworthy that irrespective of income levels, women's traditional or changing economic roles with increasing participation, higher educational attainments, across the countries of South Asia, the pervasiveness of having to confront gender ideologies that disallow women's empowerment in one or more spheres continues to be a reality they face.

South Asia is a predominantly rural, tradition-bound, culturally diverse region inhabited by a vast population that is dependent on primary sector activities based on land, forests, livestock and water. The region consists of seven independent nation-states with historical roots that are intertwined, geographical contiguity, socio-cultural similarities, especially the patriarchal domination that subordinates women through kinship ordered structures and caste-class hierarchies, as well as economic linkages fostered through the South Asian Association for Regional Cooperation (SAARC) initiative that aims to propel trade across the region and work towards enhancing the well-being of its people.

Table 2.2
Some Basic Indicators: Comparative Picture for South Asia

2004 HDI Rank	*Country/ Region*	*GDP per capita (PPP US$) 2002*	*Total population (millions) 2002*	*Urban population (% of total) 2002*	*Population under age 15 (% of total) 2002*	*Female economic activity rate (age 15 years and above) 2002*
84	Maldives	4798	0.3	28.4	43.1	65.4
89	Sri Lanka	3570	18.9	21.1	25.0	43.3
124	India	2670	1049.5	28.1	33.3	42.4
134	Bhutan	1969	2.2	8.2	41.8	57.1
138	Bangladesh	1700	143.8	23.9	38.3	66.4
140	Nepal	1370	24.6	14.6	40.2	56.8
142	Pakistan	1940	149.9	33.7	41.5	36.3
	South Asia	2658	1480.3	29.6	34.8	43.7
	Developing countries	4054	4936.9	41.4	32.2	55.8
	World	7804	6225.0	47.8	29.4	55.3

Source: UNDP, 2004.

Most of the countries of the region have opened up their economies over the last two decades or so, having initiated economic policy reforms under the structural adjustment programmes at different points of time, that have intensified over the 1990s. Industrialization, modernization, technological innovations and changes have made inroads, affecting economic growth, structures and patterns of production and employment. By the turn of the century, although different countries were located at different levels of growth and development, the growth experienced has been low in labour absorption and resulted in increasing income and social inequalities (MHHDC, 2000; Mukhopadhyay, 1999).

Each of the seven South Asian countries is at diverse junctures of economic and social development. Nepal and Bangladesh have the lowest per capita incomes, while Maldives and Sri Lanka record relatively higher per capita income (based on 2002 GDP calculations). Levels of urbanization vary, with Pakistan having one-third of its population living in urban areas, while Bhutan has over 92 per cent of its people inhabiting rural areas (see Table 2.2).

The levels of economically active female population vary across the countries, with Pakistan recording the lowest rate, while Bangladesh and Nepal are among the countries with relatively higher rates (Table 2.2). The percentage of female workers among total workers, however, is lowest in Maldives and Pakistan (see Table 2.3; ADB, 2000; UNDP, 2000, 2003). Education, early marriage and high fertility rates are often associated with changes in women's labour participation rates in the literature. Mukhopadhyay (1999), in her study based on five larger South Asian countries, notes that the age-specific labour force participation curve for women assumes a plateau-like shape suggesting continued involvement throughout the reproductive years as well. This is reflective of the necessity-based participatory behaviour of women in the region marked by the peculiar characteristics of poverty, caste and gender.

Table 2.3

Some Correlates of Women's Work: South Asian Countries

Countries	*Adult Literacy Rate (15 years and above)*		*Total Fertility Rate (2000-2005)*	*Percentage of Female Workers*
	Female	*Male*		
Maldives	97.2	97.3	5.3	22
Sri Lanka	89.6	94.7	2.0	36
India	46.4	69.0	3.0	32
Bhutan	—	—	5.0	32
Bangladesh	31.4	50.3	3.5	42
Nepal	26.4	61.6	4.3	40
Pakistan	28.5	53.4	5.1	27

Source: UNDP, 2004; MHHDC, 2000.

Despite positive indicators on gender equality in Sri Lanka stemming from the matrilineal and bilineal descent kinship (which allows for some degree of inheritance rights among women and provides considerable natal family support for daughters), late marriages and relatively high female education, indicators of women's economic roles show a less favourable picture (ADB, 1999a; Aturupane, 1996; Malhotra and DeGraff, 2000).

Demographically, the peculiarity of South Asian population is that it is largely young with 35 per cent below the age of 15 years. This implies increasing proportions of expected future entrants into the labour force.[6] Already, most of the countries of the South Asian region are facing saturation in employment generation with growth patterns being low labour absorbing (MHHDC, 2003). The challenge of generating employment and providing access to sustainable livelihood under the changing socio-economic environment wherein vulnerabilities are heightening and aspiration levels mismatch with prevailing conditions in the labour market are ominous dark clouds that need to be dispersed.

Within the South Asian countries, there are tremendous variations across regions, locations, and communities as well. The rural areas generally exhibit lower levels of human development and indicators of women-related development reflect a worse scenario. In rural areas, women experience lower life expectancy, higher mortality rates, lower ages at marriage, higher fertility rates and lower educational attainment levels. All these factors reflect the discrimination against women (UNDP, 2002).

Intra-country variations and tremendous inequalities are witnessed across the South Asian countries. In Sri Lanka, despite the strong positive gender development indicators, there are pockets within which deprivation levels remain. Apart from the ethnic conflicts that affect women and their pursuits in enhancing human capabilities, districts with plantation workers such as Nuwara Eliya, display far lower than average Sri Lankan conditions (UNDP, 1998). Despite the wide network of maternal care facilities, in Nuwara Eliya, 58 per cent births are non-institutional as opposed to Kandy where almost all births are institutional.

Even in Bhutan where basic health care is free and overall child immunization rates reveal 90 per cent coverage, institutional deliveries are very low, with 85 per cent of births being at home (see Table 2.4).

Over the years, in a number of gender-based development indicators, South Asian women are seen to be better off today than they were a few decades ago. Their survival in terms of life

Table 2.4
Survival Indicators: South Asia

Country/ Region	*Sex Ratio (females per 100 males)*	*Female Life Expectancy at Birth*	*Female Child Mortality Rate*	*Female to Male Child Mortality Rate*	*Birth Attended by Skilled Personnel (%)*
Maldives	93	66	80	1.51	70
Sri Lanka	102	76	20	0.91	97
India	94	64	97	1.18	43
Bhutan	98	64	94	0.96	15
Bangladesh	95	61	116	1.09	12
Nepal	100	59	124	1.13	11
Pakistan	92	—	99	1.14	36
South Asia	94	—	99	1.14	36

Source: MHHDC, 2000, 2003; UNFPA, 1999.

expectancy has been improving, more women are educated and working. Many of them have entered politics at least at the local governance levels[7] (MHHDC, 2000; Rustagi, 2004). There is an increasing recognition of the need to address women's issues specifically, to understand gender relations and work towards equality and empowerment for women.

These achievements are not all homogenous and tremendous degrees of variations are common across the different South Asian countries. Consider the survival indicators, although all the countries of the region display elements of gender-based discrimination, some of them are more prominent in demographic spheres as for instance, the declining sex ratios that reflect lower numbers of women in the population, especially among children and juvenile age cohorts. This is witnessed alongside improvements in life expectancy and health indicators in many parts of India. Instances of son preference are noted in other South Asian countries such as Bangladesh, Pakistan and Nepal (MHHDC, 2000; Rustagi, 2004; Arnold, 2001). Even in the other South Asian countries of Sri Lanka, Maldives, Bhutan, although no overt forms of gender-based discrimination are visible, gender stereotyping and socialization follows the male dominant norms and hierarchical thinking that treat women in subordination, assign lower worth and status to them (UNDP, 1998, 2000; RGoB, 2000).

Women located within households, with no ownership of economic assets, working mostly in unpaid family activities, are assigned lower economic worth. This, together with the already defined lower status that they wield in social contexts within patriarchal, hierarchical structures, leaves them vulnerable and disempowered. Traditionally, women have had very poor access to and ownership rights of land resources. Even in the case of matrilineal and bilateral communities where women have had greater land rights, control and management of land has remained circumscribed (Agarwal, 1994). Land reforms, wherever they have been effective even to a limited extent, continue to leave gender gaps in actual ownership and effective control of land especially for women. Thus, the ability of women to benefit from legal changes is circumscribed by a complex set of interlinked factors influenced by socio-cultural institutions. Any effort towards empowerment of women must address these power and authority relations that define institutional processes and structures.

As an achievement of the concerted efforts ongoing at international levels as well as the discourses on gender equality and empowerment world over, governments in all of the South Asian countries have evolved mechanisms to work towards empowerment of women (UNIFEM, 2003). These regional and national endeavours have gone though the processes of changing nomenclatures, making mandatory alterations in all concerned governance structures, government policy documents, plans and schemes. These have accompanied a simultaneous parallel process of monitoring, evaluation and pointing out the 'token' nature of most of these efforts (Mathema, 1998; ADB, 1999b; 2001a). The policy documents in many South Asian countries drafted on empowerment of women have only initiated the first steps. The entrenched systems that defend the status quo against improving gender balances pose many hurdles for concrete actions to take shape.

The gender ideologies that adversely impact upon women are predominant in the region in spite of the development noted by conventional well-being indicators. Thus, even in the most developed country in terms of female educational attainment, life expectancy, low fertility rates, better survival of girls and so on, Sri Lanka also witnesses certain resilient stereotypes. Many policy makers and administrators continue to view women as 'dependent wives' or 'supplementary earners' to be used as labour reserve (ADB, 1999a). Despite extension of women's economic roles and women's work participation increasing, the inequitable gender division of labour within households has changed very little. Household work is seen as 'women's work' and most women in the region tend to internalize these norms.

The responsibility of household work that is almost entirely upon women often acts as a deterrent to their participation in paid economic activities. The work burden and time taken to undertake these domestic chores, often makes the kind of regular and timely participation required within a highly competitive labour market, difficult for women. Women, in negotiating the public and private domains, are doubly burdened, and those belonging to the socio-economically backward sections of the population have an added burden borne out of caste-based subjugation. The economically active women participating in paid work spheres but out of compulsion, for survival, may be empowered to some extent, however such changes do not generate alterations in other spaces, thereby not challenging or contesting the power position bestowed upon them under patriarchal structures.

The poverty-induced, vulnerability-led economic participation of rural women in South Asian countries is often highlighted and the increasing feminization tendencies noted were used as indicators of enhancing financial crisis experienced by households ever since the economic reforms pressures intensified. In India, women belonging to the economically backward communities that coincide with the Scheduled Castes, Scheduled Tribes and Other Backward Castes (OBCs) have a significantly larger proportion of workers among them as compared to the upper castes where women are not allowed to undertake manual paid labour activities generally. The lower social position occupied by these castes, their poorer access to land and productive resources as compared to other castes leaves these households and the women with few options other than supplying their labour services for a livelihood.

The other relatively smaller segment of the organized sector employment in India, where the share of women's participation has been rising over the years, even displacing men from these coveted job spheres, is the result of the increasing educational attainment levels among women. Most of these working women belong to the socio-economically better-off sections of Indian population, while the bulk of female employment remains in the unorganized, insecure and unprotected segments.

The entry of women into paid work, the compulsions and voluntary elements that allow for its acceptance in erstwhile hostile socio-cultural environs trace the changes witnessed in the economic spheres that display seemingly more flexible regimes as compared to the complex institutions governing female bodies, marriage, reproduction, sexuality and so on. The non-linearity and disparate change in different domains—the socio-cultural as compared to the economic, for instance—add to the contradictory signals and defy simple explanations. This understanding, however, contests the notions of inflexibility and rigidity of norms and structures, and highlights the dynamism of these institutional processes and the non-fixity of how these evolve under different situations.

Instances abound across the region to indicate how changes are occurring and the conflicting outcomes for gender equality and empowerment that are witnessed. In Maldives, the traditional participation of women in public spaces was marked by the absence of overt gender discrimination and women of the archipelago have been described as the "most emancipated in the Islamic world" since they did not practice *purdah* (veiling) or seclusion (ADB, 2001a). In the changing modern context with economic development, women's traditional roles are redefined and even in spite of educational attainment, their participation in the new sectors of employment such as tourism, entertainment, mechanized fish processing remains restricted (UNDP, 2000). Gender differences and stereotypes are beginning to be noted in the current scenario quite starkly.[8] These patterns are visible in all the South Asian countries, irrespective of the varied levels of social, cultural, political, legal and economic development.

Rural Women's Work in South Asia: Issues and Challenges for Empowerment

Three basic issues define the vulnerability and lower status assigned to rural women's work in South Asia. First is the issue of invisibility, the non-recognition of women's entire contribution to the economy, since it is conceptually viewed as directed towards the household or family and hence remains unaccounted. Secondly, rural women's excessive concentration in traditional or conventional tasks and occupations, many of which tend to intermingle with their non-economic or extended economic activities (that is, extended SNA or System of National Accounting activities that have remained outside the purview of Gross Domestic Product or GDP calculations) are unpaid most of the times and this leaves such women unenumerated, that is, not counted as workers. Thirdly, the structure of the labour market and its operational dynamics, which keeps women employed predominantly in unorganized sector, in low paid, low skilled, manual and monotonous jobs. The sex role based stereotyping and gender division of labour that is prevalent in all categories of employment, irrespective of educational and skill development, exhibits resilience that is a derivative and extension of socio-cultural gender subordination experienced by women. This explains why even policy makers and administrators continue to view women as 'secondary workers' and 'supplementary earners' very often discounting or affecting their access to government programme-based employment, earnings and other benefits.

It is noteworthy that despite tremendous variations across the South Asian countries, these basic elements hold relevance for all women belonging to this region. Women are concentrated in primary sector activities, largely subsistence oriented and low in productivity. A large chunk of the women are self-employed, unpaid family workers or home-based contractual workers. The working environment is poor, and security or protection levels are non-existent. Except for a few women, who are educated, professionally qualified, employed in formal sector jobs that are secure and protected, a large mass of them are struggling for a livelihood to survive in the unorganized segments of the economy.

Before discussing the sector-specific, area or country-wise instances of rural women's economic work participation, it is worth mentioning the activities that involve women but do not get calculated as economic contribution. The role played by women in the care sector, predominantly their reproductive work (bearing, rearing, nurturing children and household maintenance), falls outside the national accounting systems that are followed by different countries. While these activities are crucial for household members' well-being and effective participation in different spheres—economic, social and political—they continue to remain non-economic activities. By virtue of women performing these roles which are statistically not counted as economic and hence not monetarily valued, women's roles and their contribution are assigned a lower status.

Efforts to prepare satellite accounts which can capture women's work through alternative methods such as time use surveys are ongoing to overcome the existing limitations. Nepal among the South Asian countries has pioneered in the preparation of such statistics as part of their national level labour force surveys (Acharya, 2000). India has also undertaken a pilot survey (CSO, 2000). HDSA (2000) based on some observations suggests that South Asian women work for 10 to 12 hours per day, which is 2-4 hours more than men's work.

Women's contribution in activities that are recognized by definition as economic activities also remains unrecognized and non-enumerated. This is due to cultural and traditional values that constrain recognition of women's economic participation. In the South Asian countries, the historically derived gender roles, spaces and stereotypes of the 'public' male breadwinner (provider) and 'private' female care-giver are espoused even under changing situations. This is due to the association of household status with women's non-work that has been perpetuated by the circumstances of women having to supply their labour in the paid market work spheres under extreme economic stress and poverty. It is ironical that at times even the opposition to changing gender roles comes from women themselves who have internalized its social construction.

In South Asia, the interaction between religious and cultural beliefs and economic forces reinforces patriarchal cultures. Clearly, value or self-worth of women might have been set very high, if measured based on their indispensability to the household. Hanna Papanek (1990), highlighting the outcome of such 'symbolic' work rather than its content, terms them as 'family status-production work'. A shift from emphasizing upon women's worth or 'value' to others in the socialization process, to focus upon their own sense of value to themselves—their sense of self-worth—are crucial to understand the persistence of inequality and evolving basic strategies for change.

Questioning why children (who are witness to the work undertaken and gender division of labour) as well as women do not unlearn these norms of inequality ingrained through the process of socialization, Papanek explains these through what she calls the existence of 'escalator hierarchies'. Age and gender differences confer power on some over others in societies such as those of South Asia, wherein the young and powerless must await their turn to enjoy control over others as they age. Rebellion endangers this possibility and hence unlearning is made more difficult (Papanek, 1990).

A large proportion of women's work undertaken within the household, for the family as unpaid workers, remains unaccounted due to the conceptual, methodological and definitional flaws. The percentage of women workers ranges from 22 in Maldives to 42 in Bangladesh (see Table 2.5). Since no comparable rural women's work participation figures are available for all the countries, the statistics used here are based on other secondary sources which follow disparate definitions.

Table 2.5
Sectoral Distribution of Labour Force in South Asia

Country	*Percentage Labour Force (Men + Women) in*			*Percentage of Female Workers*
	Agriculture	*Industry*	*Services*	
India	62	11	27	32
Pakistan	47	20	33	27
Bangladesh	59	13	28	42
Nepal	93	1	6	40
Sri Lanka	49	21	30	36
Bhutan	92	3	5	32
Maldives	25	32	43	22

Source: MHHDC, 1997, 2000.

A large majority of South Asian labour force is involved in primary sector activities—agriculture, hunting, forestry and fisheries. As per the latest comparable figures used by

Mukhopadhyay (1999), nearly 94 per cent of women in Nepal, and between 70 to 80 per cent in Bangladesh, India and Pakistan are to be found in the primary sector. Rural women in South Asia participate in crop farming, animal husbandry and a host of off-farm activities. A substantial amount of time is spent by South Asian women in looking after livestock, from rearing to protecting animals, finding and collecting fodder and water, collecting eggs, milking, ensuring the health of animals, poultry, etc.

Bhutan[9], a landlocked country, independent (never colonized), self-contained rural economy that is seeking a sustainable relationship with nature, pursuing the goal of maximizing people's happiness[10] is operating on the Buddhist philosophy of "need rather than greed". Only 8 per cent of its land is cultivated, while 70 per cent is under forest cover. An estimated 65,000 farming families own, on average, 1.5 hectares of agricultural landholdings per household (RGoB, 2000). Women's participation in traditional roles has been vital, however, their participation in government jobs remains low due to educational constraints.

The share of agriculture in GDP has been showing a declining trend in most countries of the region, however intensification in feminization of agriculture over time is noted, except in Bangladesh where share of women in agriculture declined from 50 per cent in 1991 to 47 per cent in 1995-96. In India, women workers as a percentage of total workers in agriculture rose from 37.6 per cent in 1972-73 to 39.4 per cent in 1993-94. In Pakistan, they rose from 14.3 per cent in 1984-85 to 21.1 per cent in 1993-94. In Sri Lanka, they increased from 27.6 per cent in 1953 to 34.6 per cent in 1990. In Nepal, there has been an increase of female share in the agricultural workforce—from 35.5 per cent in 1971 to a high of 45 per cent in 1991 (Mukhopadhyay, 1999). Male involvement in agriculture has undergone a rapid decline over the years. Women are entering subsistence farming activities to fill the void created by men who move to better job avenues or migrate in search of more lucrative employment.

Commercialization of agriculture and changing cropping patterns that have impacted and altered the gender division of labour and increased female labour use are noted with operation-wise changes. However, these changes have occurred strictly within the parameters of gender hierarchies. The diversification of cropping pattern and labour use systems involving women are not seen to be associated with greater control over earnings (ICIMOD, 1997). In the cotton cultivation undertaken in Pakistan, women predominantly do the job of picking cotton (UNDP, 2003). In Sri Lanka, most of the agricultural women workers are involved in the plantations sector (UNDP, 1998). In India too, women are employed in the cultivation of vegetables, floriculture and other new innovative crops.

Rural women's labour in traditional sectors such as post-harvest activities and fish processing has been affected by mechanization, modernization and automation, and very often they have been displaced. Instances of these abound across the South Asian countries. Mechanized rice mills in rural Bangladesh have displaced women involved in manual paddy pounding (*dhenki*) (Mukhopadhyay, 1999). Similar instances are also available from India. Maldivian women, known for their higher work participation, were involved in the processing of 'Maldive fish'—a delicacy exported to Sri Lanka as well. Downstream fish processing activities, such as preparation of frozen, canned, chilled/fresh and salted/dried fish for export market, occupy a bulk of local Maldivian labour force.

The point that has been highlighted and needs to be re-emphasized is that the problem or fault does not *per se* lie in technology, but with the social context of women's work in traditional systems (Sen, 1984). Technological innovations occur in tasks that are generally undertaken by men; alternatively mechanized tasks displace women replacing men instead. Associated with these changes are skill impartation and higher wages for such tasks that in effect go to men and are viewed as being usurped by them. These changes are definitely linked to the prevalent gender ideologies that undermine the significance and due returns of women's work.

The transformation of economic structures in South Asia, which have followed a shift or easing of dependence on agriculture, focusing on non-agricultural growth, have had limited impact on employment patterns, especially in rural areas and certainly in the context of women. The post-liberalization period with increased emphasis on export orientation and opening up the economy for trade have accompanied the shift of countries from being net exporters of food grains to net importers of larger quantities of food grains. The Nepal HDR, 2001 noted that 45 districts of Nepal have recently been officially declared as food deficit (UNDP, 2002). Given the household responsibility sharing, with women 'in-charge' of food preparation and home management, the inadequacy, shortage or constraints in the sphere of food consumption, often victimizes women, even resulting in domestic violence towards them.

The inequalities in landownership, trends towards concentration of landholdings pushing small and marginal farmers into a state of landlessness, have implications for food security levels within poorer households and the heightening of vulnerabilities that define livelihood strategies for majority of the rural women.

Traditional avenues in the off-farm and non-agricultural spheres that occupied women and served as buffers in times of resource constraints, if not as regular income generation activities, have also been eroded in most areas. Shift to alternative cheaper, bulk produced commodities has affected handlooms, textiles, pottery and a range of handicrafts.

Manufacturing activities in industrial enterprises and factory units under one roof or complex where workers came together to work are giving way to contractual, sub-contractual, piece rated, home-based work. This has implications for women's recognition as workers, their organization or possibility of a united voice, which in turn impact upon levels of economic empowerment.

Since the 1980s, the aggregate growth of Bangladeshi economy has been steady but slow. The share of non-agriculture in the total rural employed population rose from 29 per cent to 34 per cent (1981-1994). The rise in this share of non-agricultural employment has been higher for rural female employed population. A large number of women workers in Bangladesh are young, mainly single, although some are divorced, abandoned or married as well (ADB, 2001b). Such patterns of deployment are noted in the context of other sectors, such as fish processing, export processing zones, electronics and so on in India and Sri Lanka too.

Even in these new export-oriented industries, such as garments, footwear, electronics, pharmaceuticals, and food processing sectors, gender discriminatory practices in terms of tasks and skill levels of women workers and their pay and working conditions, remains unchanged (Unni, 2001; MHHDC, 2000).

Trading activities in certain countries, communities and specific areas within South Asia are undertaken by women (e.g., Bhutan, Manipur in north-eastern region of India, fish sellers in Maldives and other fishing communities of India and so on). Among other services, an extension of socially acceptable and traditional role stereotypes is commonly noted, as in education, health and care sectors where women are concentrated.

In Nepal, of the 7 per cent rural women workforce involved in non-agricultural activities, nearly half of them are in the services sector. Poor working environment and socially defined constraints and difficulties for women entrepreneurs are noted as additional factors delimiting women's non-agricultural participation.

Poor ownership and access to economically productive assets forms a strategic constraint affecting women's nature of economic participation in Nepal (ADB, 1999b). The unequal inheritance laws reinforced by social norms define women's limited access to productive assets. The socialization into unpaid, low productivity, low skilled and low paid work begins early in women's lives since education of females is assigned low priority. The population of girl child labourers exceeds as compared to boys (UNDP, 2002). The arguments that these are compulsions of poverty are challenged by the gender iniquitous patterns of child work participation.

In India, the impetus within governance structures to stress on economic participation of women initially began with an association to poverty reduction. The female-headed households being predominantly poverty ridden and the earnings of these women being utilized for better provisioning of basic needs, such as food, nutrition, education, health care, as opposed to their male counterparts, lends further support to encourage women undertaking paid work (Hoddinott, 1992; Kabeer, 1994). The policy shift from doling out welfare schemes to focus upon elimination of constraints such as being undertaken through provision of micro-credit and self-help group formation is one such initiative. The limitations to benefit from these effectively display multiple axes of discrimination that women face due to caste, class and gender.

In the tiny idyllic archipelago of Maldives, nearly one-third to one-half of all households are reported to be female-headed households. Women claim this is based on "their desire to be in-charge". Yet, the social norm that is applicable legally too, is that girls and women will have a legal guardian (normally the male head of the household). It is also a fact that large numbers of women are trapped in the quagmire of early marriage, with a majority of them having limited autonomy in household decision-making. The islands are also known for one of the highest rates of divorces and remarriages in the entire region with no social taboos associated to these practices. The freedom to choose partners, the social sanction for remarriage under the changing circumstances of monetary relations and market-based existences puts undue pressures that have the effect of negating the element of freedom in these choices.

The labour force participation rates (LFPR) in Maldives fell from 72 per cent in 1977 to 20 per cent in 1990. This decline can be partly explained by the reduction in women's involvement in fish preservation (dry fish) activities due to mechanization and export of raw rather than dry fish as well as the limited opportunities for higher education due to both geographical and infrastructural constraints. There has been a drastic decline in female LFPR in agriculture, and women have not been able to benefit from the boom in tourism by direct employment due to socio-cultural constraints and gender biased mindsets. The poor access to higher education as well as the social taboos against work in the entertainment industry has limited the possibility of women benefiting from tourism sector that heavily employs expatriates from other South Asian countries (ADB, 2001a). The inaccessibility to own incomes often compels the women to opt for quicker remarriages for ensuring financial security.

In Bangladesh, the government and Non-Government Organizations (NGO) sector have helped create self- and contractual employment for nearly 15 per cent of rural women (above the age of 15 years) (ADB, 2001b). There are over 1,000 local and national organizations in Bangladesh that generate self-employment opportunities for over 8 million poor, mostly women, through micro-credit, training in literacy, technical skills, and legal rights. Similar efforts are ongoing in other parts of South Asia as well.

The employment-based cooperatives, such as in dairying, textiles, specific agro-based food items that operate with assistance from government and NGOs are other efforts that are increasingly being viewed from the angle of their potential for economic empowerment of women.

In the context of declining employment avenues, and women's participation being residual in nature, the challenge is to plan for pro-poor, labour absorbing growth avenues and address the problems of underemployment and unemployment. Another critical dimension is to effectively implement minimum and gender-equal wages along with social security measures. If women workers are treated equally in the labour market, and paid fair wages, then, this can impact to a certain extent upon their economic empowerment. However, the overall structural and institutional changes to move towards greater freedom to decide, autonomy and control over earnings for women requires an overhauling of the social perceptions and mindsets within families, labour markets, the state as well as women themselves, regarding their role, status, worth or value—all of which are constituents of the process inching towards empowerment.

Concluding Remarks

In today's world, value and worth are inevitably equated with monetary calculations and considerations. As mentioned by Kelkar et al. (2004: 3638), in the context of redefining dignity ('*samman*') for women involved in the micro-credit initiatives to help generate incomes for poor, needy rural Bangladeshis: "In a cash economy, it is earning of cash income that brings respect". Various studies in the region and elsewhere have emphasized the importance of economic empowerment for improving women's status and enhancing their autonomy levels (Mukhopadhyay, 1999).

A survey-based study by PIDE, Pakistan on women's autonomy notes that paid employment and women's contribution to family income emerge as the most important determinant of women's intra-household decision-making authority (Sathar and Kazi, 1997). Even women's own perceptions about their own work and contribution changes with income or organizational mobilization and awareness generation (Antony, 2001; Kelkar et al., 2004). This has even been linked and associated with estimations of stress and tiredness experienced by women to note that there seems to be a decline in mental distress levels (Sonpar and Kanbur, 2003). However, new market roles that are expected to involve women need not necessarily bring about greater empowerment, since "the old order of hierarchies may persist and new forms of subordination may surface, reinforcing the unequal power equations between the sexes" (Mukhopadhyay and Sudarshan, 2003: 22). Instances of these have been discussed in various spheres of women's lives across the countries of the region.

South Asian social structures are indeed very complex and uniquely hierarchical. They not only define status, power and dignity, but also impinge on decisions and nature of economic participation. Therefore, women belonging to certain sections of society will not enter the labour market at all, while many others abstain from working as paid employees. The overwhelming presence of women in South Asia working as home-based informal sector workers or as self-employed is partly a derivative of the social values stemming from patriarchal norms that put limitations on women's mobility and constrain their economic participation in public spheres. To encourage women's participation, some of the South Asian countries have introduced policies of reservation in government jobs. In Bangladesh, 10 to 15 per cent and in Pakistan, 20 per cent government jobs are reserved for women (UNIFEM, 2003).

Economic empowerment clearly cannot be indicated on the basis of participation rates alone, nor is paid work by women in public spheres indicative of increasing freedom and choice for women. Education and skill development are two components that are often cited as essential for women's empowerment. In fact, the MDGs and various governmental efforts tend to delimit the approach to empowerment by emphasizing upon women's education. It is important to avoid perceiving empowerment of women as a goal or objective to be attained, since it is essentially a process and under the given circumstances within South Asia, requires multi-dimensional approaches to ensure movement towards the paths that lead to eliminating inequalities and discriminations faced by women. While there can be no denial of the positive offshoots of human capital development traits, these alone cannot transform the gender imbalances stemming from perceptions and mindsets that have not accepted women as equals in social, economic and political domains.

■ Notes

1. The seven countries are India, Pakistan, Bangladesh, Sri Lanka, Nepal, Bhutan and Maldives.
2. There is virtually no comparable data on rural women for all the countries of South Asia that can be used for purposes of this paper. Also, the definitions and categorization adopted by different countries differ.
3. There are countries and communities across parts of South Asia where matriliny is followed. Among Muslims, women do inherit a share of ancestral and parental property, albeit unequal in comparison to men, who are also legal guardians of all other dependants in the family.
4. Gender-related development index (GDI) is a composite index measuring average achievement in three basic dimensions captured in the human development index (HDI) adjusted to account for inequalities between men and women.
5. Gender-empowerment measure (GEM) is based on three dimensions of empowerment that measure gender inequality in economic participation and decision-making, political participation and decision-making and power over economic resources.
6. The HDSA, 2003 notes that in South Asia another 500 million persons will enter the labour force in the next five years which is equivalent to the total population of the European Union (expanded with 25 countries).
7. Many of them have benefited from the reservations policy of their respective governments.
8. Prior to Maldives becoming a Republic, three Maldivian queens ruled among the several monarchs, however, today as per the constitution revised in 1998, being male is a necessary qualification for being elected as President or Vice-President of Maldives. On the other hand, in the year 2000, three women were given the authority to deliver religious sermons and counseling, a role they were not entitled to perform earlier (UNDP, 2002; ADB, 2001a).
9. Bhutan is one of the least researched upon area in the region and is often left out from analysis since there is relatively very little information available.
10. Bhutan introduced a new index in its national HDR (RGOB, 2000) called the Gross National Happiness (GNH) based on the conceptual frame that development does not mean a blind expansion of commodity

production. Instead, a holistic view of life and development is called for that augments people's spiritual and emotional well-being as well.

■ References

Acharya, Meena. 2000 'Women and the Economy in Nepal'. Background Paper for the HDSA 2000 (cited in MHHDC, 2000).

ADB (Asian Development Bank). 1999a. 'Women in Sri Lanka': Country Briefing Paper. Available at http://www.adb.org/Documents/Books/Country_Briefing_Papers/default.asp

—. 1999b. 'Women in Nepal:' Country Briefing Paper. Available at http://www.adb.org/Documents/Books/Country_Briefing_Papers/Women_in_Nepal/women_nepal.pdf

—. 2000. 'Women in Pakistan:' Country Briefing paper. Available at http://www.adb.org/Documents/Books/Country_Briefing_Papers/default.asp

—. 2001a. 'Women in the Republic of Maldives:' Country Briefing Paper. Available at http://www.adb.org/Documents/Books/Country_Briefing_Papers/default.asp

—. 2001b. 'Women in Bangladesh:' Country Briefing Paper. Available at http://www.adb.org/Documents/Books/Country_Briefing_Papers/Women_in_Bangladesh/women_ban.pdf

Agarwal, B. 1994. *A Field of One's Own: Gender and Land Rights in South Asia.* Cambridge: Cambridge University Press.

Antony, Piush. 2001 *Towards Empowerment: Experiences of Organising Women Workers.* New Delhi: ILO.

Arnold, Fred. 2001. 'Son Preference in South Asia', in Sathar and Phillips (eds.), *Fertility Transition in South Asia*, pp. 281-299.

Aturupane, Harsha. 1996. *Unemployment among Educated Women in Sri Lanka.* Colombo: Department of National Planning.

Banerjee, Narayan. 2004. Nari Bikash Sangha: 'Towards Empowerment', *Indian Journal of Gender Studies*, 11(2): 179-203.

Beteille, Andre. 1994. 'Empowerment', *Economic and Political Weekly*, 34(10 &11): 589-597.

Carr, M., Chen, M. and Jhabvala, R. (eds.). 1996. *Speaking Out: Women's Economic Empowerment in South Asia.* New Delhi: Vistaar Publications.

CSO. 2000. Report of the Time Use Survey, Ministry of Statistics and Programme Implementation, New Delhi: Government of India.

Ganesh, Kamala and Risseeuw, C. 1998. 'Introduction: Gendered Change in Marriage and Family: A Policy Concern' in Risseeuw, Carla and Kamala Ganesh (eds.), *Negotiation and Social Space: A Gendered Analysis of*

Changing Kin and Security Networks in South Asia and Sub-Saharan Africa, New Delhi: Sage, pp. 11-43.

Garcia, Brigida (ed.). 2000. *Women, Poverty and Demographic Change*, New York: Oxford University Press.

GoB (Government of Bangladesh). 1996. Report on Labour Force Survey in Bangladesh, 1995-96. Dhaka: Bangladesh Bureau of Statistics (cited in Mukhopadhyay, 1999).

Hirway, Indira and Mahadevia, Darshini. 1996. 'Critique of Gender Development Index: Towards an Alternative', *Economic and Political Weekly*, 31(43): WS87-WS96.

Hoddinott, J. 1992. 'Household Economics and the Economics of the Household'. Paper presented at the IFPRI/World Bank Conference on Intra-Household Allocation, IFPRI, Washington, 12-14 February.

ICIMOD. 1997 *From Subsistence Farming to Market Oriented Enterprises: A Study of Vegetable Growing Farmers in Garampani Area*, Nainital District, India. Study by K.N. Badhani, Kathmandu: International Centre for Integrated Mountain Development (ICIMOD).

Kabeer, Naila. 1994 *Reversed Realities: Gender Hierarchies in Development Thought*, New Delhi: Kali for Women.

Kalpagam, U.2000 'Life Experiences, Resistance and Feminist Consciousness', *Indian Journal of Gender Studies*, 7(2): 167-84.

Karlekar, Malavika. 2004. 'A Note on Empowerment of Women', *Indian Journal of Gender Studies*, 11(2): 145-155.

Kelkar, Govind, Nathan, D. and Jahan, R. 2004. 'Redefining Women's 'Samman': Microcredit and Gender Relations in Rural Bangladesh', *Economic and Political Weekly*, 39(32): 3627-40.

Krishnaji, N. 1997. 'Human Development Index: A Critique', *Economic and Political Weekly*, 35(14): 1161-63.

Malhotra, Anju and DeGraff, Deborah S. 2000. *Daughters and Wives: Marital Status, Poverty and Young Women's Employment in Sri Lanka in Garcia* (ed.), pp. 145-174.

Mathema, Madhuri. 1998. Women in South Asia: Pakistan, Bangladesh, and Nepal in Stromquist (ed.), pp. 583-92.

MHHDC. 1997. *Human Development in South Asia 1997*, Karachi: Oxford University Press.

—. 2000. *Human Development in South Asia 2000: The Gender Question*, Karachi: Oxford University Press.

—. 2003. *Human Development in South Asia 2003: The Employment Challenge*, Karachi: Oxford University Press.

Mukhopadhyay, S. 1999. 'Women's Work in South Asia: A Situational Analysis and Policy Concerns'. South Asia Multidisciplinary Advisory Team (SAAT). New Delhi: ILO, June.

Mukhopadhyay, Swapna and Sundarshan, Ratna M. (eds.). 2003. *Tracking Gender Equity Under Economic Reforms: Continuity and Change in South Asia*, New Delhi: IDRC and Kali for Women.

Papanek, Hanna. 1990. 'To Each Less Than She Needs, From Each More Than She Can Do: Allocations, Entitlements, and Value' in Irene Tinker (ed.), *Persistent Inequalities: Women and World Development*, New York: Oxford, pp. 162-181.

RGoB (Royal Government of Bhutan). 2000. Bhutan National Human Development Report 2000 – Gross National Happiness and Human Development: Searching for Common Ground. Planning Commission. Available at http://www.undp.org

Rustagi, Preet. 2004. 'Women and Development in South Asia', *South Asian Journal*, No. 4, April-June, Pakistan.

Sangari, Kumkum. 1995. 'Politics of Diversity: Religious Communities and Multiple Patriarchies', *Economic and Political Weekly*, 30(51 and 52): 3287-310 and 3381-89.

Sathar, Zeba and Shahnaz Kazi. 1997. 'Women's Autonomy, Livelihood and Fertility'. PIDE. Cited in UNDP. 2003.

Sen, A.K. 1984. *Women, Technology and Sexual Divisions*, Oxford: All Souls College.

Sonpar, Shobna and Kanbur, Ravi. 2003. 'Non-Conventional Indicators of Gender Disparities Under Structural Reforms' in Mukhopadhyay and Sudarshan (eds.), pp. 24-63.

Stromquist, Nelly P. (ed.). 1998. *Women in the Third World: An Encyclopedia of Contemporary Issues*, New York and London: Garland Publishing.

UNDP (United Nations Development Programme). Various years 1990-2004. *Human Development Report.* New York: Oxford University Press.

—. 1996. Report on Human Development in Bangladesh. Dhaka: UNDP.

—. 1998. Sri Lanka Human Development Report 1998. Colombo. Available at http://www.undp.org.

—. 2000. Maldives Human Development Report: Challenges and Responses. Male: Ministry of Planning and National Development and UNDP, December. Available at http://www.undp.org

—. 2002. Nepal Human Development Report 2001: Poverty Reduction and Governance. Kathmandu: UNDP.

—. 2003. Pakistan National Human Development Report 2002. Karachi: Oxford University Press.

UNFPA. 1999. *The State of the World Population*. New York: UNFPA.

UNIFEM. 2003. *Progress of South Asian Women* 2003. New Delhi: UNIFEM.

Unni, Jeemol. 2001. 'Gender and Informality in Labour Market in South Asia', *Economic and Political Weekly*, 36(26): 2360-2377.

Chapter 3

Gender Discrimination in South Asia

Seema Joshi

The beginning of UN Decade for Women (1976-85) created a keen interest among researchers, policy makers, international organizations and economists in gender issues throughout the world. Gender equality was declared as a fundamental right in the charter of the United Nations signed in 1945. The UN General Assembly adopted "Convention on the Elimination of All Forms of Discrimination Against Women" on December 18, 1979 which came into force on September 3, 1981. Further, the target 4 of Millennium Development Goal 3 (emanating from the UN Millennium Declaration, 2000) binds all the 189 committed member-countries (of UN), including India, to do more to promote gender equality and empower women as it aims at eliminating gender disparity in primary and secondary education, preferably by 2005 and in all levels of education not later than 2015 (UNDP, 2003). In spite of many conventions, policies and goals, the world statistics present a dismal and deplorable condition of the state of women. However, the extent of anti-female bias or discrimination against women is far worse in South Asia than in most other developing countries. The fact of gender discrimination is highly despicable; female disadvantage in infant and child survival is a well documented phenomenon in the South Asian countries. It starts as soon as the girl child is conceived and becomes more visible in early childhood itself and continues in later stages of life through the unequal provision of education, health care, nutrition, to the world of work in terms of segmentation of labour market on the basis of sex, occupational segregation and male-female wage differential. There are various forms of gender inequality prevalent in this region. As has aptly been remarked by Nobel laureate Amartya Sen, "..... gender inequality is not one homogeneous phenomenon, but a collection of disparate and interlinked problems" (Sen, 2001). He points towards multi-faceted nature of gender inequality which can assume different forms varying from mortality inequality to natal inequality, basic facility inequality to special opportunity inequality, professional inequality to ownership inequality or household inequality. Studies reveal that gender discrimination (whatsoever may be its form) tends to hamper growth via creating inefficiencies (World Bank, 1995). There is strong empirical evidence showing that "investing in women will generate important benefits for society in the form of lower child mortality, educational attainment, better nutrition and slower population growth. Investing in women ensures the quality and sustainability of economic growth" (World Bank, 1995).[1]

Despite the fact that it is being globally recognized that more investment in basic services, which are used more by women and which can add to their productive capacity and thereby lead to higher capital formation and consequently to higher growth, should be done, yet intra-household gender inequalities in allocation of resources (food, health care, nutrition, etc.) are prevalent in developing countries (Dreze and Sen, 1989; Hariss, 1990; Agarwal, 1986; Sen, 1985; Agarwal, 1997) and South Asian countries are no exception to this trend. The less number of female vs male children, high female child mortality rates, adverse and even declining sex ratio of women to men reflect the discrimination and neglect of the girl child in the pre-market entry phase. It is important to point out that instead of rewarding women for combining and performing three important roles, viz., reproductive role, productive role and managing work (Moser and Levy, 1986), penalties and costs are being imposed on them in the labour market in the form of the segregation of labour market into feminine and masculine occupations, their concentration in low paid and low productivity jobs (sales and service sector) or in "atypical form of occupations" and have to undergo wage inequalities (ILO, 1995). Further, introduction of structural adjustment programme in this region has added to their woes. As has been pointed out by Heyzer (1994: 12), "for many women, structural adjustment programmes mean longer hours of work, paid and unpaid; maintaining households on reduced resources and taking more time in looking for cheap goods, setting up informal support networks etc." Besides this, to reduce cost of production, there takes place casualization of women's work in the informal sector as well as in the formal sector through sub-contracting. The tall claim of 'increased efficiency' is made by transferring cost from the paid economy to the unpaid work of women as they have to devote more time in the care of young, elderly and sick. Some studies in recent times even point towards the need for correcting certain labour market failures which penalize motherhood (Arun et al., 2004; Bittman, 1999; Dex and Joshi, 1999) for combining it with employment. Some others like Tinker (1976: 34) emphasize that "planners must not only consider and support women's economic activities but must also find ways of mitigating the drudgery of housework and the responsibility of child rearing. The roles assigned to each sex must again be made more equal—with men as well as women accepting their dual roles of work and family". It is obvious that real development cannot take place by bypassing women, who are the pillars of society and constitute half of the total world population.

It is in this context that the present study would be highly relevant and useful. Its empirical focus will be on two sets of discrimination, which women in South Asian region have to undergo or suffer:

(1) Gender discrimination at the pre-market phase: this gets reflected in lack of access to resources like education, health

care, training experience and other factors which enhance human capabilities and raise marginal productivity.

(2) Gender discrimination at post-labour market entry phase: this includes gender discrimination pervasive in specific sectors, occupations and wage differential between sexes.

Pre-entry Human Capital Discrimination in South Asia

There are a number of studies (e.g., Dreze and Sen, 1989; Anand and Ravallion, 1993) emphasizing upon the role of economic growth and state intervention in the process of human development. Economic growth helps in human development through reduction in poverty, improving access to basic social services and building up of basic capabilities in the people (Taylor, Mehrotra and Delamonica, 1997). The process of human capital formation contributes to human development and thereby to economic growth, as human development not only enhances well-being or quality of life of people, but it also adds to productive capacities of people. Therefore, economic growth and human development are interdependent. The activities covered under social sector contribute to human capital formation and thereby to human development and are, therefore, recognized as critical inputs in improving the human development index (Joshi, 2003).

It is well recognized that social infrastructure is as critical for human resource development as physical infrastructure. The crucial role played by social infrastructure in today's world can be judged from the fact that the new century opened with an unprecedented display of international commitment to improve the lives of poor people everywhere, when 189 members of the United Nations issued the Millennium Declaration at the Millennium Summit in 2000. The eight Millennium Development Goals and their 18 targets emanating from the Millennium Declaration cover the essential conditions for human development (UNDP, 2003). "Five of the eight goals and one of the two prongs (i.e., investing in people and improving the investment climate) of the (World Bank's) strategy for development concern health and education signals how central human development is to human welfare" (WDR, 2004). It has been aptly remarked in World Development Report (2004) that economic growth though essential to reach all of these goals will not be enough. Therefore, focusing on the human development goals, the WDR describes the reforms in services (especially education, health, water sanitation and electricity) to achieve them (Joshi, 2003). But no policy measure can be successful if it bypasses women. That is why, gender equality and empowerment of women has been declared as one of the eight Millennium Development Goals (MDGs). The WDR further says, "education contributes to better health, and better education and health increase the productivity that lead to economic growth. Growth then generates resources that finance improvements in people's health and education, further raising productivity. Gender equality is central in these synergies because women are the agents of development" (UNDP, 2003: 7). The WDR also stresses that since women are the primary caregivers in almost all societies, the education of current generation of women will have positive effects on the education and health of their next generation (than that of men), the result will be yet more strong if they have a strong say in family decision-making. Better educated, healthier women of second generation will help in bringing down fertility rate, raising productivity and thereby help in raising household income. Since such women work outside home and earn independent incomes, their autonomy will get enhanced. "These beneficial processes have more force when women have a voice in household decisions. And, when women can take collective action to demand more rights—to education, health care, equal employment—these positive synergies are more likely" (ibid.: 8).

As pointed out earlier, the pre-entry human capital discrimination against women refers to lack of access to education, health and other sources, which can add to their knowledge, skills and capabilities. It can be observed from the Table 3.1 that at pre-market entry phase women encounter discrimination in combined primary, secondary and tertiary enrolment ratios and in adult literacy rates.

As the table shows, the enrolment rates for all levels of education have registered an increase in all countries of the South Asian region. However, enrolments are not rising in the same proportion in which population is increasing. The table further reveals that in the year 2000-01, with the exception of Sri Lanka and Bangladesh, in rest of the sample countries Combined Enrolment Ratio (CER) for females was lower than that of males.

Table 3.1

Pre-entry Human Capital Discrimination in Enrolment Ratios and Adult Literacy

(percentage)

Country	*Combined Primary, Secondary and Tertiary Enrolment Ratios (CER) (2000-01)*		*Adult Literacy (2001)*	
	Females	*Males*	*Females*	*Males*
Bangladesh	54	54	30.8	49.9
India	49	63	46.4	69.0
Nepal	57	70	25.2	60.5
Pakistan	27	45	28.8	58.2
Sri Lanka	64	63	89.3	94.5

Source: UNDP, *Human Development Report, 2003*, pp. 311-12.

In Sri Lanka, CER for females was higher and in Bangladesh it was equal to male CER. The CER for Pakistan was the lowest in the region.

The South Asian region has registered rapid progress in the field of education. In the year 1990, adult literacy rate of this region stood at 46 per cent and by the end of the decade in 2000 it reached 54 per cent—an increase of 8 percentage points (UNDP, 1993 and 2003). However, female adult literacy rate continued to be lower than that of male adult literacy rate in the period under consideration for all the sample countries. It may be pointed out here that the experience of all the five countries under study shows that literacy attainments for women have been relatively higher now but there is no guarantee of more employment for women as the unemployment rates among educated women were noticed to be higher than that for men.

Gender-Bias Nature of Human Development[2]

The foregoing discussion thus makes it clear that women are victims of pre-entry human capital discrimination. This discrimination also gets reflected in gender-bias nature of human development. Human Development Report (HDR), prepared on the eve of Beijing Conference on Women (1995), marked a clear-cut departure from the previous reports as for the first time human development performances of various countries were compared from a gender perspective. It was being recognized that although women's capabilities were increasing, corresponding opportunities are not forthcoming in equal proportion. The construction of two new indices, namely, Gender Development Index (GDI) and Gender Empowerment Measure (GEM), was an outcome of the recognition of the existing gap between capabilities and opportunities available. "GDI measures the unequal achievements of men and women in life expectancy, education and income—the components of HDI. Thus, greater the gender disparity in a country, the lower would be its GDI value as compared to its HDI. Theoretically speaking, if there is no gender discrimination in a country, its GDI value would be equal to its HDI value. The GEM, on the other hand, reflects the opportunities available to women rather than their capabilities. It captures gender inequalities in the economic and political life of a country" (MUHHDC, 2003: 18).

Thus, these three measures, viz., HDI, GDI, GEM, present a broad picture of the state of human development in a country.[3]

Table 3.2

Indicators of Human Development (2001): A Comparison

Country	*HDI*	*GDI*	*GEM*
Bangladesh	0.502	0.495	0.218
India	0.590	0.574	0.24*
Nepal	0.499	0.479	N.A.
Pakistan	0.499	0.469	0.414
Sri Lanka	0.741	0.726	0.272
South Asia	0.560*	0.542*	0.236*
Developing Countries	0.654*	0.634*	—

* Denotes that the figures are for the year 2000. The rest are for 2003.

Sources: UNDP, *Human Development Report*, 2000, 2001, 2002 & 2003.
Mahbub Ul Haq Human Development Centre, *Human Development in South Asia, 2003.*

As the Table 3.2 shows, South Asia had a GDI value of 0.542 in 2000. This value represents 96.8 per cent of its HDI value of 0.560 of 2000. However, one can observe from the Table 3.2 sharp variations in the HDI, GDI and GEM values across the five sample countries chosen for this study. The intra-regional comparison brings out the fact that Sri Lanka had the highest GDI, whereas Pakistan had the lowest. The GEM values for the entire sample (with the exception of Bangladesh) exceeded the average for South Asian countries. It can also be observed from Table 3.2 that Pakistan had highest value of GEM indicating that women in Pakistan were having more opportunities available to them. The shortfall in GDI expressed as a percentage of HDI shows the extent which human development was gender-biased in different countries of South Asia. Table 3.3 indicates that the shortfall was largest in case of Pakistan (6%), followed by Nepal (4%) indicating development was more inequitable.

Table 3.3

GDI Values as percentage of HDI Values

Country	*GDI (% of HDI)*	*Shortfall in GDI (% of HDI)*
Bangladesh	98.6	1.4
India	97.3	2.7
Nepal	96.0	4.0
Pakistan	94.0	6.0
Sri Lanka	98.0	2.0
South Asia	96.8	3.2
Developing Countries	—	—

Source: UNDP, *Human Development Report*, 2000, 2001 and 2003.

Gender Discrimination in Labour Market

Women in South Asian region not only suffer from pre-entry human capital discrimination but they also have to encounter what is known as post-market stage employment discrimination. Irrespective of how unemployment is being defined, Table 3.4 shows that it was higher amongst women as compared to men. As has been rightly pointed out by Deshpande (1993), "all kinds of post-entry discrimination faced by them can be rationalized with the help of pre-entry discrimination".

Table 3.4

Some Indicators of Gender Discrimination in Labour Market

Countries	*Female LFPR as a Percentage of Male in South Asia, 1980-2000*	*Female Percentage of Total Employment (1995-2001)*	*Unemployment Rates (1990-2000) (%)*	*Employment by Sectors (age 10 +), 1980-90 to 1991-99*	*Occupation*	*Wage Differential in % (2001)*
	1	*2*	*3*	*4*	*5*	*6*
Bangladesh	64	37.5	2.3 (2.7)	• Decrease in share of females in agricultural employment by 8.7% • Decrease in industry by 13.6% • Increase in services by 423.8%	• Self-employment as a percentage of non-agricultural employment increased by 56.6% over the period 1980-2000.	56.41
India	50	26.8	10.0 (7.0)	• Decrease in share of females in agricultural employment by 5.9% • Increase in industry by 0.2% • Increase in services by 37.8%	• Self-employment as a percentage of non-agricultural employment decreased by 25.5% over the period 1980-2000.	37.62

Contd...

Contd...

Nepal	92	50.0	0.7 (1.5)	• Decrease in females share in agricultural employment by 7.7% • Increase in industry by 1200% • Increase in services by 331.6%		59.64
Pakistan	18	14.0	14.9 (4.2)	• Decrease in females share in agricultural employment by 8.2% • Increase in industry by 25.5% • Increase in services by 71.1%	• Self-employment as a percentage of non-agricultural employment decreased by 15% over the period 1980-2000.	32.19
Sri Lanka	50	35.2	16.2 (7.1)	• Increase in females share in agricultural employment by 14.6% • Increase in industry by 0.9% • Increase in services by 13.6%		50.01

Note: In column 3, figures in the parentheses stand for male unemployment rate and the other one for female unemployment rate.

Sources: Based on Mahbub Ul Haq Human Development Centre, *Human Development in South Asia*, 2003; UNDP, *Human Development Report*, 2003.

Various indicators of labour market discrimination are relatively low Female Labour Force Participation Rate (FLFPR), low share of females in total employment, high unemployment rates among women and concentration of women in informal sector and also wage differential between men and women. These have been elaborated below:

Relative Low FLFPR, Low Share in Employment, High Unemployment Rate (Columns 1-3)

Coming now to the indicators of labour market discrimination one by one, column 1 shows the FLFPR as a percentage of MLFPR. It varied between Pakistan's 18 per cent to Nepal's 92 per cent. Further, it is also interesting to point out here that gap between FLFPR and MLFPR has widened in India, Pakistan and Nepal and narrowed down in Bangladesh and Sri Lanka over the period 1990-2000.

Column 2 indicates that female's share in total employment was as low as 14 per cent in Pakistan and as high as 50 per cent in Nepal. The existing gap between female and male labour force participation and employment rate (columns 1 & 2) is partially due to the gender gap in education between men and women in South Asia (MUHHDC, 2003).

Column 3 exhibits that there exists a gap between unemployment rates of women and men. Unemployment rate for females was found to be higher than that for men in India, Bangladesh and Pakistan and in the remaining two countries it was just the other way round. The higher unemployment rates for women implicitly point towards the fact that access of women to employment opportunities was limited. In a study Aganon (2000) identifies certain socio-cultural factors as give in Table 3.5 affecting employment of women at three different levels, in the three countries from South Asian region.[4]

In addition to these socio-cultural factors, higher unemployment rate among educated women may be due to the reason that many of them do not take up employment of their own violation and many others take up employment intermittently while raising their families.

Table 3.5
Socio-Cultural Factors Affecting Women's Participation in Productive Work

Country	*Family-related Aspects*	*Employment-related Aspects*	*Societal Constraints*
India	• Lack of help in household for sharing domestic responsibilities.		
Pakistan	• Husband's ego would be hurt if wife works • Criticism of in-laws, neighbours • Insult to family pride • There would be less attention to children • Brother opposition: due to socialization male role to protect and care for sister • Parent's gender role stereotyping	• Employer attitude/perception that women will discontinue work after marriage	• Notions on "Shama-o-mahfil or Chiragh-okhan" (docility, humility and submission). The sharper the break, the slower acceptance of changed role of women.
Bangladesh	• General socio-economic condition in combination with patri-viri family tradition result in lower class status of women in the family. • Both men and women are reluctant to have the two genders work side-by-side together. • Rural women mostly confined to household work under the purdah system.	• Sexual harassment • Low regard for women	• Rural society's traditional value system provides superior position to men • Religious factors alongside low levels of education bar women's employment

Source: Based on Aganon (2000), Survey Report (Integrated), *Changing Labour Market and Women Employment*, Asian Productivity Organization, Japan, pp.15-16.

South Asian Women: Invisible and Unrecognized Backbone of Agriculture[5] *(Column 4)*

South Asian women have been termed as the "invisible and unrecognized backbone of agriculture". This is mainly because of the reason that agriculture continued to be mainstay of two-third women despite declining trend in agriculture (as has been shown in column 4 of Table 3.4) witnessed by all the sample countries (with the exception of Sri Lanka) taken in this study. Within this sector, women not only perform varied kinds of roles like that of agricultural labourers, managers of homesteads, landowners etc., but they also participate in all agriculture operations related to livestock management, crop production etc. To add to it they do other unpaid household jobs (unlike their male counterparts) and unpaid work on family farms. But what is really condemnable is the fact that instead of recognizing and rewarding them for bearing heavy work burdens, they are being discriminated at home front and at other levels too whether it is access to credit or to other inputs or to wages.

Growth of Informal Sector and Conditions of Women Workers[6]

Another stark reality in majority of the South Asian countries is that the informal sector has been emerging as the main source of livelihood for both male as well as female workers. In the decade of 1990s the South Asian region accounted for highest share of the informal sector in total non-agricultural employment in the world. It is important to point out here that outside agriculture, the availability of self-employment opportunities was more in industry and trade. One of the main points of differences between female and male self-employment was that women were engaged more in industry (61% during 1990-2000), followed by services (23%) and trade (17%), whereas men were absorbed in trade (42%), followed by industry (34%) and services (24%). Higher percentage of women in industry than that of men also implicitly points towards feudalistic and patriarchal structures and socio-cultural norms prevalent in many countries of the region which prevent mobility of women and limit them to home-based work in manufacturing.

Country-wise data available on self-employment as a percentage of non-agricultural employment during the period

1980-1990 reveals that it was highest in Nepal at 80 per cent, followed by India (55%), Bangladesh (53%), Pakistan (40%) and Sri Lanka (9%). However, as has been shown in column 5 of the Table 3.4, women's share in self-employment had registered a decline in case of India and Pakistan whereas the share of Bangladesh increased by 56.6 per cent over the period 1980-2000.

Informal sector activities can be broadly categorized into self-employment, casual employment and home-based workers. Coming next to casual employment, it is pertinent to point out here that data collection for this particular informal sector component is a cumbersome task because of invisibility of women's work and their exclusion from surveys. As per one estimate, this component accounts for 30-40 per cent of informal employment in the non-agricultural sector. Two countries— India and Bangladesh—collect data on this component. Both the countries have registered an upward trend in informal wage employment.

Home-based workers, though mostly invisible in South Asia, constitute a significant proportion of informal sector workers. Though exact information on this component is not available, yet information gathered from various country-level studies reveals that in the year 2000, in India, 30 million workers got employment in this segment of informal sector, out of which 75-80 per cent were women. The home-based women workers accounted for 90 per cent of total workers in case of agarbatti (incense sticks) and bidi industry in India, 80 per cent in garment industry of Bangladesh, 58 per cent in football industry in Pakistan and 10 per cent in coir-making industry of Sri Lanka.

Further, the globalization process governed by flexibility norms has resulted in creation of employment avenues for women in the informal sector in the form of casual, temporary, and contractual labour that can be hired and fired at will. Employment of this kind of labour means more profit margins as this reduces wage and non-wage costs for the firm (Deshpande, 1993). Therefore, the management prefers informal sector women workers who are more flexible to their counterparts in the formal sector (Gothoskar, 1997). However, in the flexible regime, prospect for women employment in the formal sector becomes bleak, which is not desirable. Moreover, the existing working conditions in informal sector are inhospitable, deplorable with long hours of work, low wages, and absence of job security. Moreover, lack of organizational initiative and legal protection has made them vulnerable and prone to exploitation in the labour market. The study indicates that there has taken place feminization of labour force/occupations, which is reflected in gender segregation and gender gap in wages. An eloquent evidence to feminization of paid work is provided by the free trade zones and export processing zones of South Asia where employers prefer to employ younger tribal and unmarried girls.[7]

Gender Gap in Wages

Still another indicator of labour market discrimination is the gender gap in wages. The wage differential between men and women (varying between 32.19% in Pakistan to 59.64% in Nepal) for the similar kind of jobs is closely linked to relative lack of females' access to basic services like education, health care, nutrition, training and also to less work experience. In fact, the intra-household inequalities do matter a lot as these have serious implications on living conditions and on working capacity of women. These disparities also point towards the need that the working hours for women should be flexible so that they can juggle between their job and career and reproductive and caring work in the household.

From the foregoing, it is quite evident that there has taken place 'feminization of occupations' in South Asia as is getting reflected in concentration of women in relatively low wage, low productivity segment of the labour market.[8]

Work Burden: Females vs Males

Not only are women being discriminated at pre-market and post-market phase but a cursory look at Table 3.6 provides more insights into the longer work time of the women.

As per 1993 revised UN System of National Accounts, the former activities include employment in establishments, services for income and other production of goods not in establishments, and the latter include household maintenance (cleaning, laundry and meal preparation and clean up), management and shopping for own household, care for children, the sick, the elderly and the disabled in own household, and community services.

Table 3.6

Gender Work Burden and Time Allocation

Selected South Asian Countries	*Year*	*Total Work Time (minutes per day)*		*Female Work Time as % of Male*	*Total Work Time (%)*		*Time Spent by Females (%)*		*Time Spent by Males (%)*	
		Females	*Males*		*Mkt*	*Non-mkt*	*Mkt*	*Non-mkt*	*Mkt*	*Non-mkt*
Bangladesh (rural areas)	1990	545	496	110	52	48	35	65	70	30
Nepal (rural areas)	1978	641	547	117	56	44	46	54	67	33
India (national)	2000	457	391	117	61	39	35	65	92	08

Source: UNDP, *Human Development Report*, 2003, p. 326.

Table 3.6 clearly shows that the work burden on women is more than that of men, irrespective of the fact whether that country is Bangladesh, Nepal or India or whether the area considered is rural or urban area. Further, the table also brings to light the fact that in all the three countries for which data was available on time allocated for marketing and non-marketing activities on the basis of sex, women spent relatively more time on non-marketing activities and less time on marketing activities as compared to men. Little has been done to alleviate domestic drudgery of women. If at all, the burdens have increased.

From the foregoing, it is quite clear that women are the victims of pre-entry and post-entry gender discrimination and in addition, they have to bear unequal household burden also. Further, labour flexibility, an underlying feature of globalization process, has led to feminization of occupations in South Asia as reflected in the concentration of women in relatively low wage, low productivity informal segment of the labour market.

Policy Implications and Recommendations

1. *Gender-focussed and issue-specific strategy*: Since the process of development in some of the countries has been slow and uneven, it is time for these countries to reorient their poverty

alleviation strategies by making them more gender-focused and issue-specific. Further, women-specific programmes aiming at full development and advancement of women need to be started and implemented. There is also a need to deal with all kinds of discrimination against women firmly and effectively.

2. *Gender-specific policy measures for eliminating human capital discrimination*: There is also a need to introduce gender-specific education and health sector reforms (with due emphasis on universal primary education and technical education) so that South Asian women are truly empowered with access to quality education, formal skills and good health which ensure higher productivity. These will help them to compete in the global market.
3. *Organizational initiatives*: There is also a need for organizational initiatives to mobilize and organize the women who are working in the informal sector. No doubt, it is an uphill task to develop group sensitivity among women workers in the informal sector having short-term interests (i.e., earning as much as one can) belonging to different communities, having distinct cultural and religious backgrounds.
4. *Food and nutritional security*: The study also reveals that there has taken place feminization of labour force that is reflected in gender segregation and gender gap in wages. The female marginalization in the process of development can have serious repercussions on the extent of poverty in terms of consumption distribution, calorie intake (lack of food and nutritional security), health care and education and income distribution (see Jhabvala, 1999). The lack of food and nutritional security can lead to increase in morbidity and mortality. It is, therefore, very essential that the food and nutritional security should be provided to the poor and informal sector workers on priority basis through a more effective Public Distribution System (PDS), through grain bank scheme, or through 'food for work' scheme as we find in case of India.
5. *Empowerment of women*: Above all, there is a need to identify means and ways to empower the women. Three-fold strategy for empowering all women through—(1) social empowerment,

(2) economic empowerment, and (3) gender justice[9] can play a significant role in this regard. However, there is a need to effectively implement these suggestions on priority basis through good governance. Besides, as has been rightly emphasized in WDR (2004) that gender inequality is one of the several other aspects of poverty (low income, illiteracy, ill-health, environmental degradation etc.), which is a multi-dimensional concept. To get rid of poverty and to promote development, we will have to make basic services work for people (including women) and improve their delivery through institutional reforms that will strengthen the relationship of accountability between policy makers, providers, and citizens.

6. *Greater emphasis on EQ rather than on IQ*: No policy resolution can help us in getting the desired results unless the people, who are the guiding force and provide an impetus for all the policy matters/endeavours themselves, remain self-centred, selfish and lack compassion and consideration for others. Therefore, the above-mentioned measures should be supplemented by bringing about order and love in relationship at the individual level through 'human revolution'. When we listen to our hearts and start thinking beyond our restricted, narrow confines (me, mine, "we four and no more") and devote and dedicate our lives to achieve something higher, more lofty, more profound, then takes place the human revolution, so essential for solving all the social ills afflicting our society. This change in the attitude at the individual level would spread to the level of family initially and to the societal, national and world level subsequently. Therefore, it is love which implies compassion, consideration, understanding, sympathy, real affection towards others which would help getting women their due place at the family, societal, national and world levels.[10] They will become empowered in true sense of the term when the emphasis is on raising emotional quotient (EQ) first rather than on intelligence quotient (IQ).
7. *Role of NGOs*: Women working in the informal sector lack bargaining strength. Their ignorance and illiteracy make them more vulnerable and prone to exploitation. Herein

comes the role of NGOs. It becomes essential that more interactive sessions should be organized by NGOs with the women to learn about their problems and ways of resolving them and also to sensitize them about their rights.

8. *Equality in performance of dual roles of work and family*: Not only is discriminatory treatment meted out to women at pre-market and post-market entry levels, they in addition get restricted economic opportunities and traditional household jobs of shopping, cooking, cleaning and care of the children thrust upon them leaving them overburdened. A redressal is long overdue. Otherwise inability to cope up with stresses can adversely affect their physical and mental health, lead to decline in birth rates, marital instability and may give rise to vices amongst men.[11] Therefore, as was pointed out by Tinker long back in 1976 that "the role assigned to each sex must again be made more equal—with men as well as women accepting their dual function of work and family".
9. *Flexi-working*: Flexible working hours can prove to be very useful for women as this would enable them to combine their job and a career with other family commitments including motherhood.

Conclusion

It is well documented in literature that gender discrimination tends to hamper growth via creating inefficiencies. The extent of anti-female bias or discrimination against women is far worse in South Asia than in most other developing countries. The main focus of the study is on human capital discrimination which women in South Asian region encounter at pre-market phase and labour market discrimination which they face in the post-market phase, while carrying on their traditional jobs of household management. All kinds of post-entry discrimination faced by them can be rationalized with the help of pre-entry discrimination.

The study also points out that the globalization process has further aggravated the situation by leading to 'feminization of occupations' in South Asia, where the conditions of work are inhospitable, deplorable with long hours of work, low wages, absence of job security, etc. Moreover, lack of organizational initiatives and legal protection has made them vulnerable and prone to exploitation. Hence, the study suggests for gender-focused and issue-based poverty alleviation strategies to be adopted by both governmental and non-governmental agencies.

■ Notes

1. "Three studies done in Kenya show that under investment in women's education limits agricultural productivity. Simulations based on these studies suggest that there may be significant gains from increasing women's level of physical and human capital" (World Bank, 1995).
2. See MUHHDC (2003).
3. However, there may be some countries which are achievers or good performers in terms of growth/development indicators, human development indicators and gender development indices (GDI & GEM) but these tools cannot be fully relied upon for gauging the well-being of women as it is very much possible that the women may be doing well in terms of these indicators but may be subjected to violence, mental, psychological, emotional abuse at home and at workplace or ill-treatment as is reflected in the deprivation of elderly and economically dependent widows which may not be captured by data. The rising cases of violence and crime against women, in particular has an economic cost and act as barriers to the empowerment of women and have serious consequences on women's health.
4. In her study, Aganon (2000) covers a few other countries of Asia like Vietnam, Thailand, Philippines, Singapore and Taiwan. But, for our study, only three South Asian countries are covered.
5. See MUHHDC (2003) also.
6. See MUHHDC (2003).
7. See Kalpagam (2001) and Patel (1994). In the context of India, Patel noticed that multi national companies (MNCs) employ girl children at meagre wages in free trade zones (FTZs) and export processing zones (EPZs) and set before them high production quotas which create mental and physical stresses among them. Moreover, they work under hazardous and inhuman conditions. They become victims of respiratory ailments, burns, ulcers, deteriorating eye-sights due to chemical hazards, improper ventilation, lack of health and safety provisions.
8. Also see Mitra (2000) where he has examined the change in quantum and quality of women employment in case of India since 1985-86 using both Census and NSSO data.
9. See Tinker (1976).
10. As has been emphasized in the Draft Tenth Plan in case of India.

11. Since family was regarded as the main oppressor of women and the main obstacle towards women empowerment by orthodox feminists. Therefore, to empower women efforts have to start at the family level as has been emphasized by the author.

■ References

Aganon, Marie E. 2000. Survey Report (Integrated), *Changing Labour Market and Women Employment*, Japan: Asian Productivity Organization.

Agarwal, Bina. 1986. 'Women, Poverty and Agricultural Growth in India', *The Journal of Peasant Studies*, 13(4): 165-220.

— 1997. 'Gender, Environment and Poverty Interlinks: Regional Variations and Temporal Shifts in Rural India', 1971-91, *World Development*, 25(1): 23-52.

Anand Sudhir and Martin Ravallion. 1993. 'Human Development in Poor Countries: on the Role of Private Incomes And Public Services', *Journal of Economic Perspectives*, 7(1): 133-150.

Arun, Shoba V., Thankom G. Arun and Vani K. Borooah. 2004. 'The Effects of Career Breaks On the Working Lives of Women', *Feminist Economics*, March, 10 (1): 65-84.

Bittman, Michael. 1999. 'Parenthood without Penalty: Time Use and Public Policy in Australia and Finland', *Feminist Economics* 5 (3):27-42.

Deshpande, Sudha. 1993. 'Structural Adjustment and Feminization' in Alakh Sharma and Seema Singh (eds.), *Women and Work: Changing Scenario in India,* Delhi: Indian Society of Labour Economics (Patna) and B. R. Publishing Company.

Dex, Shirley and Heather Joshi. 1999. 'Careers and Motherhood: Policies for Compatibility', *Cambridge Journal of Economics*, 23 (5): 641-59.

Dreze, Jean and Amartya Sen. 1989. *Hunger and Public Action, World Institute for Development Economic Research*, Studies in Development Economics, Oxford: Clarendon Press.

Gothoskar, Sujata. 1997. 'Women, Work and Health; An Interconnected Web—Case of Drugs and Cosmetics Industries', *Economic and Political Weekly*, 32(43).

Government of India. 2002-07. Tenth Five Year Plan, Vol. II, New Delhi: Planning Commission.

Hariss, B. 1990. 'The Intra-family Distribution of Hunger in South Asia' in J. Dreze and A. K. Sen (eds.), *The Political Economy of Hunger, Entitlement and Well-Being*, New York: Oxford University Press.

Heyzer, Noeleen and Gita Sen. 1994. *Gender, Economic Growth and Poverty: Market Growth and State Planning in Asia and the Pacific*, Asian and Pacific Development Centre.

International Labour Organization 1995. *Gender, Poverty and Employment: Turning Capabilities into Entitlements*, Geneva.

Jhabvala, Renana. 1999. 'Interventions in the Labour Market: The Case of SEWA' in T.S. Papola and Alakh N. Sharma (eds.), *Gender and Employment in India*, New Delhi: Indian Society of Labour Economics and Vikas Publishing House.

Joshi, Seema. 2003. 'Trends in Social Sector Outlays of Central and State Governments in India: A Pre-Reform and Post-Reform Comparative Analysis'. Paper presented in International Conference on Issues in Development Economics held at Burdwan University, West Bengal from December 15-17,2003.

Kalpagam, U. (2001). 'Globalisation, Liberalisation and Women Workers in the Informal Sector' in Amitabh Kundu and Alakh N. Sharma (eds.), *Informal Sector in India: Perspectives and Policies*, Delhi: Institute for Human Development and Institute of Applied Manpower Research.

Mahbub Ul Haq Human Development Centre 2003. *Human Development in South Asia* New York: Oxford University Press.

Mitra, Arup. 2000. 'Survey Report (Integrated)', *Changing Labour Market and Women Employment,* Japan: Asian Productivity Organization.

Moser, C.O.N. and Levy C. 1986. 'A Theory and Methodology of Gender Planning: Meeting Women's Practical and Strategic Needs', Development Planning Unit, Gender and Planning Working Paper No. 11, University College, London.

Patel, Vibuti. 1994. 'Women and Structural Adjustment in India', *Social Scientist*, 22(3-4):16-34.

Sen, A.K. 1985. *Commodities and Capabilities.* Amsterdam: North Holland.

— 2001. 'Many Facets of Gender Inequality', *Frontline,* 18 (22): October 27-November 09.

Sharma, Alakh N. and Seema Singh. 1993. *Women and Work: Changing Scenario in India,* Delhi: Indian Society of Labour Economics (Patna) and B.R. Publishing Company.

Taylor Lance, Santosh Mehrotra and Enrique Delamonica. 1997. 'The Links between Economic Growth, Poverty Reduction, and Social Development: Theory and Policy', in Santosh Mehrotra and Richard Jolly (eds.), *Development with a Human Face: Experiences in Social Achievement and Economic Growth,* Oxford: Clarendon Press.

Tinker, Irene. 1976. 'Adverse Impact of Development on Women', in Irene Tinker and Bo Michele (eds.), *Women and World Development*, Washington D.C.: American Association for the Advancement of Science, Overseas Development Council.

UNDP. 2003. *Human Development Report.* New York: Oxford University Press.

World Bank. 1995. *Towards Gender Equality: The Role of Public Policy,* Washington D.C.: World Bank.

—. 2004. *World Development Report,* New York: Oxford University Press.

Chapter 4

Rural Women and Empowerment

An Economic Perspective from Pakistan

Hina Nazli

Cultural and social taboos in Pakistan make the role of women in economic and political activities almost invisible. The lack of education compounds the lack of awareness about legal rights making women more subservient to and dependent on men. High illiteracy, malnutrition, lack of timely and proper medical treatment, restricted mobility and the heavy load of housework are all reflections of this subservience. Women have limited access to productive resources and only a nominal role in important household decisions, despite carrying the major workload at home and performing numerous tasks outside the home as well.

It is generally observed that women's earned income is positively and significantly related with their authority as decision-makers in the household and they usually have control over the income that they earn. However, in Pakistan, this is normally not the case. A majority of women choose to work for wages only in distress circumstances to financially support their household. Due to the extremely low levels of educational attainment, women face an extremely discriminatory and exploitative wage market, especially in the agriculture and informal sector, where they receive low rewards as compared to the time that they devote to these activities. In addition, a majority of women work as unpaid family helpers in farm as well as in non-farm activities. This work remains unnoticed and unrewarded. Despite being ruled by a female Prime Minister twice in its history, the autonomy of Pakistani women is very limited, both at the household and at national level. Their participation in economic activities is negligible and their representation in politics is merely a token. According to the ranking of Gender Development Index (GDI) of the Human Development Report (HDR), Pakistan ranked 120 amongst 144 countries in 2004. Fertility rate is 5.1 per woman; maternal mortality rate is 500 per 100,000 live births; adult female literacy rate is 28.5 per cent; female economic activity (more than 15 years of age) rate is only 36.3 per cent; and their share in earned income as per cent of males is 33 per cent.

Using nationally representative data, this paper describes the factors that determine the economic empowerment or lack thereof for rural women in Pakistan.

What is Empowerment?

Arriving at a single, comprehensive definition of 'empowerment' is a formidable task, given that empowerment is a multi-layered concept. There are different behavioural norms and power structures in the societal fabric, and these govern individual actions at each level. Given the multiplicity of power structures, the concept of empowerment applies to all the various levels and thereby its definition can fluctuate according to context and perspective.

Generally, women empowerment is defined as a process by which women take ownership of their lives and through the expansion of their choices (ESCAP, 2002). Kabeer (2001) points out that the ability to define one's goals and act upon these, and, awareness and self-esteem are the core elements of empowerment. A similar definition is adopted by UNIFEM that is based on the ability to generate choices, the sense of self-worth and the right to control one's life. These definitions essentially imply that empowerment entails (a) increase in choices, and (b) increase in the ability to exercise those choices. Increase in choices is a function of access to resources (such as capital, physical infrastructure, schools, education and health facilities etc.), and increase in the ability to exercise those choices depends on abolition of inhibiting political, legal and social practices. This brings us to various dimensions of empowerment, namely, *physical*, related to the protection against any physical violence; *economic*, related to the access to and control over resources and income; *legal*, related to the access and participation in the legal system; and *political*, related to the participation in the political process.

Discourse on empowerment and the requirement of targeted policies to increase empowerment gave rise to the need for developing indicators for measuring empowerment. One such indicator is the Gender Empowerment Measure (GEM), which focuses on females' participation and measures gender inequality in key areas of economic and political decision-making. According to the ranking based on the GEM, Pakistan ranked 64 out of 78 countries in 2004. This rank is better than the ranks of two South Asian countries, Sri Lanka and Bangladesh, and other Islamic countries such as Turkey, Iran, Egypt, Saudi Arabia, and Yemen. Pakistan's GEM ranking has improved[1] in recent years, however this improvement has mainly been a result of increased women participation in recent elections[2] with little change in the economic status of women.

In all practical terms, different aspects of empowerment are inseparable and according to Cheston and Kuhn (2002), "...it is very difficult to move far ahead in any one area without corresponding changes in other areas". While there is no doubt in the interconnectedness of these aspects, this paper focuses mainly on economic empowerment of Pakistani women in rural areas. This is done in the belief that the major obstacle to women's empowerment is economic. However, linkages are drawn with other aspects wherever necessary.

Empowerment of Rural Women in Pakistan

In Pakistan, women are far behind men in all walks of life. Their role is mostly confined only to the household chores and childcare. They rarely have access to productive resources and have very limited participation in important household decisions. Even most of the important decisions in a woman's life, such as education, work, marriage, major purchases, number of children, and those relating to the education of children and their marriages are taken by the male members. In order to examine the role of women in household decision-making, the Pakistan Integrated Household Survey (PIHS) asked several questions from women aged 15 to 49 years. Table 4.1 presents the summary statistics of the participation of the 15,348 rural women in the sample in household decision-making.

This table shows that most of the decisions about a woman's education, employment, purchases of food and clothing, medical treatment and recreations are taken by the head of the household alone. In some cases, especially those related to medical treatment and recreation, he does consult his spouse. Women's role in deciding about the purchases of food and clothing is however found to be quite significant. It is interesting to note that women have lesser autonomy for the decisions that are directly related to them, such as education, employment, medical treatment and recreation. But, they can decide themselves about the tasks that are mostly related to household, such as purchases of food and clothing.

In responding to the question "why you are not seeking paid work", most women said that their husbands did not permit them; only 19 per cent responded that they were too busy in household work, and 9 per cent reported that no work was available. When asked about "who decides where and when you should be married", 70 per cent women did not respond. Among the 4,748 women who responded, 41 per cent said that the head of the household alone decides, 30 per cent reported that head of household in consultation with his spouse decides and 15 per cent said that head of the household in consultation with other male members decides. These findings are similar to Sathar and Kazi (1997) who observed that in rural areas of Punjab, women's involvement in economic decisions is extremely limited. The majority of women participate only in decisions related to the purchase of food. In all other decisions, either domestic or economic, they are consulted but do not act as major decision-makers.

Table 4.1

Proportion of Women in Household Decision-making in Rural Pakistan

Who decides	*About education*	*About employment*	*About food purchases*	*About purchases of clothing*	*About medical treatment*	*About recreation*
Women herself	7.0	7.7	27.1	22.6	8.9	5.8
Head alone	54.3	53.2	40.0	38.3	40.2	41.1
Head and his spouse	13.4	15.5	14.8	17.9	25.3	25.6
Head and concerned woman	2.6	3.0	1.5	4.3	7.4	7.2
Head and spouse with concerned woman	1.9	2.1	2.8	4.6	5.4	5.4
Head and other male members	4.6	5.5	6.1	5.8	6.3	8.5
Others	12.0	8.8	3.3	2.1	2.2	2.1

Source: Computed from PIHS (2001-02).

These results indicate that despite a considerable improvement in gender-related indicators over time in Pakistan, women are not independent in making most of the decisions, even those that are directly related to their own life. Most of the time of their lives, they serve the household as a major comfort provider at the cost of their education, employment, leisure and pleasure.

The PIHS (2001-02) observed that the women who participate in wage market have some autonomy in the decision-making processes at household level as compared to those who do not take part in wage employment. In this context, the next section focuses on the dynamics of rural labour market and female participation.

Structure of Rural Labour Market in Pakistan

The size of the labour force, its distribution amongst various sectors, the levels of unemployment and underemployment all have an important bearing on the human as well as economic development of a country. The estimated population of Pakistan in 2003 was 148 million and estimated labour force was 42.75 million. Out of this, 39.41 million were employed—34 per cent in urban areas and 42 per cent in rural areas. The labour force participation rate, measured in terms of crude activity rate (unadjusted for age), was 29.61 per cent—29.85 per cent in rural areas and 29.10 per cent in urban areas.

The Labour Force Survey does not show an encouraging trend for female labour force participation in rural Pakistan. In the last five years, this rate has fluctuated around 11 per cent (see Table 4.2). Arif and Sheikh (2002) have identified a lower female labour force participation rate at younger ages. This indicates that household responsibilities and cultural and family norms keep most of the females away from taking part in wage market at younger age. The computation of the female labour force participation rate generally excludes all females who participate in such household activities that produce goods or services at home which are available in the market.[3] Considering those women who participate in such activities as employed, the female labour force participation rate increases from 11 per cent to 32 per cent (Labour Force Survey, 2001-02).

Table 4.2

*Labour Force Participation, Crude Activity Rate (CAR), Unemployment and Underemployment Rate in Rural Pakistan**

Years	Labour force (million)		Labour force participation rate		Unemployment rate		Under-employment rate	
	Male	Female	Male	Female	Male	Female	Male	Female
1997-98	21.67	4.79	48.4	11.5	3.46	11.86	9.20	47.67
1999-00	22.86	4.85	48.2	10.7	5.43	14.04	10.95	43.44
2001-02	24.05	5.31	47.6	11.1	6.11	14.12	10.32	41.08

* All these rates are for age 10 and above.

Source: Labour Force Survey (various issues), Government of Pakistan.

Unemployment and Underemployment

The unemployment rate in Pakistan has increased rapidly after the mid-1990s. In rural areas, this rate has increased by 14 per cent during 1996-97 to 2001-02 (from 4.98% to 8.27%). The incidence of unemployment in rural Pakistan is significantly higher amongst women as compared to men. For example, in 2001-02, the female unemployment rate exceeded male unemployment rate by 8 percentage points (see Table 4.2).

Unemployment alone fails to present the true picture of the rural labour market. A very large segment of the labour force is characterized by 'disguised unemployment' also referred to as underemployment. This phenomenon is most common in agricultural and informal sectors. According to the official classification, persons working less than 35 hours per week are considered underemployed. Based on this classification, female underemployment has been persistently four times as high as that of male underemployment from 1997 to 2002. Table 4.2 indicates that during 2001-02, nearly 41.08 per cent of employed females in rural Pakistan worked less than 35 hours a week as compared to 10.32 per cent males. Although the female under-employment rate has declined in the past four years, this decline has been marginal.

Employment by Occupation and Employment Status

Agriculture sector is the largest employer of rural labour force. In 1982-83, 68 per cent of employed persons were engaged in this sector. This proportion has declined to 59 per cent in 2001-02. Other important sectors are manufacturing, construction, wholesale and retail trade, and social services sectors where nearly 35 per cent labour force was employed (see Table 4.3). A majority of employed females are concentrated in agriculture (80%), followed by manufacturing (11%) and services (8%). This means that 99 per cent rural females choose to work in these three sectors.

Table 4.3

Percentage Distribution of Rural Employed Persons by Major Industries and Gender (2001-02)

	Both	*Male*	*Female*
All sectors	100.00	100.00	100.00
Agriculture, forestry, hunting and fishing	59.01	54.86	79.58
Mining and quarrying	0.07	0.09	0.00
Manufacturing	8.68	8.31	10.51
Electricity, gas and water	0.57	0.67	0.00
Construction	6.23	7.43	0.26
Wholesale and retail, trade and restaurants and hotels	9.20	10.82	1.22
Transport, storage and communication	4.81	5.71	0.35
Financing, insurance, real estate and business services	0.29	0.35	0.00
Community, social and personal services	11.13	11.78	7.91

Source: Labour Force Survey (2001-02), Government of Pakistan.

A majority of rural females were found working as unpaid family helpers (56%), followed by employees (29%) and self-employed (15%). This pattern was reverse among males, i.e., 48 per cent males were self-employed, 32 per cent employees and 20 per cent were unpaid family helpers. Out of total working women, only 1 per cent belonged to professional category and 1 per cent worked as administrative and managerial workers. A majority was found concentrated either in agricultural (54%), craft-related work (11%) or in elementary occupations (27%). Once again, concentration of women in these sectors points out their lack of skills and resources that pose a hindrance in their opting for sectors such as community, social and personal services or financing, insurance and business services that demand high levels of skill, education and/or capital. The following section explains more about female concentration in the informal sector.

Employment in the Informal Sector

Labour absorption has declined in many sectors due to the increasing reliance on capital intensive techniques. The formal sector generally demands educated and skilled manpower. A large proportion of Pakistan's population consisting of the uneducated and the unskilled labour force, therefore, tend to seek jobs in the informal sector. The informal sector as defined by the structure of the organization and the size of the establishment includes family enterprise/industrial establishment with less than 10 workers and non-industrial establishments with workers not more than 20.

According to the Labour Force Survey (2001-02), on the whole, females' strength in this sector was 8 per cent. Various independently conducted studies[4] in the cities of Pakistan, categorize the informal sector workforce as consisting of self-employed, regular workers, family helpers and *shagirds* (apprentices who are generally given board and lodge at the work sites). This is also true for the rural informal sector. Table 4 shows that the informal sector is composed of either self-employed or wage employees. The proportion of unpaid family helpers is very low in the informal sector as compared to the agricultural sector. A majority of males is found concentrated in self-employed category whereas most of the females worked as wage employees (see Table 4.4).

Table 4.4

Percentage Distribution of Employed Persons Engaged in Informal Sector by Employment Status and Gender in Rural Areas (2001-02)

Employment status	*Both sexes*	*Male*	*Female*
Total	100.00	91.96	8.04
Employer	0.77	0.77	0.00
Self-employed	44.4	41.8	2.60
Unpaid family helper	10.48	8.59	1.89
Employee	44.34	40.70	3.64

Source: Labour Force Survey (2001-02).

A majority of males was found involved in wholesale, trade and related work as managers while females in manufacturing sector as craft and related workers. As has already been argued, this is basically a result of low levels of skills and capital as well as cultural inhibitions faced by female workers.

Working Hours and Monetary Reward

Informal sector is characterized by long working hours and low wage rate. The data of Labour Force Survey, 2001-02 shows that average working hours per week in the informal sector are 50-52 for males and 37 for females. Among working females in this sector, 40 per cent work 25-39 hours and 21 per cent work 42-48 hours per week. The data of Labour Force Survey allows calculation of weekly income for males and females separately. This variable reveals very obvious gender disparity in the monetary reward for an equal length of work (see Table 4.5).

Table 4.5

Weekly Income by Working Hours, Gender and Formal/Informal Sector (2001-02)

Groups of working hours	*Formal sector (Rs/hour/week)*		*Informal sector (Rs/hour/week)*	
	Males	*Females*	*Males*	*Females*
15-24 hours	316	186	184	117
24-34 hours	697	534	233	159
35-39 hours	740	507	191	189
40-48 hours	718	582	366	241
49-55 hours	409	309	264	189
56 and above	420	463	291	251

Source: Computed from Labour Force Survey (2001-02).

There are significant differences not only within sectors but also across genders. On average males get higher reward in both formal as well as informal sectors than females. In the informal sector, this difference is highest for the working groups 15-24 hours and 40-48 hours. This, however, essentially underestimates the actual working hours of females since it does not include the time they spend in conducting their daily household chores. Also, when remunerative work is done within the boundary of the household, it ends up being treated as part of 'female work' like the regular household chores of cooking, washing etc. And not always does it carry the respect or empowerment that entails working in the formal sector. The following section attempts to consider this statistical bias and estimates the monetary value of what is generally considered as female housework.

Time Use Analysis

As discussed above, Pakistani women play a major role in agricultural production, livestock care and craft-related work in rural areas. They often devote more time to these tasks than men do. They participate in sowing, transplanting, weeding and harvesting, and post-harvest operations, such as threshing, drying, grinding, husking and storage (including making mud bins for storage). In addition, they carry out their regular household chores and care of children and the elderly.

In barani (rainfed) agriculture, where crop production is not sufficient to meet subsistence needs of the households, men have traditionally sought employment in the non-farm sector. As a result, women have to take over a substantial burden of the work in agricultural production (GoP, 1995). In barani Punjab, women contribute to almost all of 22 identified crop tasks with the major contribution to seed preparation, collection and application of farmyard manure, husking maize and storage (FAO, 1998). Men's involvement is higher in the early stages of cultivation such as field preparation. Men also monopolize mechanical work. For example, they carry out mechanical threshing (with animal or fuel-powered machines), while hand-threshing is mostly a women's task. Driving tractors and watering the fields are also men's job. Food processing and storage is an area where women's participation is considerably higher than that of men's (Mumtaz, 1995).

Livestock is another major activity that is conducted by women. Women's significant role in livestock care and production has been highlighted by many studies. Women's active involvement includes a variety of tasks, such as making feed concentrates, feeding, collecting fodder, grazing, cleaning animals and their sheds, making dung cakes, collecting manure for organic fertilizer, in some cases milking, processing and marketing of animal products (making ghee, selling eggs, etc.) (Sultana, Nazli and Malik, 1994; ESCAP, 1997).

Various studies estimated the hours spent on different activities performed by rural women. Some studies found that on average they spend at least 15 hours per day in household chores (Khan and Bilquees, 1976; Shah, 1986; Ahmad, Asghar and Khan, 1993; ESCAP, 1997; World Bank, 1990). Alderman and Chishti (1989) observe that the average rural woman worked between 25 to 35 hours per week in household activities excluding childcare. If market-oriented activities and childcare are also included, then their workload and time both increase notably. Because of the incompatible nature of available jobs for the women of rural areas, the educated women are found less likely to participate in market-oriented activities. Sarwar and Saleem (1993) noted that in rural areas, females of the farm households spend 54.9 per cent of their time on domestic work, 22.4 per cent on livestock, and 9.2 per cent on crops.

In examining the time allocation of rural women in different activities, Sultana, Nazli and Malik (1994) divided their sample into wage-earners and non-working women. They found that the wage-earner women bear a larger burden of household work. On average, working women spend 19 hours per week on market-oriented work and 28 hours per week on household chores. On the other hand, non-working women spend 16 hours per week on domestic work. This reflects the economic condition of the working and non-working women in the selected sample of that study. The women who stay at home are found to be wealthier and afford to take leisure. This study also estimated the determinants of female time allocation and observed a negative and significant association between women's reservation wage rate and decision to participate in labour market. However, education and market wage rate are found to have positive impact on this decision. All these studies suggest that making education accessible for the females, especially in rural areas, and provision of employment opportunities in public as well as in private sector, would encourage them to participate in economic activities.

The Labour Force Survey provides information on the hours worked in different household activities for the females who are classified as unemployed. Columns 2 and 3 of Table 4.6 show the hours worked in a respective activity by those women who are

Table 4.6
Average Hours Worked in Different Household Activities by Unemployed Females

	Average hrs/week in listed household activities (hours)	*Number of females in listed household activities (#)*	*Proportion of females in listed household activities (%)*	*Average hrs/week by all females (hours)*
1	*2*	*3*	*4*	*5*
Agricultural activities	9.66	1,039	6.70	0.65
Food processing activities	7.95	1,431	9.23	0.73
Livestock care	8.26	5,235	33.76	2.79
Poultry raising	4.13	1,015	6.55	0.27
Construction work	5.57	1,422	9.17	0.51
Firewood collection	5.49	2,043	13.18	0.72
Fetching water	6.96	2,787	17.97	1.25
Stitching/sewing clothes	6.27	5,800	37.40	2.35
Shopping	5.3	3,087	19.91	1.06
Washing clothes	7.14	14,467	93.30	6.66
Child/elderly care	10.69	8,635	55.69	5.95
Help in children education/homework	8.48	947	6.11	0.52
House cleaning	8.28	14,640	94.42	7.82
Other activities	14.41	11,795	76.07	10.96
Total		15,506		42.24

Source: Computed from Labour Force Survey (2001-02).

actually involved in those activities. For example, among 15,506 females, 1,039 are involved in agricultural activities and they spend nearly 10 hours per week in this activity. Similarly, livestock activity keeps engaged 5,235 women who work eight hours per week in this activity. According to this estimation, childcare appeared as the most time demanding activity. In this 8,635 (i.e., 56% of sample) women are involved, and spend 11 hours per week. Among others, agricultural, food processing, livestock care and house cleaning appeared as activities that keep rural women very busy (see Table 4.6, column 2). Column 4 of this table shows that among 15,506 unemployed females, 94 per cent are involved in house cleaning activities, 93 per cent in washing clothes, 56 per cent in child/elderly care and 37 per cent in stitching/sewing. As mentioned earlier, the estimation of hours worked per week (column 2) in different activities includes only those females who are involved in these activities. However, including all unemployed females in the estimation of hours worked per week in different activities indicates that house cleaning, washing clothes, childcare, livestock care and other activities are the most important activities for all females. They spend nearly 35 hours per week in these five activities (see Table 4.6, column 5). On an average, a typical rural female spends 42 hours per week in activities that are although a part of house work but produce goods and services that are available in the market.[5]

By applying average market wage rate we can compute the money value of time that females devote to housework. According to the data of Labour Force Survey, on an average, females' weekly income for those who work for at least 42 hours per week is Rs 346: Rs 279 in informal sector and Rs 382 in formal sector. Applying this average weekly income (Rs 346) implies that the minimum money values of a typical rural woman's house work is Rs 1500 per month. This means that if there are 16.9 million rural females not working in market for wages, they are still contributing a worth of approximately Rs 304 billion per year to the economy.[6] This estimate would be even higher if male wage rate had been applied to compute it. It is important to note that the questions related to time usage on household chores are not asked to employed females. Whereas these females, in some cases, are more vulnerable in terms of load of work, they work outside home, earn wages and in addition fulfil household responsibilities and thus are left with a little time for leisure. Including these females would increase the time devoted to household work per week per female and hence its money value.

Globalization, Rural Economy and Rural Women

The decade of the 1990s witnessed an increasing volume of agricultural products in total international trade in this region. More than two-thirds of intra-developing country trade originated from and was destined to developing Asia. Four countries of South Asian sub-region (Bangladesh, India, Pakistan and Nepal) were net importers of agricultural products with a considerably higher share of all major agricultural products while the opposite holds for Bhutan and Sri Lanka.

The World Trade Report (2003) indicates that the agricultural products of developing countries are less competitive in the world market because of the disproportionate impact of tariff barriers. In addition, because of the rising importance of food safety, food exports of these countries are suffering. The requirements of the Agreement on Agriculture (AoA) increase the need for specific institutions to support developing countries' agriculture and enable these countries to maximize the gains from international trade in agricultural products. The experience of East and South-East Asia indicates that globalization provides opportunities to the developing countries to reduce poverty and boost economic growth. At the same time, the East Asian financial crisis highlights the various risks and uncertainties and the potential economic volatility underlying the process.

Trade liberalization, with a reduction in tariff and non-tariff barriers and market deregulation, has direct impact on domestic production and hence on employment. However, research on the effects of globalization on gender is lacking. Vijfhuizen, Braga, Artur and Kanji (2003) examined the impact of liberalization on the working men and women in cashew industry in Mozambique in the 1990s. They conclude that liberalization will result in job losses and subsequent impoverishment for some women and the women who will remain in the market will face decline in wages and deteriorating working conditions. However, for Pakistan, Siddiqui (2003) found contrasting results while examining the effects of trade liberalization on time allocation by men and women among market, household and leisure by using the GCGE (gender computable general equilibrium) model. She finds that trade liberalization, both with and without compensatory measures, leads to an increase in female paid work. A rise in the demand for female labour in market leads to drop in female leisure time. However, with fiscal adjustments, female paid employment drops but household work rises as households substitute household produced goods for the market goods.

Role of Micro-credit and Women Empowerment

In recent years micro-finance is considered as a powerful tool of poverty alleviation that empowers individuals through sustainable livelihood. Although Europe is the origin of micro-finance but in recent years 76 per cent of total micro-loans are in Asia, followed by Latin America (21%) and Africa (3%) (Khandker, 1999). Since the early 1970s micro-credit and savings have been used by many women's organizations as a way of increasing women's incomes. During the 1980s institutions such as Grameen Bank, Bangladesh and Bank Rakyat, Indonesia (BRI) emerged as poverty targeting micro-finance institutions (MFIs). These institutions have adopted an 'empowerment' approach to credit delivery. Various MFIs around the world have learned from their experiences. Since then, MFIs have received both cynicism and accolades in the development discourse as empowerment tools for rural women. In this section we shall briefly overview both positive and negative dimensions of micro-credit and its relation to empowering women.

Empowering Impact of Micro-credit

Studies advocating the positive impact of micro-credit programmes point out numerous empowerment indicators such as increase in household assets, consumption smoothing, increase in intra-household bargaining power and improvement in the self-esteem of women.

Decrease in the levels of poverty and increase in incomes are some of the most popular indicators of empowerment. For instance, in 2000, the United Nations Common Country Assessment for Bangladesh reported that micro-credit resulted in an increase of per household income by 29 per cent. Similarly, the World Bank reported that a 10 per cent increase in loan from Grameen bank increased women's non-land assets by 2 per cent, whereas a similar increase in the loan from BRAC increased these assets by 1.2 per cent (see World Bank, 1998). The Women's Empowerment Programme in Nepal carried out a study according to which 68 per cent of the women involved in the programme reported an enhancement in the decision-making behaviour in areas such as family planning, children's marriage, property transactions and schooling of their daughters (Ashe and Parrott, 2001). Similarly, Kabeer (1996) points out that just the process of bringing credit to the house helped a majority of the women in gaining some benefit.

Some studies even find a positive relationship between membership in a credit organization and reduction in domestic violence (Hashemi et al., 1996). Although this relationship is debatable, however, numerous studies carry anecdotes relating to borrowing behaviour to decrease in the incidence of physical abuse.

Debilitating Impact of Micro-credit

Taking credit is a risky decision, since it entails the possibility of default. This risk exists whether the borrower is male or female. However, since females generally have fewer resources to pay back a loan than men, therefore, they face a greater credit risk than their male counterparts. Some challengers of the use of micro-credit as an empowerment tool argue that the empowerment enhancing qualities of micro-credit are not long lasting and are less likely to continue after the project completion.

Loan taking activities also impact woman's work time and therefore overall work burden. In most cases, women mention a greater burden of work due to added activity. However, such burden need not be debilitating at all times. Kabeer (1996), for instance, noted that women borrowers of the Small Enterprise Development Programme in Bangladesh reported an increase in workload with a simultaneous increase in satisfaction as a result of improved self-esteem and better household bargaining power.

While scholars continue to debate the effect of micro-credit on empowerment, the precise impact is hard to measure. The success of micro-credit or any other development initiative for that matter is affected by numerous factors, a lot of which are not even quantifiable. Success of a programme in one country does not necessarily imply success in other parts, and hence all micro-finance (MF) programmes ought to be carefully dissected and analyzed before replication in another country or region. Nevertheless important lessons can be drawn from successful MF programmes across countries. Some of these, as pointed out by Cheston and Kuhn (2002), are discussed below:

- Carefully planned training should be an integral part of MF for women entrepreneurs. MF recipient clients from Costa Rica termed that other than credit, training was the most important component of their programme.
- Special emphasis ought to be placed on education, since lack of literacy can limit the prospects of participation in the formal market. Although this is a daunting task, however it would ensure long-term benefits of the MF programme.
- Any empowerment initiative cannot be imposed from outside. It is therefore extremely important for women to be aware of their legal rights. Increasing awareness should be an integral component of MF programmes.
- Finally, institutional structures ought to promote empowerment of women by not only acting as facilitators, but also including women in decision-making at the institutional level. Women gain encouragement to see other women making independent choices in life and asserting their rights. Hence, interaction with women field officers and women officials at higher ranks within MF organizations can boost confidence of poor rural women to a large extent.

Micro-credit in Pakistan

In Pakistan, informal money-lenders are the main source of credit to a larger proportion of population in rural areas. The Pakistan Rural Household Survey (2001), conducted in selected districts of all provinces of Pakistan, noted the dominant role of informal lenders in rural credit market[7], the high share of Agricultural Development Bank of Pakistan (ADBP) (88%) in formal loans, and the dominance of friends and relatives (61%) in informal lending. The share of shopkeepers and landlords was also found significant (18% and 16%, respectively) (see World Bank, 2002).

In Pakistan, the micro-finance sector is in the initial stages of development. Three different types of institutions are involved in the service delivery of credit to the needy. These include: specialized micro-finance institutions (MFIs) including commercial banks; rural support programme; and NGO micro-finance institutions.

Specialized Micro-Finance Institutions

Khushali Bank and First Micro-Finance Bank are the specialized MFIs, set up by the Government of Pakistan in 2000 and 2001, respectively. In addition, First Women Bank also disburses micro-credit to women.

Khushali Bank aims to promote self-employment. This provides loans up to Rs 30,000 to poor people to set up their own business. The Bank's social sector services package includes women development, capacity building services for skill development and the provision of basic infrastructure services such as health, education, drinking water, sanitation and communication etc. Up to March 2004, the Bank had disbursed loans amounting to Rs 2.135 billion to 210,784 people. Women constitute 35 per cent of the Bank's clients. Nearly 80 per cent of the lending activity remains in the rural areas and 20 per cent in urban areas. The Bank plans to access over 56,000 people by the year 2006 (Pakistan Economic Survey, 2003-04).

The main objective of the First Micro-Finance Bank is to provide financial services to the needy, especially to the women, in urban as well as in rural areas.

Rural Support Programmes (RSPs)

The RSPs are some of the pioneering initiatives undertaken in Pakistan for micro-credit schemes to the poor. The RSPs function on the basis of a community model, which uses the community organization forum for delivering credit.

NGO Micro-Finance Institutions: Pakistan Poverty Alleviation Fund (PPAF)

In order to enhance the access of the poorer households and communities to socio-economic services and hence their empowerment, the Government of Pakistan set up Pakistan Poverty Alleviation Fund (PPAF) in February 1997. PPAF funds for income generation activities and improved community physical infrastructure are disbursed through its three main units, viz., (1) Credit and Enterprise Development Unit, (2) Community Physical Infrastructure Unit, and (3) Human and Institutional Development Unit. PPAF aims to reach the poor and disadvantaged communities in both rural and urban areas through NGOs and the community-based organizations (CBOs).

The Pakistan Microfinance Network (PMN) is the representative body of MFIs in Pakistan that includes formal sector financial institutions, NGOs and RSPs. According to the PMN, nearly 5.6 million individuals in Pakistan are in need of credit services. However, the outreach of present services fulfils the needs of only 1 per cent.

According to the Annual Report of PPAF (2004), micro-credit loans of PPAF have increased from Rs 35.6 million to Rs 2,814 million between the financial year 2000 and the financial year 2003. The bulk of the micro-credit is disbursed under the Credit and Enterprise Development Unit with disbursements in the financial year 2003 of Rs 1,314 million, 47 per cent of the total PPAF disbursement. This amount was equivalent to 4.8 per cent of the total institutional loans disbursed during that year. In 2003, the 119,196 borrowers received an average loan of Rs 8,816. Nearly 44 per cent loans went to women. Most of the loans (38%) were disbursed for livestock, followed by agriculture (32%), and enterprise development and commerce and trade (30%).

Gallup Pakistan (2003) evaluated the functioning of PPAF through a survey of 1,700 borrower and non-borrower households in 140 community organizations of 17 districts in all the four provinces of Pakistan. This study found that borrowing households were better off than those that had not borrowed. On the average their incomes and consumption had increased and there was an improvement in their personal and business assets, housing facilities and other amenities/services, and also in their social status (especially for women borrowers). Borrowers were, however, not able to obtain as much credit as they wanted. In the survey sample, the mean value of loans received by the borrower group was Rs 9,138, 53 per cent of their desired amount (Rs 17,136). This survey asked several questions related to the change in personal social status by men and women. These results are summarized in Table 4.7.

The table shows a significant and positive change in the personal social status of women who obtained and utilized loans. It can be concluded that participation in micro-credit improves the level of empowerment of Pakistani women.

Table 4.7

Perception about Change in Personal Social Status

Questions	*Change*	*Total (%)*	*Male %*	*Female %*
How has your social status been affected after taking loan?	Increased	45	39	60
	Decreased	4	5	1
	Unchanged	51	56	39
Has the importance of your opinion regarding children marriages....	Increased	37	33	46
	Decreased	1	1	0
	Unchanged	63	67	54
Has the importance of your opinion regarding decisions on education of children....	Increased	31	27	40
	Decreased	3	3	2
	Unchanged	66	70	58
Has the importance of your opinion in resolving family disputes....	Increased	19	18	20
	Decreased	12	10	15
	Unchanged	70	72	65
Has the importance of your opinion in business decisions....	Increased	37	32	48
	Decreased	3	3	3
	Unchanged	60	65	49
Has the importance of your opinion in purchase or sale of household items....	Increased	25	22	31
	Decreased	3	4	2
	Unchanged	72	74	67
Has the importance of your opinion in purchase and sale of property....	Increased	21	20	22
	Decreased	2	2	2
	Unchanged	78	79	75

Source: Gallup (2003).

According to the data provided by the PMN, during past four years, the proportion of women savers increased from 30 per cent to 34 per cent. In 2002, the average female savings were Rs 842 against male savings of Rs 1129. By the end of 2003, there were 71,595 individuals who took loans from specialized MFIs/banks, among them 84.11 per cent were females. Similarly, the proportion of female borrowers in total borrowers from RSPs and NGO MFIs was 35.4 per cent and 72.62 per cent, respectively.

The concept of micro-credit for women development is fairly new in Pakistan and it may be too early to examine its impact on their social status and empowerment. However, based on the available data published by the PMN and PPAF, case studies done by some NGOs, and the assessment report of the Gallup Pakistan, we can conclude that micro-credit is serving as an effective tool of women empowerment.

Conclusions

This paper examined the economic empowerment of Pakistan's women in rural areas by looking at their participation in the labour market. Using a nationally representative data set and applying statistical techniques, we draw five main conclusions:

- *Limited role of rural women in household decision-making*: The head of the household appeared as major decision-maker in the family. However, the women who participate in wage market have some autonomy in the decision-making processes at household level as compared to those women who do not take part in wage employment.
- *Extremely low participation of rural women in labour market*: Rural labour market is characterized by low female labour force participation rates. This is primarily not only due to social and cultural taboos but also because of fewer job opportunities for females in rural areas. In most instances this may also be due to the under-reporting of female work as most of the female activities may easily pass off as household chores. Because of low levels of education, a majority of women are found concentrated either in agricultural sector or non-agricultural informal sector. Most of the females are working as unpaid family helpers or wage employees.
- *Rural women face extremely discriminatory wage rate in the informal sector*: The informal sector generally demands less educated and low skilled manpower. A larger proportion of women, who involve in non-farm activities in rural Pakistan, are found concentrated in the informal sector where they receive much lower wages as compared to men for similar activities and same working hours. On an average males get higher reward in both formal as well as informal sectors than females. In the informal sector, this difference is highest for the working groups 15-24 hours and 40-48 hours. This, however, essentially underestimates the actual working hours of females since it does not include the time they devote in the

production of goods and services at home that are otherwise available in the market.

- *Women contribute a significant amount in the economy if their housework is valued in monetary terms*: Women spend a large portion of their time in household chores, which goes unnoticed and to-date there have been no attempts to measure their housework in monetary terms. A typical rural woman contributes Rs. 1,500 per month in her household if we apply a discriminatory prevailing rural market wage rate. Considering only those rural females who are categorized as unemployed, they are contributing a worth of approximately Rs. 304 billion every year to Pakistan's economy that remains unnoticed. This amount would increase considerably if all women from rural as well as urban areas were included.
- *Micro-credit plays an important role in improving the social status of women*: Despite being at a transition stage, the role of micro-credit is found to be very positive in empowering women in Pakistan. The experiences of many NGOs and rural support programmes indicate a significant and positive change in the social status of Pakistani rural women who obtained loans to generate income for their household.

In Pakistani society, women's decision to participate in the labour force is governed by cultural, social and economic factors, it is not straightforward to say that employed and earning women are 'empowered women'. This argument ought to be considered in relation to the conditions of the working women as well as the factors that force them to work. In this regard micro-credit has gained a lot of popularity as an empowerment tool during the last two decades. Empowerment is not a spontaneous phenomenon and nor is it one that can be imposed from outside. However, policy can certainly create an environment to facilitate and promote women empowerment. Some of the policy measures that can promote women empowerment are as follows:

- Data and research (especially on working hours for women).
- Labour laws for the informal sector (strict implementation of labour laws).
- Investment in girls education and health.
- Comprehensive micro-credit programmes with broader outreach.

■ Notes

1. Pakistan ranked 92 out of 94 countries in 1997.
2. Women's participation in the general election of 2002 was 46.14 per cent only as compared to developed countries where women's participation in the electoral process exceeds 90 per cent. In the elections of 1996-97, women's legislative representation remained extremely low (only 1.4%) with highest representation in National Assembly (3.2%). The elections of 2002 showed a remarkable increase in women's legislative representation, i.e., from 1.4 per cent to 19.9 per cent. In National Assembly, this proportion was 21.6 per cent. In Provincial Assemblies and Senate, this proportion remained in the range of 18 to 19.7 per cent.
3. These activities are: agricultural operations such as ploughing, sowing, transplanting rice, cotton picking, etc.; processing food such as grinding, drying seeds; livestock operations; poultry raising; construction work such as mud plaster, etc.; collection of firewood; fetching water; stitching/sewing; shopping; washing clothes; child care; helping in children's homework; house cleaning; etc.
4. For a detailed review see Nazli (2003).
5. Computation of average working hours in the listed fourteen activities gives 42 hours per week. It can be higher if we consider only those women who are involved in all fourteen activities. In our sample, however, we have not found any case in which a woman is involved in all fourteen activities.
6. This amount is equivalent to US$ 5 billion.
7. Only 8 per cent households borrowed from the formal sources of credit during 2001.

■ References

Ahmad, Munir, Asghar, C. and Khan, N.A., 1993. 'Participation of Rural Women in Agricultural and Household Activities: A Micro-level Analysis'. In A.S. Haider, Z. Hussain, R. McConnen, and S.J. Malik (ed.). *Agriculture Strategies in the 1990s: Issues and Policies*, Islamabad: Pakistan Association of Agricultural Social Scientists.

Alderman, H. and Chishti, S., 1989. 'Simultaneous Determination of Household and Market Oriented Activities of Women in Rural Pakistan', *Research in Population Economics,* Vol. 17.

Arif, G.M.F. and Sheik K.H., 2002. 'Women's Employment Concerns and Working Conditions in Pakistan', *PIDE Workshop Paper*.

Ashe, Jefferey and Parrott, L., 2001. 'Impact Evaluation of PACT's Women's Empowerment Program in Nepal: A Savings and Literacy Led

Alternative to Financial Institution Building' (Cambridge, Mass.: Brandeis University).

Chaudary, M.A., F. Azim and A. Burki, 1989. 'Skill Generation and Entrepreneurship Development under *Ustad Shagird* System in Pakistan', National Manpower Commission and FES.

Chaudhry, M. Ghaffar and Khan, Z., 1987. 'Female Labour Force Participation Rates in Rural Pakistan: Some Fundamental Explanations and Policy Implications', *The Pakistan Development Review,* Vol. 26, No. 4, Part II.

Cheston, S. and Kuhn, L., 2002. 'Empowering Women through Micro-finance'. A draft paper commissioned by the Microcredit Summit Campaign. http://www.microfinancegateway.org/content/article/detail/3240_cheston_2002.DOC

ESCAP, 1997. *Rural Poverty Alleviation and Sustainable Development in Asia and the Pacific*, United Nations, New York.

—, 2002. Bulletin on Asia-Pacific Perspectives Asia-Pacific Economies: Sustaining Growth Amidst Uncertainties, United Nations, New York.

FAO, 1998. Women in Agriculture, Environment and Rural Production—Fact Sheet Pakistan. FAO, Bangkok.

Gallup Pakistan, 2003. PPAF Micro-Credit Financing: Assessment of Outcome, Islamabad.

Government of Pakistan, 1995. Fourth World Conference on Women, Beijing, September, Pakistan, National Report, Ministry of Women Development and Youth Affairs, Government of Pakistan, Pakistan.

Government of Pakistan (various issues), Labour Force Survey. Federal Bureau of Statistics, Statistics Division, Islamabad.

Guisinger S. and Irfan, M., 1974. 'Real Wages of Industrial Workers in Pakistan: 1954-1970', *The Pakistan Development Review,* Vol. 8, No. 4.

Hamida, B., Essma, 2000. 'Empowering Women through Micro-Credit: A Case Study from Tunisia'.

Hashemi, S.M., R.R. Schuler, and A.P. Riley, 1996. 'Rural Credit Programs and Women's Empowerment in Bangladesh', *World Development,* 24, No. 4: 635-53.

Kabeer, N., 1996. 'Agency, Well-being & Inequality: Reflections on the Gender Dimensions of Poverty', *IDS Bulletin,* 27, No.1: 11-21.

Khan, S.A. and F. Bilquees, 1976. 'The Attitude, Environment and Activities of Rural Economy: Study of Jhok Sayal', Pakistan Institute of Development Economics Research Report No. 98, Islamabad.

Khandker, Shahidur R., 1999. *Fighting Poverty with Micro-credit: Experience in Bangladesh* New York: Oxford University Press.

Mumtaz, Khawar, 1995. 'Gender issues in agricultural and rural development' in *Gender Issues in Agricultural and Rural Development Policy in Asia and the Pacific*, RAPA Publication 1995/2, Regional Office for Asia and the Pacific (RAPA), Food and Agricultural Organization of the United Nations, Bangkok.

Nazli, H., 2003. 'Rural Labour Markets in Pakistan: Institutions and Constraints'. Background Paper prepared for the Rural Factor Market Study, The World Bank, Washington D.C.

Pakistan Microfinance Network, 2003. Performance Indicators Report, Islamabad.

Pakistan Rural Household Survey, 2001. Pakistan Rural Household Survey. PIDE/World Bank presented at the *Civil Society Workshop Rehearsal, Cairo, Egypt,* March 2000, 7.

Sarwar, M. and Saleem, M.A., 1993, *Baseline Study of Punjab Small Holders Dairy Development Project in Gujranwala,* Punjab Economic Research Institute, Lahore.

Sather, Z. and S. Kazi, 1997. 'Women's Autonomy, Livelihood and Fertility: A Case of Rural Punjab', Pakistan Institute of Development Economics. Islamabad.

Shah, Nasira (ed.), 1989. *Pakistani Women: A Socio-economic & Demographic Profile,* Pakistan Institute of Development Economics, Islamabad and East-West Population Institute Honolulu, Hawaii.

Siddiqui, R., 2003. 'Modeling Gender Dimensions of the Impact of Economic Reforms on Time Allocation Among Market Work, Household Work and Leisure'. Paper presented at PIDE internal seminar.

Sultana, N., Nazli, H. and Malik, S.J., 1994. 'Determinants of Female Time Allocation in Selected Districts of Pakistan', *The Pakistan Development Review,* Vol. 33, No. 4.

UNDP, 2004. *Human Development Report,* Oxford University Press, New York.

Vijfhuizen, Carin, Carla Braga, Luis Artur and Nazneen Kanji, 2003. 'Gender, Markets and Livelihoods in the Context of Globalisation: A Study of the Cashew Sector in Mozambique'. Main Report. International Institute of Environment and Development.

World Bank, 1990. *Women in Pakistan: An Economic and Social Strategy,* A World Bank Country Study, Washington, D.C.

—, 1998. *PREM Notes,* No. 8 (Washington, World Bank).

—, 2001. *Engendering Development: Through Gender Equality in Rights, Resources, and Voice*—Summary (Washington, D.C.: World Bank, 2001); www.worldbank.org/gender/prr/engendersummary. pdf.

—, 2002. *Pakistan Poverty Assessment: Poverty in Pakistan: Vulnerabilities, Social Gaps, and Rural Dynamics,* The World Bank, Washington D.C.

World Trade Report 2003. *Annual Report 2003,* World Trade Organization.

Websites consulted

www.google.com
www.pak.gov.pk
www.pmn.org.pk
www.ppaf.org.pk
www.ifpri.org
www.worldbank.org
www.adb.org
www.fmb.org.pk
www.nrsp.org.pk

Chapter 5

Micro-Credit Programmes and Rural Women

A Case Study of Lalitpur District of Nepal

Puspa Ghimere Niraula

The population of Nepal is 23.15 million, of which women constitute 50.1 per cent (Population Census, 2001). The growth rate of population is 2.27 per cent whereas GDP growth rate is 3.1 per cent only (HMG Economic Survey, 2003-04). Around 80 per cent of the population is dependent on agriculture, where growth depends on the vagaries of monsoon. A recent estimate made by the National Planning Commission shows the extent of poverty at 38 per cent (living on a dollar or less a day). Since more than 90 per cent of the country's population is living in rural areas, the nature of income-based poverty is also rural-oriented (Economic Survey, 2003-04). It is more intense and severe in the villages of the hilly regions of the mid-western and far-western development regions of Nepal (Economic Survey, 2003-04). Analyzing from a gender perspective, poverty affects women's lives more than men, which are reflected in gender-based economic and social indicators of the country as shown in Table 5.1 below:

Table 5.1

Changing Gender Status: Selected Socio-Economic Indicators

Indicators/Years	*1981*	*1991*	*2001*
Economically active (age of 10 years and above)			
(i) Female	46.2	45.5	55.3
(ii) Male	83.1	68.7	71.7
Women in total economically active population (per cent)	34.6	40.4	43.4
Women in agriculture (per cent)	36.4	45.0	48.1
Women in non-agriculture jobs (per cent)	14.3	20.2	34.4
Literacy in 6 years + age group (per cent)			
(i) Female	12	24.7	42.5
(ii) Male	34	54.1	65.1
Female in total school enrolment			
(i) Primary		37.2	44.1
(ii) Secondary		31.5	41.5
(iii) Higher Secondary		28.7	40.6
Life expectancy at birth (years)			
(i) Female	48.1	53.5	61.7
(ii) Male	50.9	55.0	60.1
MMR per 100,000 delivery (number)		850	539
Female/male wage ratio in:			
(i) Agriculture			4/5
(ii) Non-agriculture			3/4
HDI Index	0.328	0.416	0.490
GDI Index	—	0.312	0.470

Source: Acharya, 2003 and Population Census, 2001, HMG/N Economic Survey, 2003/04.

The table shows that women's labour force participation is increasing between 1981 and 2001. Women fare worse than men in all indicators, although over time there is an overall improvement for both men and women.

Background of Micro-Credit Programmes in Nepal

In Nepal, although development programmes targeted to women existed since the inception of the planned development during mid-1950s, those programmes mostly catered to address the reproductive roles of women as mothers and homemakers (Bhadra, 2003). The productive role of women has been recognized only after the landmark study of the status of women in Nepal in 1979.[1]

The Government of Nepal incorporated a separate chapter on women in development (WID) in its Sixth Five-Year Plan (1980-1985). After that, provisions have been made to mobilize and involve women, both as agents and beneficiaries, of the nation's development process (Acharya, 2003). Several women targeted programmes are initiated in sectors like education, health and micro-credit for income generation. Women targeted micro-credit programmes are Women Development Programme/Small Farmer Development Programme of ADB/N (1981), and Production Credit for Rural Women (1982) of the Ministry of Panchayat and Local Government (Bhadra, 2003). In 1993, effectiveness of PCRW programme resulted in another ADB-funded Micro-Credit Project for Women to be delivered by the NGOs.[2]

After the restoration of democracy in 1990 and the constitutional mandate for gender equality, Nepal became a signatory of CEDAW in 1991. The Convention (CEDAW) as a human rights document calls for empowerment of women through development deliveries (Women's Studies Programme, TU, 2003). In 1995, Nepal ratified Beijing Platform for Action to address the 12 critical areas of concern for women and girls. In line with Beijing declarations, the Ninth (1997-2002) and current Tenth (2002-2007) Five-Year Plans have aimed to achieve the goal of poverty alleviation through mainstreaming and eliminating gender inequality and empowerment of women (Acharya, 2003).

In 1999, the Women Development Division in Ministry of Local Development was transferred to the Ministry of Women, Children and Social Welfare. In fiscal year 1999-2000 Women's Awareness and Income Generation Programme, known as Jagriti, was initiated with a goal of mobilizing community-based women's organizations.[3] Nepal has endorsed the UN Millennium Assembly Declaration in 2001 and endorsed for promotion of gender equality and empowerment of women.[4]

In the education sector, girls' scholarship programmes had been in operation in the Ministry of Education and Sports (MOES) for a long time. Under the Women's Education Section of Department of Education, various women and girls targeted educational programmes are being implemented such as girls scholarships, feeder hostels and female teachers programmes, textbooks, uniforms and food distribution programmes, non-formal education, and out of school education.[5]

In health sector, during 1960s and 1970s, health programmes targeted at women were mostly related to family planning. During 1980s maternal and child health programmes were launched with a view to curtail maternal and child mortality. During 1990s, especially after the Cairo Conference on Population and Development and the Beijing Conference, focus on women's health has shifted to women's reproductive health and safer motherhood programmes.[6]

At present, under the umbrella of Women Development Programme of the Ministry of Women, Children and Social Welfare, the main micro-credit programmes in operation are:[7]

1. Production Credit for Rural Women (PCRW),
2. Micro-Credit Project for Women (MCPW), and
3. Women's Awareness and Income Generation Programme (Jagriti).

Production Credit for Rural Women

PCRW programme was launched in 1982 with an objective of women's socio-economic development with provisions for micro-credit, extension services, drinking water, health services and skill development trainings. The main focus of the programme is to raise the economic status of group members. The programme is initiated in all 75 districts under the umbrella of Women Development Programme. The main activities under PCRW are:[8]

(i) *Training*: basic training, enterprise development, gender sensitization, institutional development, reproductive health and legal awareness training.
(ii) *Income-Generation Activities*: on-farm—crop development and off-farm activities—cottage industries, retail shop and saving and credit management.
(iii) *Community Development Programme*: Non-formal education and early child development, drinking water and sanitation,

improved stoves, *Sulav* toilets, improved water-mill, reproductive health and family planning.

(iv) *Institutional Development Programme*: women's groups are facilitated to organize into ward-level committees, Village Development Committees (VDCs) women's cooperatives formation, and capacity building of existing cooperatives.

Micro-Credit Project for Women

A decade's successful experience of PCRW programme made the government launched MCPW in 1993. Currently, such projects are conducted in 12 districts and five municipalities with 95 NGO partners. The project has already formed 10 women's development cooperatives. MCPW differs from PCRW as it is conducted by NGOs at the supervision of Women Development Section offices. The main focus of this programme is to raise the economic status of group members. The main programmes under MCPW are:[9]

(i) Women's group formation and training,
(ii) Strengthening of NGO capacity, and
(iii) Micro-credit for women.

Women's Awareness and Income Generation Programme – Jagriti

This programme is lunched by HMG/N, as extension to replicate the successes of PCRW and MCPW programmes. The main focus of the Jagriti programme is social, economic and political empowerment of women. Jagriti differs from PCRW and MCPW in its focus and modality. It is a type of institutionalized self-help group at the grassroots level for which local level social worker work as a volunteer and facilitate the social mobilization of women and saving and credit activities. The main activities of Jagriti programme are:[10]

(i) Institutional development,
(ii) Training,
(iii) Saving and credit programme,
(iv) Income generation, and
(v) Women's awareness programme.

With these introductions to various micro-credit programmes, launched by the Nepalese government, the study aims to highlight the effectiveness of women-targeted programmes on women's socio-economic empowerment, especially on three aspects, viz., income generation, employment, and education and health. To assess the impact of PCRW, MCPW and Jagriti programmes, a case study of Lalitpur district was undertaken in 2003. The findings of these programmes are based on the study done by Central Department of Home Science and Women's Studies, Tribhuvan University (2003). It was a team research conducted in five sample districts in five development regions of the country, with the author as the team leader of Lalitpur district.

Both qualitative and quantitative techniques were used to collect primary information. Focused group discussion, key informant interviews and observation methods were used for obtaining qualitative information. Survey method with structured questionnaire was used to collect quantitative information. To assess the real impact of women-targeted programmes on women, an experimental method was used. The PCRW, MCPW and Jagriti programme members were taken as the experimental groups and those women who were not members of any such programmes were taken as the control group. Gender analysis tools were used to analyze gender differentials in roles, access, control, decision-making and participation between the experimental and control groups of women.

Lalitpur district lies in Central Development Region of Nepal. It is one of the three districts of Kathmandu valley. Total population of the district is 3,37,785. Of them, 48.9 per cent is female population (Census, 2001). According to the District Profile (2001),[11] major ethnic groups of Lalitpur district are Brahmin/Chhetri, Newar and Tamang. There were two government hospitals, nine private hospitals, 10 health posts and 30 sub-health posts in Lalitpur up to the year 1998-99.[12] According to the Ministry of Education and Sports (2001), total educational institutes in Lalitpur district were 740. Of them, pre-primary schools were 108, primary schools 310, lower secondary 172, secondary 126, higher secondary 13 and campus were 11.[13] Development indicators of Lalitpur district are[14]: HDI ranking is 2nd, GDI ranking is 3rd and GEM ranking is 1st.

In Lalitpur, the proportion of female-headed households is 14.2. Overall literacy rate of women in the district is 42 per cent and number of girls receiving scholarships are 255. Similarly, total girls' enrolment at primary, lower secondary and secondary levels is 49.1 per cent. In health aspect, 78 per cent of couples are found to practise family planning and 45 per cent of the deliveries are found to be assisted by trained health personnel.[15]

In Lalitpur district, there are mix-ethnic groups (mainly Brahmin/Chhetri, Newar and Tamang) but the women who were the members of PCRW, MCPW and Jagriti groups were mostly from Brahmin/Chhetri and Newar ethnic groups. This may affect the utilization of programme benefits, as these groups in the Lalitpur districts are comparatively well-off. Besides, the Women Development Offices (WDOs) might have purposively identified some successful groups for conducting Focus Group Discussions (FGDs) and questionnaire surveys.

Programme Impact

In Nepal, women-targeted micro-credit programmes are although in operation in all 75 districts, but not in all the Village Development Committees (VDCs) of the districts. So, in Lalitpur, women development officials and social mobilizers were consulted to identify the programme VDCs and women's groups.

In Lalitpur district, eight FGDs were conducted among 108 participants. In order to find the age differentials in income, health, literacy/education, political participation and legal awareness, age stratification was done while conducting FGDs, which were:

(i) Below 19 to 34 years
(ii) 35 to 50 years
(iii) Above 50 years

In Lalitpur district 65-70 questionnaires were administered proportionately—50 per cent for experimental group and 50 per cent for control group. Information obtained from FGDs and survey was supplemented by seven key informants interviews and observation of health posts and schools. Further, women's cooperatives were visited while participating in their monthly meetings. The research team spent nine days in Lalitpur district for collecting field information.

The findings showed that in Lalitpur PCRW and MCPW groups are more organized in terms of rules and regulations, saving and lending processes, organizing monthly meeting, etc. Women's groups in the VDCs have already formed their own cooperatives and were provided some seed money (around Rs 50,000) from the WDOs. In Jagriti groups also they collect savings and lend money among group members, the group was less organized and had not formed cooperatives. They used to say that as in other groups the WDO did not provide seed money to their groups.

In spite of some differences between the PCRW/MCPW and Jagriti groups, their working pattern (e.g., identification of the potential groups, organizing them with raising awareness, group formation, saving habit development and lending money) is similar.

Thus, the findings of FGDs in all the three groups are also much similar. Here are the major benefits of PCRW, MCPW and Jagriti programmes on women's lives as perceived by the women themselves.

Group dynamism and organizational development: All group members responded that they have got the opportunity to be organized in the groups. Now, they can share their feelings, experiences and problems with each other and understand each other.

Increased mobility: To participate in organizational activities, they are coming out from the household chores. Thus, the programmes have increased their mobility.

Development of saving habits: Previously, they did not have the idea of small savings, so they used to spend whatever money they had in hand. After joining the group they knew the importance of small savings and its credit potentialities. Thus, the programme has developed their saving habits and prevented them from unnecessary spending.

Availability of credits at low interest and without collateral: Now, they are getting loans at low interest rates through group guarantees.

Skill development: The group members are provided different types of skill development trainings, e.g., livestock and vegetable farming, training about soap making, candle, *tika, agarbatti* making and so on. Especially, training about livestock and vegetable farming are very helpful to them because Lalitpur has high potential for farm production and there is easy access to marketing also.

Capacity development: WDO is frequently providing different types of social mobilization and capacity building training to the group members, such as non-formal education classes, awareness about ante-natal care (ANC) and post-natal care (PNC) and family planning services, political participation and leadership development, etc., which are much helpful for socio-economic empowerment of programme women.

Legal awareness: WDO has also provided legal and reproductive health awareness trainings to the group members in their VDCs. Now, they came to know that before three months of conceiving, abortion is legal, but still they have doubts whether this would bring other negative consequences, especially to young girls. Some members knew that in case of rape and more children, abortion is legal. Earlier, there were many members, who did not know under which conditions abortion is legal.

Self-reliance, self-confidence and independence: With increased mobility, their self-reliance, self-confidence and independence (economic and social) have also increased. They are becoming vocal and able to talk with other people and/or share their problems openly.

As a result of self-reliance and socio-economic independence, the members feel that now they should not depend on husband or other family members to buy small personal needs. They can afford to buy basic needs such as medicine, food, clothes and stationery for their children too.

Family, community support: Slowly, they are getting support and respect from the family members and community people also.

Collective action against social evils: Now, they are able to take collective action against social evils. In some cases they have already taken action against alcoholism, domestic violence (wife beating), etc. Most importantly, they are confident enough to take action against such social problems.

Health Awareness

Women although were found aware of family planning, anti-natal and post-natal care, they were found less aware about their personal health care. Basically, they used to hide their reproductive health problems. Most of the women (below 50 years) were facing the problems of white water discharge and smelling, irregular menstruation, no menstruation (their menstruation had been stopped for some years)[16] and abdomen pain during menstruation. When the situation used to get critical, only then they share their problems with family members and would visit city hospitals.

Since the members were given legal awareness training, some of them were found aware of legalization of abortion. Still, there were some practices of unsafe abortions among the women like eating mirror dust, 'Kuvindo' (a kind of vegetable), turmeric and honey, drinking kerosene and eating dangerous herbs and using them in the vagina.

Health problems faced by the women above 50 years were poor eyesight, white water discharge, excessive bleeding, waist ache, backache and headache, disease related to uterus and prolapsed uterus. Thus, reproductive health issue is still a neglected issue among the women of this district.

Government health delivery system had also not adequately addressed women's reproductive health problems. In case of bleeding, they had to visit city hospitals. Group members also opined that health workers are generally male and there is lack of separate child delivery room in the health post. So people prefer to go to city hospitals rather than village health posts. During the observation of a health post, it was found that the personnel have maintained the privacy by keeping a cupboard in front of the checking bed.

Education Awareness

In Lalitpur most of the respondents below 50 years had attended primary level education or some kind of non-formal education. All the members were sending their daughters to school. They had the view that educating girls is necessary for their future development. However, due to the gendered division of labour, mostly girls have to help their mother in the household chores.

Group members further responded that in spite of the provisions of scholarships and other incentives at school, especially for girls and other disadvantaged children, there are problems of non-availability of textbooks in time, drinking water and other physical facilities at school.

Thus, the government service (especially educational and health) delivery system had not adequately addressed the problems of girls/women even in the more accessible district.

Economic Benefits

Saving credit mobilization: Women of all three groups opined that now they have learned to save money, so they feel safe that they can use their savings whenever needed. They further opined that through this process of saving credit mobilization, they are getting credit at low interest rates.

Skill development and income generation: One of the main activities conducted/practised through the micro-credit programmes in Lalitpur district was skill development and income generation. Therefore, almost all old members had been provided training about livestock raising, vegetable farming and small-scale entrepreneurship development (e.g., making tika, dhup, petty shops, etc.) depending upon the potentiality of the locality. Many group members have started livestock and vegetable farming whereas some of them had opened small tea shop and other retail shops. Their income has been increased from selling agriculture products (milk and vegetables) and shopkeeping. As a result, the purchasing power capacity of their family has also been increased.

Among other economic benefits included development of collective bargaining capacity among the group members. Now, they are able to take decisions independently and felt economically secured for their old ages.

Social Benefits

Development of group dynamism is one of the main social benefits of the programme. They opined that organizing in groups means possibility of meeting friends, sharing and interaction with each other, discussion on any issues and getting together for collective action. They feel secured that they have strong organizational structure, feeling of collectiveness and unity. They also feel that their individual status in the family has become much better as their family members are recognizing the economic potentialities of saving-credit activities. Their saving habit has been developed. They are also getting loans at cheap interest rates through group guarantees and have already started different income-generating activities. Thus, through micro-credit activities, their status in the family, community as well as at larger societal level has been improved. Now, they feel they are able to solve problems through group efforts.

Weaknesses

Low saving and low investment: The group members opined that their small savings are not sufficient to meet their demands for money. Although the Women Development Office has provided some seed money to the PCRW and MCPW members after they formed their cooperatives, that was not enough to meet their demands. The members require money for livestock farming (which usually cost Rs 15-25,000), whereas the maximum limit of providing loan is only Rs 15,000. Thus, many group members feel it is very difficult to get loan, particularly if other members have already taken. Due to limited credit facilities some of them could not conduct big enterprises even if they have potential, skill and market for the products. As a result of low investment, the profit remained low, thus income status of the women did not improve as expected.

Increased workload of women: The women who are involved in any income-generating activities, like vegetable farming, livestock farming, petty shop, etc., should devote extra time in addition to their regular household (including reproductive) responsibilities. Therefore, in spite of increased self-confidence and awareness (in economic, social and legal aspects), their workload has increased. Thus, one of the main weaknesses of micro-credit programmes all over the country is that they have increased workload of women. Still they have no programmes of changing social perceptions about gender roles.[17] Although group members say that they are getting family support, that is generally limited to moral support only. Thus, due to increased workload, some of them reported that they could not even find time to visit their parents.

There are some members in the groups, who even do not get moral support from their male members, especially from their husbands. Sometimes, they had to pretend or say something else to attend monthly meeting, especially when their male members stay at home.

Low support from the community people: The upper caste community leaders and elites, mainly male, are not very cooperative or supportive to women's groups. Sometimes, they feel threatened due to their collectiveness and solidarity. Here is an illustration.

Women's groups were collecting monthly Rs 5 extra (as a community saving)[18] since the beginning of group activities. The money was collected to spend in some community activities. After some years of collection of extra money, they built a temple from that money in a nearby village. Actually, they wanted to save their time visiting temples during festivals. They contributed their labour too for constructing the temple. When the temple was ready, at the beginning, no men of the community wanted to visit the temple. They were saying that it was women's temple. Rather, they wanted to construct a separate temple for men. Later, due to their collective efforts, the misunderstanding was solved and now there is no such situation and men of the community did not construct separate temple for themselves.

Inadequate income-generating training days, training quotas and the types of training: The group members opined that limited quotas for skill development and income-generation training are inadequate as compared to their increasing numbers. Some new members have not even got 7 days' basic training. Those who have got some sort of training felt that training days are insufficient because for them, to start any sort of business and manage it properly they need detailed information/knowledge about it. Besides, those who had got training about making soap, tika, candle and agarbatti (mainly those from the Jagriti group), felt problems of procurement of raw materials and market for their products. Thus, they need different types of training, according to availability of raw materials and potentiality of local/domestic markets.

Some group members also feel discriminated, while distributing skill development training quotas. They were saying that some active members are taking training opportunities several times and some were not getting chance even once.

Lack of educated members in the groups, especially to maintain accounts: After formation of cooperatives, the group members of Lalitpur district were facing severely the problem of keeping accounts properly. The main reason is that there are no educated members in the group. Before forming cooperatives, the members were provided non-formal education classes and were made to read and write. Besides, some members had also been given training about book-keeping and other financial activities but in the absence of WDO members they still feel the problem of keeping accounts properly.

A specific problem felt by Jagriti group members is the problem of depositing money regularly. Some members find it a burden to deposit even Rs 25 per month due to their poverty. Those members, who have already taken income-generation training and also started some sort of business for some time, felt they lacked marketing information and linkages.

Suggestions to Overcome the Weaknesses

The members of all three groups were also asked to suggest some measures to overcome the weaknesses. Some of the suggestions that we received are as under:

(1) Non-formal education programmes to those who could not read and write. The members opined that literate and/or educated members understand financial and other official matters easily and would be able to mobilize other women outside the programme.

(2) There are some educated women in the VDCs, who are not involved in groups due to their own time and work schedules. Group members opined that if the educated women of the VDC would be encouraged to join the group, they would not have problems of book-keeping. Therefore, in this regard, they had needed some support from women's development workers or women's development offices to mobilize educated women.

(3) Training:
   - Each and every group member should be provided at least basic training of 7 days.
   - Educated members should be provided training about book-keeping, balance-sheet preparation and other financial management.
   - Skill development and income-generation training should be provided to all members according to their needs and capacities.

(4) Group members also suggested that each and every member should get opportunities of skill development and income-generation training. Thus, available training quotas should be fairly distributed.

(5) Group members of MCPW suggested that there should be a women's library in the village equipped with sufficient reading materials, especially the holy books and other books related to saving-credit management, so that the adult women of the village should not always listen from others, rather they can read and get knowledge by themselves.

(6) Since members of the Jagriti groups were facing problems of utilizing their skills due to the lack of raw materials and marketing of the products, they suggested the WDOs should support to explore sources of raw materials and marketing of the products at least in the starting phases.

(7) Members of all three groups suggested that in order to ensure girls' access to at least primary education, they should be provided free education, including free uniform and textbooks, and drinking water facilities at school.

Gender Analysis of Programmes' Impact

Some gender analysis tools were used to analyse gender differentials in mobility, access and control over household resources and decision-making. This is also to test if women development programmes have led to any gender transformation. The major findings of the gender analysis were:

Mobility

Women from the different programme groups are found to have more mobility in terms of distance and frequency of visit outside their homes and villages.

Access and Control over Resources

With regard to household resources, women from the programmes are found to have more access in terms of labour, time, land, livestock and income. Regarding control over resources, however, they have less control than their male counterparts.

Regarding community resources the women from the programmes have more access in grazing land, forest, water resource, saving and credit, etc. than women outside the programmes. Women in both the groups did not have any access to the state level resources, especially in planning and budgeting process.

Decision-Making

Women from the programmes have greater decision-making power in terms of family planning, seeking medical care, participation in meeting/trainings, etc. than women outside the programmes. In family matters, women from programmes are found to have greater decision-making power in terms of expenditure on children's education, seeking medical care for family members, purchase and share of livestock, etc.

In agricultural matters also women from the programmes have greater decision-making power in terms of labour allocation, crop selection, livestock selection and input-output marketing. However, in case of output marketing, women of both groups, have less decision-making power than their male counterparts.

Analysis of Gender Roles

Reproductive role: For both groups of women, there is still no sharing of household and other reproductive works, e.g., rearing and caring of children, old and sick people by their male counterparts. So, the women from the programmes are suffering from excessive workload.

Productive role: Women from both groups are heavily engaged in agriculture and livestock activities but they have no control over marketing of products. Some women from programmes have started retail shops and they are making good income and also controlling their earned income to some extent. Women outside the programmes were generally engaged in construction works as wage labour. Some of the women from the programmes (e.g., Jagriti) have taken skill development training on making agarbatti, candle, tika, etc., but due to non-availability of raw materials and proper information about marketing channels, they are unable to start business or continue it if already started.

Community role: Women from the programmes are found to participate more in community level activities than women outside the programmes in activities like community forestry, saving and credit, fund collection for social and cultural activities. In ward-level politics, generally, men involve more than women. Women from both groups are found to contribute voluntary labour in community development activities.

Some Best Practices

(1) Women' groups collected money and constructed a temple in the nearby village so that they could save their time and labour in visiting temples of city areas during festivals. They had the opinion that instead of walking (or travelling by vehicle) long distances, they can entertain themselves in their own villages.

(2) Similarly, women from one VDC (Bodikhel) collected money to enrol a girl in a private school and also made the school to grant scholarship for her study.

(3) The Jagriti group of women in Godamchaur VDC raised voice against alcoholism and protected a woman from regular beating by her husband. When her husband put her outside the home, they themselves made a house in a public land and ensured her settlement.

Concluding Remarks

In spite of the weaknesses and limitations, the micro-credit programmes implemented in Lalitpur district are quite successful in social mobilization and empowerment of women. In this regard, Acharya (2003) writes: "The micro-credit programmes, widely in vogue, have been designed to fit the traditional roles of women. They do not empower women or provide a better ground for equality directly, but indirectly they do strengthen women's self-confidence and capacity for collective action."[19]

During FGDs the members of Jagriti group were found less organized in terms of saving and credit mobilization as this has only four years of implementation.

As compared to economic independence and group solidarity women's groups were found less aware about their personal as well reproductive health matters. Although they share their problems among themselves (group members) and become friends, they hardly share their problems with their male counterparts. When the situation gets critical, only then do they share their problems with their male family members and visit city hospitals. Although male members of the family were not consulted during research, the health post personnel had the opinion that for ANC and PNC services women consult the health personnel frequently, but still tended to conceal any problem in their reproductive organs until it gets serious. Thus, they need special awareness programme in their reproductive health matters.

Micro-credit programmes will be an effective tool for social mobilization and women's empowerment if all the male members of the community/VDCs are equally mobilized or made aware about social, legal, political and economic aspects of gender equity together with their female counterparts.

At VDC or community level there should be interaction or talk programmes organized by WDOs at least once a month inviting all local community people, guardians, male/female intellectuals and resource persons. The issues for discussion should be women's workload and its consequences to their reproductive health (both physical and mental health), equal distribution of housework between women and men, gender equity in the distribution of household resources, role of both women and men in household decision-making and effective participation in local level governance.

■ Notes

1. *Gender Issues in Micro-Finance Management* by Bhadra (2003, p. 1) and *Study on the Effectiveness of Programs Targeted to Women*, Women's Studies Program, Tribhuvan University (2003, pp. 1 and 3).
2. Efforts at Promotion of Women in Nepal, Acharya, (2003, pp. 15-18) and *Gender Issues in Micro-Finance Management* by Bhadra (2003, p. 1).
3. *Nepalma Mahila Bikash: Awadharana, Sansthagat Byawastha, Karya Pragati Ra Chunautiharu*, Women's Development Division (2003, p. 43).
4. *Study on the Effectiveness of Programs Targeted to Women*, Women's Studies Program, Tribhuvan University (2003, pp. 1 and 3).
5. *Study on the Effectiveness of Programs Targeted to Women*, Women's Studies Program, Tribhuvan University (2003, pp. 1 and 3), *Gender Assessment in the Education Sector*, New ERA (2001, pp. 45-52) and Gender Budget Audit in Nepal, IIDS (2002, pp. 58-67).
6. *Study on the Effectiveness of Programs Targeted to Women*, ibid.
7. For detail please see *Nepalma Mahila Bikash: Awadharana, Sansthagat Byawastha, Karya Pragati Ra Chunautiharu*, Women's Development Division (2003, p. 46).

8. ibid (pp. 50-62).
9. ibid (pp. 65-68).
10. *Nepalma Mahila Bikash: Awadharana, Sansthagat Byawastha, Karya Pragati Ra Chunautiharu*, Women's Development Division (2003, pp. 63-65).
11. District Profile, Informal Sector Research and Study Center (2001).
12. ibid.
13. School Level Educational Statistics of Nepal (2001), DOE/MOES.
14. *Study on the Effectiveness of Programs Targeted to Women*, Women's Studies Program, Tribhuvan University (2003, pp. 10 and 11).
15. Sources: Census (2001), Annual Report of DOE/MOES (2000) and Annual Report of DOH/MOH cited by Women's Studies Program, TU (2003, p. 14).
16. All those whose menstruation had stopped since 1 to 5 years or becoming irregular were found taking Depo-Provera injection for family planning.
17. For detail please see the study report on "Gender Assessment and Gender Budget Audit of the Ministry of Local Development" conducted by SAHAVAGI team for Mainstreaming Gender Equity Program of the Ministry of Women Children and Social Welfare (2004).
18. *Nepalma Mahila Bikash: Awadharana, Sansthagat Byawastha, Karya Pragati Ra Chunautiharu*, Women's Development Division (2003, p.46).
19. Efforts at Promotion of Women in Nepal, Acharya (2003, p. 12).

■ References

Acharya, M., 2003. *Efforts at Promotion of Women in Nepal*, Tanka Prasad Acharya Memorial Foundation in cooperation with Friedrich-Ebert Stiftung, Kathmandu, Nepal.

Bhadra, C., 2003. 'Gender Issues in Micro-Finance Management', a paper presented in *Training on Principle and Management of Micro-Finance Institutes* conducted by Center for Micro-Finance Pvt. Ltd.

HMGN/NPC, 2002. *Population Census 2001*: National Report, National Planning Commission Secretariat, Central Bureau of Statistics in collaboration with UNFPA, Nepal.

HMGN/MOES, 2001. *School Level Educational Statistics of Nepal*, Ministry of Education and Sports, Department of Education, Statistics Section, Bhaktpur.

—, 1999. *Basic and Primary Education Program (BPEP II) 1999-2004*, Program Implementation Plan (Main Report), Ministry of Education, His Majesty's Government of Nepal.

HMG/NPC, 2002. *Tenth Plan 2002-2007*, His Majesty's Government, National Planning Commission, Kathmandu, Nepal.

IIDS, 2002. *Gender Budget Audit in Nepal, published by UNIFEM* 'Follow the Money' Series, South Asia in 2003.

Informal Sector Research and Study Center, 2001. *District Profile*, Kathmandu, Nepal.

New ERA, 2001. *Gender Assessment in the Education Sector, Mainstreaming Gender Equity Program* (MGEP)/UNDP, Lalitpur.

SAHAVAGI, 2003. *Gender Assessment and Gender Budget Audit of the MLD*, conducted for the MOWCSW and MGEP/UNDP, Kathmandu, Nepal.

WES/DOE/MOES, *Mahila Shikshya*, annual production 2000 to 2004.

Women's Studies Programme, Tribhuvan University, 2003. *Study on the Effectiveness of Programs Targeted to Women*, conducted for the Monitoring and Evaluation Division of National Planning Commission, Kathmandu, Nepal.

Chapter 6

Rural Women of Bangladesh

From Home to Market

Nazneen Ahmed

Traditionally, rural Bangladesh is described as agro-based economy with poor infrastructure, huge dependence on natural resources for livelihoods, little connection of farmers and artisans with formal market and scarce facilities of modern life. For the last one-and-a-half-decade such realities are increasingly being altered by new perceptions of livelihoods for the rural people. New opportunities and challenges, born out of the new realities, are influencing the rural women of Bangladesh—both their outer and inner states.

Since independence in 1971, the economy of Bangladesh went through massive changes in terms of both politics and development policy. The state-controlled economy that emerged after independence was reversed with private sector led economy since late 70s. The next decade experienced a series of deregulation and liberalization endeavours. Structural adjustment programmes of 1980s and massive liberalization (trade, finance and investment) attempts throughout 1990s have endured notable impacts all over the economy. New forms of cooperation between activities of government and non-government organizations (NGOs), evolution of micro-credit programmes, migration of people from rural area to the urban areas or even to another country, technological advancement in agriculture, newer business opportunities, education opportunities, infrastructural development—all these have led to new visions of livelihood in rural Bangladesh. The wind of changes has also blown over the rural women and has generated new dynamics in their livelihoods. The women are increasingly participating in formal market-based activities, altering the traditional view that they should only engage themselves in household duties. It has been, for a long time, common in rural Bangladesh for very poor women to engage themselves in paid work outside home. However, the new opportunities in livelihood have brought larger number of women to the paid work—even from the non-poor families. As a result, the power status of the women is also going through changes. The changing rural economy is posing new opportunities as well as new challenges to the rural women's life. Moreover, not all women have experienced the changes in the same way. In many cases new challenges are exposing women to new sources of vulnerability. There are innate crisis in women's livelihood in a country like Bangladesh and all is not just "gone with the wind".

This chapter will explore how participation in income generating activities is affecting the lives of rural women of Bangladesh. This will be performed by looking into two dimensions of the issue: (i) changes that are arising out of the utilization of the new opportunities available within the rural economy and (ii) impact of female participation in urban-based manufacturing sector, mainly in the readymade garment sector. While looking at the impacts of income generating work, the paper will explore the actors stimulating the rural women to participate in those activities.

Section 2 provides a brief profile of rural women of Bangladesh and section 3 describes some notable aspects of recent changes in the rural economy and the actors behind such changes. The nature of rural women's employment in the urban manufacturing sector is presented in section 4; the empowerment status of the rural women under the changing circumstances is analysed in section 5 while section 6 incorporates concluding remarks.

Women of Bangladesh: A General Profile

According to the World Bank statistics, 49.6 per cent of total population of Bangladesh in 2000 is women. Proportion of women in total population has increased over the years. Table 6.1 presents some selected gender statistics of Bangladesh. Proportion of female population is found to be 1 percentage point higher in Bangladesh compared to the South Asian average. Life expectancy at birth is higher for females compared to their male counterpart.

Table 6.1

Selected Gender Profile of Bangladesh

Indicators	*Bangladesh*				*South Asia*	
	1980	*1990*	*1995*	*2000*	*1980*	*2000*
GNP per capita(US$)	210	280	330	380	260	440
Population						
Total (millions)	85.4	110.0	120.1	131.1	901.3	1,354.2
Female population (% of total)	47.9	48.2	48.3	49.6	48.2	48.5
Life expectancy at birth (years)						
Male	49	55	58	61	54	62
Female	48	55	59	62	53	63

Source: Genderstat, World Bank, 2002.

According to FAO (2000), women constitute 45.6 per cent of the farming population of Bangladesh and they have extensive workloads with dual responsibility for farm and household production. It is also noted that the role of women in rice production is already substantial and expanding further. However, women's contribution to agriculture, which is counted as unpaid family labour, is grossly underestimated. Moreover, women are actively involved in forestry, fisheries and livestock production.

Table 6.2 shows that only 23 per cent of the rural women are engaged in income generating activities. About 59.3 per cent of them are engaged in agricultural work. However non-agricultural sector is also an important source of their income.

Table 6.2
Major Occupation of Rural Labour Force

(in percentage)

	Both Sex	*Male*	*Female*
Labour force participation rate (as % of total rural population)	54.6	84.0	23.1
Major occupation of the employed people			
Total	100	100	100
Professional, technical	3.2	3.2	2.9
Administration, managerial, clerical	1.9	2.1	6.4
Service workers	12.2	13.9	5.4
Agriculture, forestry, fisheries and related work	62.2	63.0	59.3
Production, transport labourers and others	15.9	15.5	17.6

Source: Labour Force Survey of Bangladesh, 2002.[1]

The majority of women workers are primarily involved in the informal sector of the economy. Bangladesh is a highly patriarchal society. This characteristic is more prominent in the rural areas. In households and through local and legal decision-making bodies, men exercise control over women's labour, their choice of marriage partner, their access to labour and other markets, and their income and assets. Women's access to legal, social, health, economic and political institutions is mediated by men. They are dependent on men throughout their lives, from father through husbands to sons. State legislation and institutions underpin this gender subordination and dependence, in spite of constitutional affirmations of sex equality.[2]

Changing Rural Economy: New Opportunities and Challenges for Rural Women

Nature of Changes in Rural Economy: Some Notable Features

Rural economy of Bangladesh has been experiencing rapid changes for the last one and a half-decade. Direct and indirect affects of globalization and various structural adjustment programmes are visible in many parts of rural Bangladesh though not in the same pace. According to Toufique and Turton (2002) the new rural scenario is one in which urbanization is an important demographic feature and where agriculture is one activity amongst many other actual and potential rural and non-rural activities. Income from non-agricultural sector is rising significantly. The proportion of income derived from non-agricultural activities broadly follows the pattern of increasing employment in the non-agricultural sector (Toufique, 2001). During the 1990s contribution of agriculture in the Gross Domestic Product (GDP) gradually declined (from 29% to 26% from early to late 1990s). Over the same time span, however, industrial sector's importance in GDP increased from 21 per cent to 26 per cent while the real GDP in this sector was rising by 86 per cent (World Bank, 2002). Share of rural household income derived from agriculture decreased from about 63 per cent in 1987 to 54 per cent in 1994 while the share derived from non-agricultural activities increased from 37 per cent to about 48 per cent. Market forces are evolving as important dictators of rural life. Roads, bridges and electrification have notably changed the rural physical and socio-economic infrastructure. Multinational and national suppliers and wholesalers are active even in remote areas. Thus rural livelihood opportunities are emerging often from outside the villages. In such a society human capital is becoming an important source of income generation instead of land (Toufique and Turton, 2002).

The rural women of Bangladesh are increasingly involved in paid work outside the home. Not only in economic activities but also the rural women are more visible in rural leadership. They are participating in rural elections, not only as voters but also as candidates. Many of them are elected to different positions of the local government. In Bangladesh, every 'Union Parishad' (UP), the lowest tier of local government, has to have at least three women members out of a total of 13. Rural women are participating as candidates for both reserved seats and open seats. In 1997 about 4,483 women participated (as candidates) in the election of 4,283 UPs. Out of this, 110 women were elected as members, and, of these, 20 women were elected as UP Chairmen (the highest position in UP). This was the first time when women stood for election in open seats of rural bodies.

Women are finding work as health and family planning visitors, teachers, and workers of income generating projects. In many cases the traditional employment of the women are altered. For example, women who were traditionally employed in *dheki* (indigenous home based manual rice milling) are now getting employment in the *chatals* (mechanized rice milling). They are even starting small businesses. A notable feature of the changes in rural women's life in the last decade was their participation in the micro-credit programmes operated by various NGOs. Because of inherent better management capacity of the females, micro-credit is often allocated to the women (though often the ultimate user is the man). Not only through micro-credit programme, but also through various health, development, education and social awareness programmes, NGOs are playing vital roles in bringing changes in the rural life. All these are having impacts that are more visible on women's life. Rozario (2002) has presented the following picture of new rural Bangladesh: (i) women play a more notable role in the cash economy as a result of the monetization of the village economy; (ii) villagers are more dependant on credit for all aspects of subsistence; (iii) women are mobile and have greater presence in public spaces and in formal paid labour.

Migration and greater mobility are playing a critical role in shaping the rural livelihood in Bangladesh. A number of people are migrating from the rural area to the urban area, even to the foreign countries. According to Afsar (2002) approximately 3 million Bangladeshi nationals were employed abroad between 1976-99, all of them temporary migrants. New migrants are mostly young adults. The traditional picture of only males leaving their village to find work to support the families is changing as rising number of women are joining their rank. A part of the rural women is moving to the urban manufacturing sector. Through such involvements, they now have better linkage with the global economy.

Main Actors Behind Recent Changes in the Rural Economy

There are broadly three actors in bringing changes in the rural economy: government, non-government organizations and market. The mechanism through which these actors are functioning is summarized in Figure 6.1.

Improved rural infrastructure has generated revolutionary impact on rural economy not only by improving the standard of living but also by stimulating market activities. It has made

Figure 6.1

Main Actors Behind Recent Rural Changes

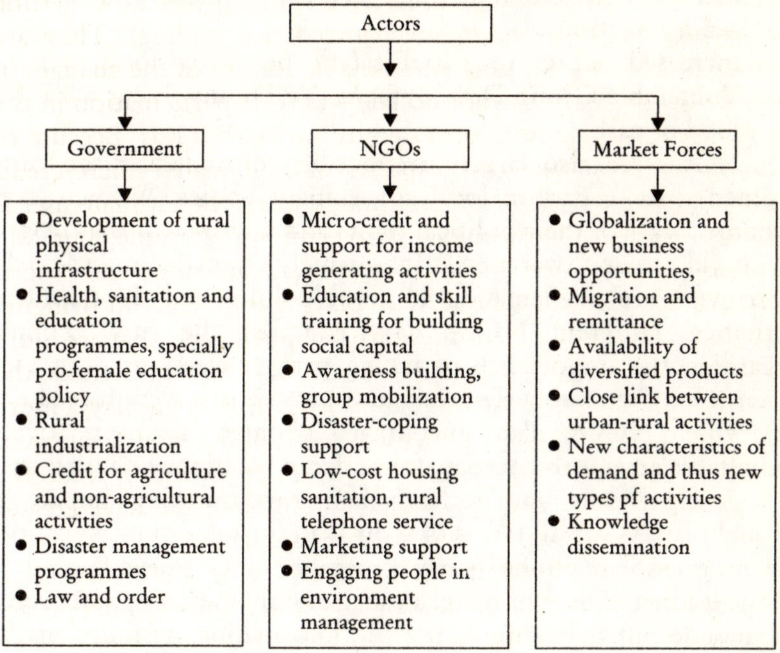

movements of both goods and people faster. Electricity has made it possible to adopt new technology. NGOs have become a new source of employment for rural women. Greater market opportunities are also enabling the rural women to move out of the traditional closed society. Women are increasingly absorbed in manufacturing sectors like Ready-made Garment (RMG) industry, jute handicrafts, tobacco processing, paper bag making, etc. NGO programmes are also improving the awareness of the women regarding health, legal rights, etc. Though there are shortcomings and several criticisms, there is no doubt that micro credit schemes of the NGOs have significantly improved the lives of thousands of women. NGO interventions have also succeeded in mitigating gender imbalance. According to Rozario (2002) some positive implications of such interventions are:

- Increased school attendance among females and the poor.

- Increased access to finance, which has increased women's financial independence.
- Increased pressure, through NGOs to modify aspects of gender relations.
- Increased access to social safety net provisions such as Vulnerable Group Development (VGD), involving work for food or cash.

NGOs are also largely responsible for inducing the rural women to take part in local government bodies. Women have become aware of their political rights and micro-credit has helped to build their awareness. Increasingly, female micro-credit borrowers are participating in local politics and development activities. Different NGOs have educated the rural women regarding the importance of taking part in elections even as a voter. Many women were reluctant to (sometime were forced not to) vote. NGOs also encouraged women from relatively vulnerable groups to compete for and win positions of authority.

A significant and rather silent revolutionary impact is brought by NGOs in terms of their loan for tele-communication. Owning a mobile phone by many members of Grameen Bank (one of the leading NGOs of Bangladesh) not only means a good source of income but it is stimulating the information mobility in the rural economy. In many remote regions in Bangladesh workers get informed about work through mobile phones. In many areas, mobile phone business has become a good source of income for women.

It is widely recognized now that the government-sponsored scholarship programme for secondary school education of the female students is having positive impacts on girls' enrolment and continuation in secondary education. Under this scheme girls receive a full tuition subsidy and a stipend to cover additional school expenses. No such facility is given to the boys. Such opportunity has succeeded in delaying the early marriages for the girls attending school. However, survey by Amin, Mahmud and Huq (2002) suggests that such delay in marriage ultimately increases the amount of dowry. Traditionally, more the age of a girl the more will be the dowry. Even the better qualification of the girls is failing to alter this. Therefore, the family of an 'aged' educated girl still has to pay higher dowry.

The expansion of the service sector and new market opportunities are involving women in new professions. Still there are some activities, which are considered to be men's job. For example women, specially, young ones do not go to run a shop in the market area nor do they become petty traders. Keeping 'good' reputation in the society is very important. Still an increasing number of rural women are participating in economic activities once considered unusual for women. Many of them are migrating to the urban manufacturing sector.

Rural Women in the Urban Manufacturing Sector: Becoming a Garment Worker

It is evident from the last section that a new livelihood opportunity for the rural women of Bangladesh is to join the urban manufacturing sector. In many cases these rural women have no previous experience of formal work, nor even any training. There are many sectors where women are joining (pharmaceuticals, shrimp processing, readymade garments etc). The present paper is concentrating on the women participation in the most important export sector of Bangladesh – the RMG sector.

Starting as a non-traditional export item in late 1970s, RMG sector evolved as the main export sector of Bangladesh by early 1990s. While the export earning from this sector was only $1 million in 1978, it became more than $4 billion in 2000. It is now quite an established fact that availability of cheap labour was the main pillar behind such a rapid flourish of this sector. While apparel sector employed 0.2 million people in 1985-86, it was employing 1.5 million in 1997-98 (Zohir, 2000). The current employment is 1.8 million and 80 per cent of them are females (Khundker, 2002). It is observed that almost all the women workers in the garment manufacturing industry originate in the rural areas and rural women's entrepreneurial role has expanded significantly in the recent past (Mahmud, 2001). Different studies on the female garment workers have found some common characteristics in them.

Thus we see from Table 6.3 that the female RMG workers are mostly young, unmarried and possess only 1-5 years of education. Such women are mainly from poor families. Traditionally, single rural women who migrate to urban areas alone

Table 6.3
Characteristics of Female RMG Workers in Different Studies with Respective Samples

Characteristics	*Kibria, 2001 (%)*	*Zohir, 2000 (%)*	*Zohir and Majumder, 1996 (%)*
Age Group (years)			
Below 15	16	—	16
15-19	45	54	39
20-24	26	23	24
25-29	9	14	11
30+	4	9	10
Marital Status			
Never-Married	50	50	54
Married	20	39	38
Widowed/separated/ Abandoned/Divorced	30	11	8
Education (years)			
No Education	24	27	29
1-5	47	40	35
6-10	29	30	27
10+	—	2	9

have been destitute and impoverished from the lowest socio-economic segment of the society. However, with emergence of garment industry, solo migration of rural women from a more diverse array of socio-economic background is observed (Kibria, 2001). The previous studies found the following reasons to be stimulating a rural woman's decision to work in RMG factories:

- Some women have to earn cash out of necessity in order to survive. These women are not dealing with the question of whether or not to work but what type of work is available at hand.
- For some better-off married women, factory work offers an acceptable way to earn cash to improve the living standards of their families. Particularly common is the earmarking of income for the current or future needs of children or younger siblings.

A large group of females consider the job in a RMG factory to be a way to financially take care of oneself and build one's own future, thus reducing the burden and responsibility of the family for one's upkeep and well-being. They think that one can make far more money on a regular basis than other available activities in the rural areas. Besides financial incentives, the nature of garment work and the social image that it holds seem to create some attractions over the more traditional forms of income generation. One important issue that influences their decision to work in garments is, they think that the job will remove the burden of the parents for arranging and paying for their marriage and dowry.

A job in a RMG factory means not only income for the females but greater freedom and more importance in the family. In most cases, the payment in a factory is much higher than that could be earned in the rural area. Zohir and Paul Majumder (1996) have noted that the women's work and thereby income-earning from the RMG factory has brought important social changes. A large proportion of the workers have gained the power to use their income as they wish, though in many cases the male family member (husband or the father) gets hold of the income. Such new income source of the females has extended effects on the status of the whole family and their living condition.

Not everything is positive of being a garment worker. Studies mentioned above have found that most of the female workers face various health problems because of overwork. They are often paid less than their male counterpart, often they work with no payment during the maternity period. Discrimination in terms of gender is clearly visible in the RMG sector. The workers who receive appointment letters at all are mostly supervisors, quality controllers or cutters and were predominantly male (Majumder, 2003). Wage of the female workers is also less than their male counterpart in many factories, even for same skill, experience and education level. Paul Majumder (2003) has identified that for the education level of class XI and above, wage of female RMG worker is 72 per cent of her male counterpart; in case of education level of class I to class V, it is only 58 per cent. The study has also found that in case of males and females both working in the factory for about 14 months, the female wage is only 46 per cent of the respective male wages.[3]

The female workers are often exposed to sexual harassment both in the work place and on the street to the work factory. This also poses negative impact on their reputation and social image back home. Without safe transport and safe housing, female garment workers are exposed to a greater insecurity. On their way to the factory, which is usually long, they often have to hear lots of 'bad' comments from the men around. They are considered to be 'available' by many of those men and they even offer 'rates' for them. Safe transportation and safe, clean and hygienic accommodation are the rights most urgently required by garment workers. The findings of the study by Paul Majumder have shown that 77 per cent of the surveyed female garment workers in her research, live in temporary houses. These houses are low-lying and always musty and damp, surroundings are filthy. Most of them use unsanitary toilets sharing with 20-40 persons. There is no adequate supply of water. Workers also face different types of problems on their way to the factory. Paul Majumder has also mentioned that the root cause of 75 per cent of sexual harassment of women workers is the absence of safe transportation and safe living areas/accommodation.

Women's Empowerment: Changes Matter or Not?

After all the changes mentioned above, the obvious question that arises is to look into whether women are empowered now than before or not. An important indicator of empowerment is to look at the participation in decision-making by the females. Mujeri (2002) has presented the status of rural women's decision-making from an extensive village level survey. The study has noted both economic decision-making and other household decision-making. It is observed that the husband strongly dominates in economic decision-making. The dominance is mostly observed in case of the decisions like choice of crop production, receiving/providing credit, investment of credit funds and sale of produced crops. Women's role is restricted mostly within their own domain. Even in case of spending earned income and involving in NGO activities, only around one half of the surveyed women are able to take decisions by themselves. The husband and the wife jointly take decisions mostly on purchase of daily necessities. In case of other household decision-making the husband also has the dominance. Such decisions include purchase of clothing, treatment during illness, children's education, repair of houses, adoption of family planning measures, immunization and marriage of children. Women have dominance only in case of immunization. In case of family planning and marriage of children, the decision is taken jointly.

Even after various incentives for the females the opinion is still quite widespread that education spoils a girl's character and undermines her willingness to fulfil her traditional role. Early marriage and the importance of preserving a girl's good reputation lead to widespread withdrawal of girls from school at puberty, especially if they attend co-educational institutions. The evidence of higher dowry for 'aged' educated (at least up to secondary level) girls' support such social attitude.

Afsar (2002) has noted that formal employment of the women is generating positive impact on poverty alleviation. Specially semi-literate and unskilled women from rural poor families are entering the formal manufacturing sector that was previously opened only to a few educated and upper middle-class women (Afsar, 2000). It is enabling the young unmarried women of landless families to defer marriage. But it may also burden women with a double workload of home and factory work. The study by Zohir and Majumder (1996) has shown that almost half of the female workers gave their income to the parents or to the husband. Only one-third of the females decide alone on spending their income. Still a job in the garment industry empowers the female workers both socially and economically. They have gained better status in their family. Working in a garment industry also enables them to improve their consumption level and housing condition. Also the unmarried workers are empowered in the sense that they have greater say regarding their marriage. Many of them even contribute in paying their dowry.

Rozario (2002) has looked into the issue of women's empowerment in terms of women's ability to exert influence within and beyond the household. The question is whether increased presence of the women in paid work outside home/village or their access to micro–credit has increased such influence or not. In that connection, the income of the women is contributing much for the welfare of the family and the family is appreciating that much. At the same time the traditional role of the male as the sole bread-earner for the family is threatened. The family and the woman herself are also concerned of the social reputation all the time. Therefore, the rural women of Bangladesh are facing a new type of inner conflict. Their feeling of whether they are better off in such an outset may differ from person to person.

In case of the micro-credit fund of the women, often the husband is the decision-maker in spending that. However, this may not be bad if the husband is the better decision maker and the decision is taken for the betterment of the family as a whole. Ultimately, the women are taking the loan for the welfare of the family. It is observed that despite the increased participation of women in paid employment, ingrained gender values are still dominant in the rural society of Bangladesh. It is a very common practice by the working-women to wear a veil in the rural area for keeping their safety and reputation. They might not be even interested to contest the norms of *parda* (covering the body with a veil) by undertaking outside income generating work. They may even use the micro-credit to withdraw from work outside the home, which they often see as dishonourable and embarrassing, so as to conform better to gender norms (Kabeer, 1998). But this feeling does not prevent the women from improving their livelihood by exercising new opportunities. They are increasingly taking part in decision-making and they are also implementing their choices more. A survey conducted by ASA (a large MFI with 1.5 million borrowers) among 1,200 women micro-credit borrowers in 1998 conclusively shows that the borrowers' capacity has increased; their awareness has improved and the women are now empowered in economic and social matters (Figure 6.2). Therefore, micro-credit is not merely an instrument for credit extension to the poor borrowers. It is a movement to emancipate the poor—especially women—to alleviate their poverty, improve their quality of life, and build their capacity and awareness and to integrate them economically and socially into the mainstream of the economy.

Dowry is still a very strong phenomenon in the rural economy. Even after actively participating in income generating activities, women consider dowry to be an obvious issue. Dowry remains unchallenged in the rural society. Moreover it is increasing over time (Rozario, 2002). While purity, honour and

Figure 6.2
Micro-credit and Women's Awareness Development

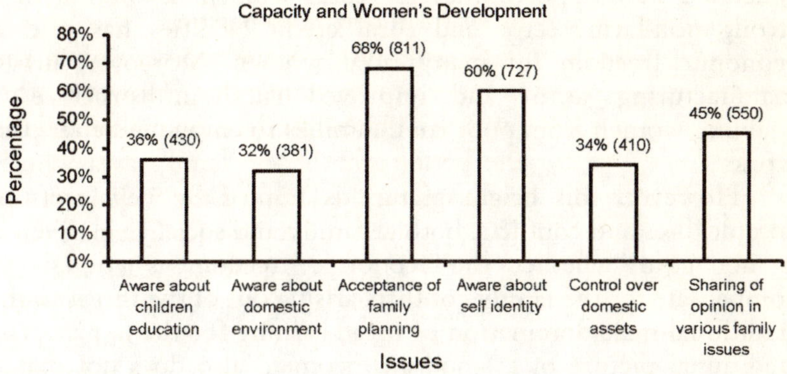

Source: Ahmed (2003).

shame continue to mandate early marriage for women in the rural areas, men marry at a considerably later age, leading to a disparity between the available numbers of men and women.

Greater participation of the women in local government has some positive empowerment effect for the rural areas where they belong, however the wider impact is yet to be observed. The elected women members of the UP are often deployed to perform only welfare-oriented works like education and health care and are kept away from major development projects (Haq and Mohiuddin, 2000, as cited in Rozario, 2002).

Conclusion

Empowerment is a broad and complex concept. Kabeer (1999) has identified empowerment as more than just participation in decision-making; rather it includes the processes that lead women to perceive themselves as able and entitled to make decisions. Therefore, collective action is important for ensuring social and political empowerment. Sen (1990) refers to this issue as a change in the self-perception of women. In this connection the empowerment process needs to include the eradication of negative social structure, so that women can discover their inner capacity and right to influence decisions. Here lies the limitation of empowerment in rural Bangladesh.

It is observed in this paper that there have been a number of changes in the rural economy, which, in many cases have generated new opportunities for rural women. Evolution of a strong non-farm sector and rural credit facilities has offered economic freedom for many rural women. Moreover, urban manufacturing sector and improved rural infrastructure is enabling women from poor rural families to engage in better-paid works.

However, this bright picture is framed by new sorts of complexities and conflicts, both at family and social level. Even it is not clear whether the economic freedom is enough to compensate for the family conflicts arising out of the threat to the traditional male domination of bread-earning for the family. The traditional picture of a 'good girl/women' also does not match with the new mobility and activities of the women. It is obvious that deep-rooted traditional attitudes towards women will not change in a day or month. The good news is that women of rural Bangladesh have at least started thinking of themselves, of their separate identity as a human being. Moreover, women's new ability to contribute significantly to economic resources to the marriage can lead to an increased sense of self-esteem and to a greater effective voice in household decision-making (Kabeer, 1998). They have started getting used to spending their own income, to the power of their educational attainment, to the new awareness and knowledge within themselves.

The support from the government in terms of ensuring their security, implementing equal right laws, increasing social awareness and skill development programmes, is what is required to boost up their new vision of rural women's life. The NGOs should also stress on building up solidarity among the rural women to influence community views on women. In that way women's role as a significant income earner of the family will be valued with greater honour and ultimately this will alter the social attitude towards rural women as a whole. Social attitudes cannot be expected to change immediately. But facilitation of the continuation of the positive changes in rural women's life will expand the horizon and nature of 'acceptable' female etiquette.

Notes

1. The Labour Force Survey (LFS) of Bangladesh is conducted by the Bangladesh Bureau of Statistics, the government body to collect, process and present statistics of diverse economic and national issues.

   In the statistics used here, Labour includes any person aged 15 years and over. It excludes own household activities. According to LFS, an employed person is one who was either working one or more hours for pay or profit or working without pay in a family farm or enterprise or organization during the reference period or found not working but had a job or business from which he/she was temporarily absent during the reference period.
2. Article 28 of the Bangladesh Constitution states that "women shall have equal rights with men in all spheres of state and public life".
3. Wage gap between male and female workers is prevailing in the whole economy. In 1999-2000 according to the Labour Force Survey (LFS) of the Bangladesh Bureau of Statistics, 41.7 per cent of women drew salaries of less than 750 taka per month compared to 7.3 per cent of men, and 71.5 per cent of women were earning less than 1,500 taka per month compared to only 26.4 per cent of men. Women are also concentrated in low or unpaid agricultural work in rural areas with almost 75 per cent reporting underemployment (working less than 35 hours per week).

References

Afsar, R. 2000. 'Gender, Labour market and Demographic change: a case study of Women's entry into formal manufacturing sector of Bangladesh' in B. Garcia, R. Anker and A. Pinnelli (eds.) *Women in Labour Market in Changing Economies: Demographic Issues.* Oxford: Oxford University Press,

Afsar, R. 2002. 'Migration and Rural Livelihoods' in Toufique, K.A. and Turton, C. (eds.) *Hands Not Land: How Livelihoods are Changing in Rural Bangladesh*, Bangladesh Institute of Development Studies (BIDS) and Department for International Development (DFID).

Ahmed, K.F. 2003. *Micro-credit as a Tool for Women Empowerment: The Case of Bangladesh*, Internet publication (www.foreignaid.com/thinktank/microcredit.html).

Amin, S. Mahmud, S. and Huq, L. 2002. *Baseline Survey Report on Rural Adolescents in Bangladesh: 'Marriage'*, Kishori Abhijan Project of Ministry of Women and Children Affairs of Bangladesh.

FAO 2000. http://www.fao.org/sd/WPdirect/WPre0104.htm

Kabeer, N. 1998. 'Money Can't Buy me love?: Re–Evaluating Gender, Credit and Empowerment in Rural Bangladesh', *IDS Discussion Paper* 363, Institute of Development Studies at the University of Sussex, UK.

Kabeer, N. 1999. 'Resources, Agency, Achievements: Reflections on the Measurement of Women's Empowerment', *Development and Change*, Vol. 30, No 3.

Khundker, N. 2002. *Globalization, competitiveness and job quality in the Garment Industries in Bangladesh*, Bangladesh Economic and Social Challenges of Globalisation, UPL, Dhaka.

Kibria, N. 2001. 'Becoming a Garments Worker: The Mobilisation of Women into the Garment Factories of Bangladesh', in R. Sobhan and N. Khundker (eds.), *Globalisation and Gender: Changing Patterns of Women's Employment in Bangladesh,* Centre for Policy Dialogue and The University Press Ltd. pp. 61-90.

Mahmud, S. 2001. 'The Labour Use of Women in Rural Bangladesh,' in R. Sobhan and N. Khundker (eds.), *Globalisation and Gender: Changing Patterns of Women's Employment in Bangladesh*, Centre for Policy Dialogue and The University Press Ltd. pp. 25-60.

Majumder, P.P. 2003. 'Gender Discrimination in Bangladesh Labour Market', in Shahiduzzaman and Mahfuzur Rahman (ed.) *Gender Equality in Bangladesh – Still a long Way to Go*, News network, Dhaka.

Mujeri, M.K. 2002. 'Gender Issues at the Local Level: Summary Results of a Pilot Survey in Bangladesh', Working Paper no 11, under Micro Impacts of Macroeconomic and Adjustment Policies in Bangladesh (MIMAP) project.

Rozario, S. 2002. 'Gender Dimensions of Rural Change' in Toufique, K. A. and Turton, C. (eds.) *Hands Not Land: How Livelihoods are Changing in Rural Bangladesh*, Bangladesh Institute of Development Studies (BIDS) and Department for International Development (DFID).

Sen, A. 1990. *Development as Freedom*, Oxford University Press, Oxford.

Toufique, K.A. 2001. 'Sustainable Rural Livelihoods in Bangladesh', *IDS Research Report 45,* Institute of Development Studies at the University of Sussex, UK.

Toufique, K.A. and Turton, C. 2002. *Hands Not Land: How Livelihoods are Changing in Rural Bangladesh*, Bangladesh Institute of Development Studies (BIDS) and Department for International Development (DFID), Chapters 1 and 2.

World Bank 2002. 'Bangladesh: Progress in Poverty Reduction', Background Paper, Bangladesh Development Forum, Paris, March 13 – 15, 2002.

Zohir, S.C. 2000. *Social Dimensions of the Growth of Garment Industry in Bangladesh*: 1990-1997. BIDS, Dhaka, Bangladesh (MIMEO).

Zohir, S.C., Majumder, P.P. 1996. *Garment Workers in Bangladesh: Economic, Social and Health Condition, Research Monograph*, Bangladesh Institute of Development Studies. No. 18.

Chapter 7

Poverty and Women in Rural Labour Markets of North-Eastern Bangladesh

Fazila Banu Lily

In the study of poverty it is necessary to incorporate both the viewpoints of the poor, as persons who are affected, as well as the views of the institutions involved in analysing and working with the objective to change the poverty situation. Similarly, it is important to understand the framework conditions under which poverty perpetuates its course as well as to alleviate the situations for some fortunate ones. The framework conditions include the social (physical security, health, demography, gender), cultural (education, cultural identity, communication), economic (market, production, services, infrastructure), ecological (environmental and natural resources), and political (human rights, good governance, democratic institutions). Under these framework conditions, the poor are most susceptible to vulnerability caused by human made or ecological change in the livelihood situations of an area. Women of the poor strata in north-eastern region of Bangladesh live their lives in a condition in which they are at the interface of survival of their own and struggle to keep alive their future generations. This study examines how poverty intertwined with vulnerability, affect women in rural areas of the north-eastern part of Bangladesh and how they cope with this situation in order to live their lives.

Methodology

Systemic analysis method is applied to carry out the field research. The method refers to analysis of the evolution of rural realities and the analysis is systemic as it tries to understand the society in its integrity. The tools examine the link between income scales and access levels to social services. It captures the analysis of the effects on lives and livelihood by abandoning the static picture framework and favouring an evolutionary paradigm of a rural society, congruent with its heterogeneity and micro-to-macro linkages (Wennubst, 2002). The methodology helps to understand how and why individual or groups' livelihood strategies change or evolve.

This approach is a socio-economic vision of societies and remains in essence qualitative by grasping the dynamic evolution of the society and drawing causal-effects of the groups' behaviour. It is based on the concepts of evolution of the agrarian system and sustainable livelihood strategies of the people. The agrarian system constitutes the canvas, from which society's structure and sustainable livelihood strategies are woven.

The tools to collect information include case studies and focus group discussion to collect qualitative information within a short period. A set of guiding questions is used while conducting selected case studies and focus group discussions. The study area is the north-eastern district of Bangladesh called Sunamganj. The poorest section of female labour force engaged in stone breaking and coal collection were selected for case studies. The focus group discussion included the people who are engaged in agriculture, stone and coal businesses.

Sunamganj district is located in the foothills of Meghalaya State of India. The area consists of 37 big swamps and over 700 rivers and water bodies. Less than one-sixth of the area under this district composed of highland on which the people live. Thus, the villages look like small islands within the large swamps and lakes.

Understanding Poverty

As is stated in the Poverty Well-being Study (SDC, 2000) there is no generally applicable definition of poverty. Poverty itself in Dreze's and Sen's (1999) view is a severe failure of basic capacities. Poverty relates to the failure of the ability to achieve presently those things that are ultimately important. On the other hand, the more common definition of poverty is in terms of inadequacy of incomes, e.g., a person's income level falling below the 'poverty line'. As they argue, the failure of basic capacities must ultimately be the central concern. In the context of this analysis "a person is poor if she has too low an income" i.e., causal and also "she is poor when she has to lead a very deprived life" (ibid.: 14). Thus poverty is identified with the deprivation itself and lack of economic means to escape that deprivation.

Descriptions and perceptions of poverty and its myriad dimensions are as many and varied as the ways in which poverty affects the daily lives of the poor. To date such descriptions and perceptions have been dominated by the external viewpoints of the actors in the fight against poverty, who in principle adopt two different approaches:

- The purely quantitative one-dimensional approach whereby poverty is measured exclusively in figures (income, calorie).
- The qualitative multidimensional approach, which also takes into account socio-cultural categories of poverty (for example, participation in social life, special occupational group, women).

Poverty is differentiated between:

- Absolute poverty as a threshold in which a specific value is assigned to the poverty line in which poor are defined as all those with less than 1 US dollar at their disposal to cover daily needs.[1] Owing to its comparability, this benchmark is widely used world wide and simultaneously the most restricting definition of poverty.
- The second is the relative poverty indicating social disparities. This is based on available resources and compares their

distribution. The best known is income quintiles, which compare the income of the poorest fifth of the population with the richest fifth.

For the purposes of understanding poverty we can additionally distinguish between:

- The subjective concept of poverty, which draws on the personal as well as collective, culturally-related values and preferences of those affected. This concept of poverty involves selection, ranking and evaluation according to individual benefits.
- The objective concept of poverty, which is based on norms and criteria defined by experts. One example of the objective approach is the 21 core indicators devised by the World Bank, UNDP, OECD for measuring development.

Poverty distinguishes two types of deprivation:

- Physiological, i.e., the ability to cover basic needs (income, nutrition, clothing, shelter).
- Sociological, i.e., the way in which the poor are disadvantaged due to structural inequities such as access to land, credit, and services. The reasons for these aspects of poverty are to be found in social power structures, governance and macro-economic conditions. Efforts to promote empowerment and the participation of the poor constitute key elements of this approach.

In practice, the various perceptions and concepts of poverty are not always easy to separate.

The reality of poverty is most readily measured in terms of the livelihoods of the poor. Besides quantitative dimensions, this measure also determines the qualitative dimension of life during the life cycle. Livelihood is used in attempts to record several dimensions of poverty and incorporate them within a holistic view. Determining these quantitative and qualitative data is a complex and difficult task.

Poverty cannot be considered in isolation. It must always be seen as part of a dynamic relationship involving other social phenomena such as:

— Inequality: Inequality constitutes unfair distribution within a population group whereby the poor have no equitable or reasonable share of goods.

- Vulnerability: Vulnerability expresses exposure to risk based on factors such as race, religion, sex, age, etc. It involves a combination of factors that determine the degree to which someone's life and livelihood is put at risk by a discrete and identifiable event in nature or in society.
- Exclusion: The extent of social exclusion is a key element of poverty.
- Underdevelopment: Poverty refers to the individual domain. Underdevelopment is the aggregate of individual poverty.

Perception of the People

How the poor perceive the causes of their poverty situation does not necessarily vary from one region to another. However, how they prioritize the causes may differ depending on ecological, political and social conditions of that place. Illness and death of a family member, climate-induced or natural disasters such as drought, floods, storms and earthquakes, conflicts or an unfavourable market can destabilize the balance under which people live and put them in vulnerable situations. But primary causes are not solely responsible for the process of impoverishment. Numerous other factors support and accelerate it, prime among which are the rapid pace of social and economic change and the inability of poor households and those at risk of poverty to respond to such changes. As stated in the Poverty Well-being Study (SDC, 2000) this is attributable to the lack of reliable and understandable information concerning alternative approaches, the lack of alternatives which would allow poor people to sell their only asset, their labour power at better conditions, the growing deficit in available natural resources such as soil, water, fauna and flora, the lack of viable social safety nets which would provide the needy with a period of recuperation and reflection, and the lack of reliable partners, i.e., the support group from public and civil society organizations for people and communities in need.

Household and communities who are currently regarded as still intact to meet their subsistence needs comfortably can become poor overnight for the unfavourable conditions stated above. When people describe their poverty situations, the following key words predominate: dependence, loss of self-worth and self-esteem, isolation, patronage and deprivation of rights, no recognition, no gainful employment opportunities, stress, lack of security and safety, loss of cultural identity, lack of basic education and vocational training, loss of perspective and fear of the future, hunger, inadequate housing and clothing. Social and material needs are often given equal emphasis in the eyes of the people who live under poverty. The causes of poverty are difficult to identify accurately for most of the people who live under poverty. Mostly they consist of a combination of unfavourable circumstances which set a fateful dynamism in motion. When the person or a community can identify the major causes of poverty, make prioritization of the causes and take up steps accordingly, they bring the changes towards alleviating their situations. However, poverty is closely linked to issues and problems associated with gender, which brings another aspect in the multidimensional nature of poverty as women have different strategic needs than men that make them more susceptible to falling into poverty than men.

Poverty in Rural Bangladesh

In Bangladesh, since 1980s a moderate acceleration in the growth process has been observed. A slight decline in poverty at roughly one percentage point a year has been happening, but this still leaves over 40 per cent of the population in poverty. Concurrently, a rising problem of inequality continues which is more pronounced in the urban areas (Rahman, 2004) mainly due to migration of rural poor to the urban areas for employment. Migration of the educated rural rich to urban areas continues due to better health facilities in cities, better education for their children and to be closer to state power. The industries are also centred in and around the towns and cities. Like many cities elsewhere in South Asian countries, the rural poor in Bangladesh move to the cities to occupy the service sector to cater to the rich. Similarly, they are absorbed in the industries that engage the unskilled labour force.

While discussing the issue of poverty in rural Bangladesh, we have to take into account the agricultural production systems, which is still the dominant sector where a total of 63 per cent population of the country are dependent for their livelihood in rural areas. The pattern of wealth distribution among this population is crucial for our understanding. A total of 48 per cent of these people are landless and work as agriculture wage labour, 42 per cent are marginal, small and medium farm owners having land up to 3.5 acres. On the other hand about 10 per cent population have land of an average size of 12 acres. The distribution of cultivable land reveals the inequality among different categories of the people living on farming; 10 per cent farmers own 63.2 per cent of total cultivable land while 43 per cent poor, marginal and medium farmers own 36 per cent of the cultivable land of the area under study.

Participation in agriculture production systems even as landless wage labourers and share croppers is important for a rural family as it provides food reserve for a certain period of time that allows them to maintain the basic subsistence food requirements and not fall into starvation when wage labour is not available during the lean season or illness. Therefore, the landless families fall in deprivation and suffer from vulnerability in case of any ecological or human made disaster that destroys crop and hence reduce or eliminate their livelihood opportunities to work in the agriculture sector.

The major ecological disaster in Sunamganj region is recurring floods. Flood is a regular occurrence in Bangladesh due to its geographical location in which all big rivers from India flow to the Bay of Bengal. During monsoon the onrush of water from upper regions of India inundate the lower parts of Bangladesh and cause numerous losses of crops, livestock, damages of houses and erosion of homestead land. Land erosion due to wave action in swamp areas of Sunamganj region is one of the major factors contributing to landlessness, specially homestead land. The study area of Sunamganj experiences floods every year as the water from Assam and Meghalaya flows through Sunamganj region to the Meghna River. The depressed low lying area of Sunamganj district produces enough quantity of paddy, which is the major cereal crop of this area. In the years when flood occurs before the crop is harvested, people lose their food for the whole year. The poor subsequently lose their opportunity to work as wage labour in agriculture and make a food reserve for number of months. It is important to note that for harvesting of paddy the wage is usually paid in kind, that is in paddy.

The population pressure on natural resources and very limited absorption of labour power in the industrial sector make the poor more vulnerable to meet their livelihood need. Even though Bangladesh has made a progress in reducing the birth rate to 1.5 per family, it is however, compared to the already existing density of population to the available land area of the country, far behind to bring any impact on the land-people ratio. The present density of the population in Bangladesh is 834 per sq km, which is the highest in the world. The study area of Sunamganj has an average family size of 6 that is much higher than the national average of 4.9. Considering available resources in the area that is land, water, sand and stone, losses of resources due to floods in most years, having no industrial production systems in place, the area is unable to provide the livelihood opportunities to the people here. This scenario further depresses the labour market and makes people go for seasonal migration leaving their family behind. But the female labour force and especially if she is the sole income earner of the family, cannot afford to go for seasonal migration.

Where the Women are Placed in the Poverty Context

The poverty literature of the 1970s in Bangladesh as stated by Rahman (2004) was replete with references to analytical categories such as interlocked markets and personal dependence. These described a situation where the poor households were enmeshed in interlocking ties of dependence in land, labour and credit markets. Poor households were effectively subservient to the class of landlords and creditors even in their social and political choices. Agriculture having been the major sector for ensuring the food security, the poor section of the population were primarily dependent on the landlords as employers and users of their land as share croppers. Numerous evidences were there in which the poor were totally under the grip of landlords in terms of accepting any conditions set by them as regards wages, working hours and benefits such as food, clothing and advance to meet their family needs. In some cases the poor sold their labour in advance to meet the family crisis and worked as bonded labour until the money was repaid. In the case of women they worked for rich landlords for the full harvesting season in exchange of food and clothes. Even women within poor strata who worked, were often the young unmarried girls or divorced women and widows but not the married women. The main reason was that when the husband was alive, his community and their society did not encourage the women to work for others even when the husband was not able to fully meet the subsistence needs of the family. Consequently the women suffered being at home but could not work for earning an income.

In recent years the spread of high-yield agriculture and better road infrastructure has significantly contributed to weakening personal dependence of the agricultural labour on the landlords. High input costs for agricultural production and gradual mechanization bring the landlords and labours into more interdependent relationship. Women's reproductive burden too has gone down indicating a noticeable lowering of the population growth rate. However, while types of constraints such as personal dependence and extreme vulnerability have weakened, socio-political constraints have been much more resistant to change.

The poor women in rural Bangladesh being the sole or main person responsible for securing the subsistence needs of her family, always not by choice but as survivors of circumstances, fall in the level of poorest of the poor. The north-eastern region of Bangladesh, i.e., Sylhet division where the rural labour market is predominantly occupied by agriculture and natural resource sector, i.e., fisheries, sand and stone collection from rivers, does not allow women to take part in them. The main reason is that the activities take place away from home and involve long travelling which do not permit the women to leave their children and family unattended. At the same time the traditional norm of the society here is yet to make the change where women would go for some 'gainful' employment such as working in the agricultural field, fishing and operating boats to collect sand and stone. Another aspect we need to keep in mind in the analysis of women's engagement in the rural labour market even with our well-known extensive micro-credit programme to widen the labour market is that for women in the rural areas, the women who take up wage labour job in public sphere, are the ones who have no other income option left to remain within the household domain (Wennubst, 2002).

Here we must mention about the recipients of micro-credits provided by the large and small micro-credit institutions. More than eighty per cent of the recipients of micro-credit are women and belong to the poorer strata that have one or two male members in the family to earn an income through wage labour and are considered as endowment security for the credit organization. But the women who are the head of the household due to being divorced, separated or widowed and in some cases women who are defacto head of household, and have no one to supplement an income to their families usually do not get an access to micro-credit. For them as Dreze and Sen (1999) stated, poverty itself manifests as a severe failure of acute vulnerability of wage labourers in a market economy. It is a problem as wage labourers have little ability to survive on their own when unemployment develops rapidly.

The importance of the vulnerability of wage labourers to livelihood[2] can be particularly acute when the class of wage labourers has become large but a social security has not yet developed. As Dreze and Sen observe, it is not always true that traditional means of social security in pre-wage economies are typically adequate. In fact, they are often altogether insufficient and meagre. The social security that exists in the study area does not fall under the present definition of 'social security'. It is the community support that facilitates the women to participate in the labour market by looking after their children, guarding their house and looking after their physical security. At the same time the wage system has added a particular system of vulnerability, that is these labours are seen as wage earners and accounted as potential labour force. However, their meagre income is still remaining below the threshold level and often not enough to meet basic livelihood requirements of their families.

Female Labour in North-eastern Region of Bangladesh

Case Study of a Stone-Breaker

Ms. Rabiya Khatun: Age 64 Years

Rabiya is from Uttar Badaghat village. Her parents migrated here from Kishoreganj when she was a child. Rabiya's husband died in 1974. He was a day labourer and had only the homestead land with a thatch house. She became a widow with 4 daughters and 2 sons. Two daughters were young and waiting to get married while the other children were small. Rabiya first tried to work at people's house as domestic labour but the wage was either only food or 250 grams of rice a day, she could not feed her children and herself with that job. She started stone-breaking work. Initially she took her sons along and dug the sands to collect stone, break those stone and sold to the contractors. In this way she could earn more. When the sons grew adolescent, they took wage labour jobs in agriculture and sand collection. Rabiya continued to collect stone and breaking it. Since the last 8-9 years she stopped collecting stone as she became weak of old age. For the last one year she has not been able to walk herself to the stone-breaking yard, her grand daughter (elder son's daughter) accompanies her.

Rabiya earns Tk. 30-35 a day. When she was strong at her young age, she could earn double the amount. She is living with her son who is also a stone-breaker. The son has 2 daughters from his first wife who died and 1 son from his second wife. Rabiya's first granddaughter used to break stone until she was married. Her second grand daughter is 11 years old; she also breaks stone with her.

Rabiya borrows money from the contractors for whom she breaks stone when she cannot work and in need of money. They don't charge any interest. She does not borrow big sum of money, as she knows she will not be able to return the money.

Rabiya has a small hammer of her own, which costs Tk. 50. All stone-breakers should have this hammer. But for breaking bolder stone one needs a bigger sized hammer that costs Tk. 300-350. The contractors lend this hammer to the stone-breakers who work for them free of charge.

The Obstacles Women Face in the Rural Markets

We have examined the issue of women in the rural market in the context of the north-eastern part of Bangladesh where the women who join the rural labour force are the poorest ones in the community. If we look at the evolution process of the area, we see two different patterns in the rural production systems under which the women labour force emerges as they are today. The area is a low-lying swamp; thus it has got two distinct production systems and seasonal characters. In the wet season people mainly live on fishing, sand and stone collection from the riverbed and transportation in waterways. In contrast, during dry season the swamps and lakes dry up and paddy cultivation becomes the main occupation of the people. More than 60 per cent of the people are migrants coming here from other parts of the country. Migration to this area started about 5 generations ago when people saw the opportunities that existed here in its abundance of resources. But like in many societies all migrants could not make better fortune as some others did.

One pattern among the female labour force is observed that they are the destitute of the three main production systems, i.e., agriculture, fishing and mixture of agriculture and fishing. When one came from Muslim fishing families, and their families were the last ones to migrate in this region, they had to take the worse location, in the marginal areas that are prone to flood, living on small islands susceptible to erosion. They are not skilled and they have less access to livelihood assets from the beginning of the settlement in this area. Often they are women headed families, who have no linkages or contact with other trades which plunge them in a poorer situation, while the men from similar material base being the main income earners have the trade links and networks with diverse wage earning groups. The seasonal poverty is touching everybody who are at the bottom of the production systems. It is the seasonality of not accessing cash due to scarcity of wage employment and no other formal or informal system to access cash in this region except the traditional money lender who charges 120-365 per cent interest on loans.

The second pattern is formed by the people who migrated here 30-40 years ago and from the beginning took the lowest work, like stone-breaking, sand and coal collection. But the female labour force do not take part in sand and stone collection as traditionally they do not operate boats that are the only transportation used to carry sand and stone from the river bed.

The labour market for woman here is limited to post-harvesting activities, stone-breaking, earth-cutting and coal collection. In post-harvesting work, only very few farmers who do not have enough family labour hire female labourers. At the same time the wage is the lowest of all activities stated above. However, female labourers especially the young girls and wives prefer this work as it is done within the household domain. The other important aspect is that these labour forces often are supplementary income earners for their families and the work is also seasonal. But when the women are the sole earners of their family, they go for more regular income such as stone-breaking. The greater vulnerability of women is closely connected with lesser opportunities for getting outside work and paid employment, therefore they go for such activities that are in the close proximity of their homes[3] and bring them regular income although the amount appears to be significantly low.

These labourers in all respects, work in the most difficult conditions in terms of workplace, payments and social services rendered by the state, local government and the employer. The stone breakers work on the bank of the river flows by the foothills of the Meghalaya State of India. They come in the morning, often from the other side of the river by paying boat fare of Tk. 10/- to Tk. 20/- [4] depending on the weather. They work in the rain and under the sun for the whole day. Before dusk the volume of the stone they break is measured by the contractors and paid. During the day they have no interaction with the contractors or with the local authority such as Union Parishad members or rural health workers.

Physical insecurity is often present that makes them more vulnerable when taking jobs in the public sphere in which the labour have no or a meagre bargaining power with the employer and at the same time which is internal and an autonomous labour market, area-specific and non-competeing. The female labourers are forced to take up this job as they have no other option for livelihood. Without this meagre income by selling of their labour they would starve along with their children. For these women begging is not an option, as being at young or middle age and able to carry out physical work, people would not support her with alms. In this rural labour market, ownership of the means of production does not entail direct control of labour in the production process as labourers are controlled with the volume of their products.

As there are unemployed workers and their numbers continuously renewed within natural resource based production systems, which by competition for jobs help to depress wages. The existence of this group is held to force wages down to subsistence or below subsistence levels. The unemployment remains a factor in the bargaining power possessed by the labour. These labourers who posses basically no means of production excepting their own labour power, which they try to sell for a wage in order to earn an adequate income to buy enough food, are particularly vulnerable to changes in labour market conditions. A decline in wages vis-à-vis food prices, or increase in unemployment, can spell disaster for this class, especially in case of natural calamities and serious illness in the family.

It is a deprived region in terms of lack of policy advocacy for the development of the area to have better communication and good governance; as a result the area remains remote from the Centre as well as divisional city. Due to the remoteness of the area, the public services are very poor even though some of the infrastructures are in place. For instance the government primary schools, rural health centres, family welfare centres exist in the area. However, the personnel to provide services are often not available. The female labour force with long hours of work and no one back home cannot send their children to school. Similarly with their inadequate income they are not able to buy whatever poor health services are available in their area. Furthermore, the service providers especially the health and family welfare workers come to the field only when their supervisors pay visits to the rural centres from cities to monitor their work. It is important to note that there are no pro-poor and specifically pro-poor women mechanisms in these two sectors.

The Opportunities for Women

With all vulnerabilities and precariousness, the women in rural labour markets have secured some important victories with regard to their greater mobility and visibility in the public sphere. One dominant reason is that having no livelihood options other than joining the labour force, women have been forced to come to the public space. At the same time in the larger society through programmes of micro-credit, programmes focused on girls' education, safety net programmes specially focused on women[5] have no doubt made impact on the patriarchal society where women have traditionally been secluded in the private sphere. This change has made the participation of women in the rural labour market relatively easy. However, education for the children of the poor female labourers of this region is nearly impossible, as the existing public sector education systems have no scope to cater them. Therefore, a different approach is required to integrate these children in the government-supported primary schools.

The idea of 'social security' as observed by Dreze and Sen (1999) is that of using social means to prevent deprivation and vulnerability. The connection of deprivation in terms of the biological results in falling into illness and malnutrition. The appropriation of social means help to come out of that state. Social means can be providing direct support to the vulnerable population to acquire the means to basic capacities. Providing free food or cash to potential victims of illness, and those who are flood affected is an obvious example of this. On a more regular basis, providing unemployment insurance, free health services and basic education are examples of such direct support to have long-term impact on alleviating the vulnerable conditions of these people.

These female labourers possess the naturally acquired skills that they have learned from their ancestors and by observing others. These women have huge potentials to learn other skills that can widen their opportunities to do the existing job with more efficiency and go for other kinds of work. Under the present situation they cannot diversify their job and extend their market possibilities. Due to lack of skills they suffer from insecurity to search for new jobs that offer them better wages. They have high resilience to overcome natural calamities like floods, erosion of homestead land, personal catastrophes such as death of husband or abandoned by husband who had been once the sole income earner of the family and death of children. They have overcome the social barriers by taking up jobs in the public domain and have made their place accepted by the society. With all these strengths, new skills would expand their horizon in the rural market and alleviate their situation.

Considering the vulnerability of the rural female labour force of this region due to its precarious nature of the labour market as well as illness and natural calamities a special credit facility is necessary.[6] They are outside of the existing micro-credit systems as they do not meet the criteria of the recipients of such credit. This kind of credit assistance would reduce their vulnerability in case of crisis situation. At the same time it would facilitate the process of risk minimization through diversification of fields of activity to increase an income with the help of the knowledge and support services that are integrated with the credit.

Future Potentials

Mathie and Cunningham (2003: 479) state that "social capital is present in the networks, norms, and social trust inherent in associations whose members work together in concerted collaborative action". This female labour force too may form networks and associations among them that bind them together and they can build on their common understanding and interests. Since they have very minimal income and have no savings to meet any incidental events, they fall into further deprivation. Generation of savings funds as a security to meet such situation is necessary and in doing so their own network and association is necessary. Socio-organizational measures aimed at limiting expenditure and increasing income are important for alleviating their situation.

Importance of female participation in gainful economic activities as a material factor in combating the special deprivation of women involves policy reforms. These women labour force is unskilled in any trade and often illiterate. Therefore, to make them skilled, both formal and non-formal transfer of knowledge and skills is essential for them to enter into the gainful employment market.

At the same time enhancing their present positions and conditions in the rural labour market requires as Hossain Rahman (2004) states, targeted resource delivery to women, transforming entrenched patriarchal attitudes which seek to limit women's spaces and deny their needs, and eliminating the insecurities of public spaces which inhibit women's engagement within such spaces and render violence a recurring threat.

Notes

1. The World Bank initially brought this indicator to define the poverty at individual level. Later, many institutions and researchers have adopted this indicator for analysis of poverty in their respective areas.
2. Livelihood entails sustainable employment and income to meet the basic needs of the poor (UN, 2000).
3. Mainly they consider about their children who are often left unattended or with the neighbour or relatives while they are at work.
4. US $1=Tk. 60/- and some times women pay one-third or even of their one day wage.
5. Examples of such programmes are Vulnerable Group Development Programme for women, Pension Scheme for Widow introduced by the Government in recent years.
6. Bangladesh Rural Advancement Committee (BRAC)—a national Non-Government Organization has introduced a special credit programme for the 'Ultra Poor'—who are beggars and unable to work due to physical disability and old age. The conditions to receive and payment of such loan are made on the basic needs and priorities of these groups of people.

References

Dreze, J. and Sen, A. 1999. *Hunger and Public Action*, Oxford University Press, New Delhi.

Marx, K. 1857. *Grundrisse – Foundations of a Critique of Political Economy*, Harmondsworth: Penguin (1973).

Mathie, Alison and Cunningham, G. 2003. 'From clients to citizens: Asset-based Community Development as a strategy for community-driven development', in *Development in Practice*, 13, 5, Carfax Publishing.

Rahman, Islam, R. and Islam, K.M.N. 2003. *Employment Poverty Linkages*, Bangladesh, ILO, Geneva.

Rahman, Zillur, H. 2004. The Review of Strategy Paper – 'Action Aid Bangladesh 1999-2003', Action Aid Bangladesh, Dhaka.

Swiss Agency for Development and Cooperation (SDC), 2000. *Poverty Wellbeing: An Orientation, Learning and Working Tool for Fighting Poverty*, Swiss Agency for Development and Cooperation (SDC), 3003 Bern, (Switzerland).

UNDP, 1999. *Review of Poverty Concepts and Indicators*, Lok-Dessallien, Renata.

UN, 2000. *The Common Country Assessment: Bangladesh*, University Press Limited, Dhaka.

Wennubst, Pius. 2002. *Sunamganj Rural Assessment: Getting to know actors and their stake*, Social Development Division, Department of Foreign Affaires, SDC, Bern, (Switzerland).

Chapter 8

Women in Non-Farm Activities in Sri Lanka

Are Women Empowered or Not?

Ramanie Jayatilaka

Sri Lanka is considered as an agricultural country and it will remain so even though non-agricultural activities are receiving importance in the country. The country does not have a proper industrial policy and there is no indication of the country moving towards industrial development. A majority of the population is engaged in agriculture. Agriculture provides employment to over 36 per cent of the labour force and it exceeds the contribution of any other sector. It is estimated that 1.8 million families are engaged in agriculture (Pussepitiya, 2002).

The majority of the country's population lives in rural areas and their main economic activity is agriculture. Rural women throughout history were engaged in agriculture. Like their male counterpart, they too contributed to both paddy and *Chena* (slash and burn) cultivation. However, their contribution is invisible.

National statistics do not provide a correct picture, as it does not show women's contribution. But many micro level studies have documented women's contribution to agricultural work. Women are not often remunerated and their work is seen as helping in the family farm. Often, women are not the owners of land.

Today, rural population in Sri Lanka is faced with the problem of underemployment and poverty due to the slow growth of agricultural sector in the last few decades. Rural women are more and more attracted to non-farm activities to earn a living to augment the family income. Although men are seen as bread-winners in families, women throughout history have shouldered the burden of maintaining the subsistence of the household. This is truer in rural and urban poor households. This study discusses the experiences that women have gained by engaging in two non-farm activities introduced by the Participatory Rural Development Programme initiated by the University of Colombo. The study will highlight that although women have improved their capabilities and gained strength and confidence, still patriarchal values in the society are too strong to make a difference in gender relations. We begin with a brief description of the status of women in agricultural activities.

Women in Agriculture

The national statistics point out that 75 per cent of the population live in rural areas. In 1997, over 36 per cent of the workforce was in agriculture and agriculture contributed 18 per cent share in GDP (ibid.). This shows that although agriculture has not developed, the proportion of the population that finds its employment in agriculture has not fallen rapidly. Agriculture in Sri Lanka could be categorized under two main sectors, plantation and subsistence agriculture. While tea, rubber and coconut are the main crops under the plantation sector, paddy is dominant in the subsistence sector.

Paddy and highland crops such as millet, grains, vegetables, chillies, etc., are cultivated in rural areas. While paddy is the main cultivated crop, it is dominated by small sector cultivation. As much as 99.5 per cent of paddy farms are less than 2.02 per cent hectares (5 acres) in size. Approximately, 42 per cent of all paddy holdings are under 0.4 hectares (1 acre) in size and a further 9 per cent between 2.02 - 8.09 hectares (5 and 20 acres) (Tennakoon, 2000).

Women, throughout history participated in agricultural activities. Historical writings have documented women's participation in agricultural activities. Robert Knox's *An Historical Relation of Ceylon,* (1981) provides a vivid picture of agricultural activities in ancient Sri Lanka. Knox explains the gender division of labour in the agricultural activities. He says:

> Then when the corn is grown about a span high, women come and weed it, and pull it up where it grew too thick, and transplant it where it wants....The women's work is to gather up the corn after Reapers, and carry it all together (page 15).

In traditional agriculture reciprocity was an accepted norm. People were paid in kind and not in money. Knox's account shows that women's labour was rewarded, in kind. Indrani Munasinghe (1998) writing on *Women in Ancient Ceylon* (Sri Lanka was known as Ceylon) shows that like at present women were engaged in specific agricultural activities. As is today, gender division of labour in agriculture was also evident in the past.

Women's participation in agriculture continues to present times. Looking at women's participation in different economic sectors in Sri Lanka it is evident that agriculture, forestry and fishing had the highest number until recently where the manufacturing sector took the first place as shown in Table 8.1.

Although women engage in agriculture, more than 70 per cent of the women agricultural workers render their services without receiving a pay or profit whereas only 29 per cent of male workers are found in this category as revealed in Table 8.2.

This is because most women do not own agricultural land. Owning agricultural land brings social status and power in the village and it structures relationship both within and outside the household. Even though agriculture may not bring much profit, people wish to own and control land as it gives prestige and power. I wish to argue here that women are marginalized in agriculture due to not owning land although they contribute an equal share in agricultural activities. Agriculture is therefore seen as a man's activity and it gives men power both within and outside family.

Table 8.1

Women's Participation in Major Different Divisions of Industry

Major Divisions of Industry	Percentage of Women Employees to Total Employees								
	1972	1976	1980	1985	1988	1989	1990	1991	1992
Total	36.7	34.0	33.7	36.7	41.8	38.0	44.3	43.8	46.3
Agriculture, Forestry & Fishing	50.2	51.7	49.1	51.0	50.7	51.1	51.4	50.4	51.9
Mining and Quarrying	13.0	15.4	8.0	9.6	14.1	16.0	11.0	14.8	18.7
Manufacturing	35.6	31.4	31.3	39.4	49.2	33.9	53.3	57.6	60.5
Electricity Gas & Water	1.2	3.2	2.2	4.3	13.0	7.7	6.0	7.5	7.7
Construction	0.9	5.3	9.7	7.8	12.2	11.6	17.9	18.1	18.6
Wholesale & Retail Trade and Restaurants & Hotels	10.5	16.9	18.3	20.3	27.6	25.8	25.7	24.3	24.7
Transport and Storage	1.5	1.7	3.5	3.0	12.5	3.3	3.1	8.7	11.1
Financing, Insurance Real Estate and Business Services	10.9	16.8	19.5	25.0	27.0	29.3	28.7	29.8	30.3
Community Social and Personal Services	6.8	14.8	18.4	22.9	23.2	22.1	30.4	31.7	28.0

Source: Department of Census and Statistics 1997.

Table 8.2

Agricultural Workers by Employment Status

Employment Status	*Women %*	*Men %*
Employer	1.6	2.8
Own Account Worker	24.6	64.7
Unpaid Family	70.6	29.0
Agricultural Labourer	2.2	3.6

Source: Department of Census and Statistics 1997.

Women receive a secondary place in agriculture and Agarwal (1994) correctly argues in her book *A Field of One's Own,* that if women are to be empowered then it is critical for them to own land. It is therefore important to understand Sri Lankan women's access to land.

Studies on Sri Lanka, (de Zoysa, 1995, Risseeuw, 1988) have shown the detrimental effect of the colonial policies on women's rights to land. Sri Lanka was under the influence of Portuguese (1505-1658), Dutch (1658-1796) and British (1796-1948). The British who ruled the whole country until 1948 had a greater influence than other colonial regimes by bringing structural changes in the country. The British introduced several land legislations and marriage ordinance, which had far reaching effects on the Sri Lankan peasantry. The British rulers whose primary intentions were to exploit land for cash crops were not happy with the existing land tenure patterns. The British also were not happy with the existing marriage system, which was conflicting with the concept of monogamous marriage bound by law. Therefore, the British introduced legislations on marriage and land, such as 1899 Ordinance (No. 13) on marriage, Crown Lands Encroachment Ordinance (No. 12) of 1840 and Waste Lands Ordinance, (No. 1) of 1839.

The ordinance on marriage prohibited the traditional marriage systems, polyandry and polygyny and made monogamous marriage legal. Also registering marriages became the accepted norm in the society. The two legislations on land had immediate effect on the peasant society. The British who were responsible for introducing capitalist relations, were keen to promote a land owning class and to create a land market. The two legislations on land required clear land rights and individual ownership within the family. These legislations indeed created a propertied class and fragmented land within the ranks of poor peasants. This in return had a detrimental effect on women's access to land. As de Zoysa (1995: 96) says, the development of a land market under the Waste Lands Ordinance demanded a monogamous system of marriage founded on a patrilineal descent and inheritance of land, and decision-making had to be compressed within the nuclear family headed by a single individual. Therefore, she says, "Marriage and land policies were ubiquitously linked, and all like Siamese twins, stood together in the years that followed".

In the post-colonial society, monogamous marriage and nuclear family are important. Ethnographic studies on Sri Lankan rural society reveal the inferior status received by women in family, where men have been favoured against women in inheriting land (Thambiah, 1958; Leach, 1971; Robinson, 1975; de Zoysa, 1995). The law itself may not be discriminatory against gender on land rights, but social norms and practices are more effective in determining who should own family property. In this regard sons are more favoured than daughters.

Men's favourable position in society with regard to inheritance of land is further seen in state allocations of land. In the 'Village Expansion Scheme' and in the dry zone settlement schemes women hardly received land. The State policy on land alienation is very much gender biased, where men are seen as breadwinners and women as their dependents (Agarwal, 1994; de Zoysa, 1995; Schrijevers, 1985).

This account clearly points out that women hardly received land rights in both private and state lands. This disadvantaged position also disqualified women to receive agricultural extension services and credit facilities offered by the State from time to time. Thus I wish to argue here that women are pushed to a state of powerlessness within and outside the household due to not owning land, which is the main resource in agriculture. Gender hierarchy is maintained through the existing patriarchal attitudes toward land ownership.

Women in Non-Farm Activities

Non-farm activities comprise of diverse categories of employment. According to Binswagner (1983) "non-farm activities refer to employment beyond that required to produce crops and raise livestock". Therefore all activities other than crop cultivation and rearing livestock would fall under the category of non-farm activities. An enormous diversity also lies in the area of productivity from one area to another. As quoted from Ho, Dunham (1992:6) identified three types of non-farming activities. They are:

(a) part time, often seasonal work that is undertaken by agricultural household members to supplement income;

(b) rural non-factory production—a specialized (full time) occupation for the operator and helpers—carried out by artisans though still depending primarily on family members for labour; and
(c) factory production which is full-time employment in the organized sector using hired labour.

In rural Sri Lanka it is the first two categories, which are more important. As explained in the previous section, rural underemployment and poverty are increasing due to agriculture not expanding. Agriculture today is not profitable due to the high cost of production. Therefore, rural non-farm activities are increasingly becoming important in easing the problems of underemployment and poverty. Land tenure arrangements, fragmentation of land; low productivity in agriculture and the relative return from farming being unattractive compared to other sources, all have contributed for people to opt for non-farm activities. In many farming households, family members engage in both agriculture and non-farming agriculture (Senanyake and Dissanayake, 1999).

Rural women play a significant role in non-farm activities as Senanyake and Dissanayake say, "Our focus group discussions with women reveal that, poor women who are bound to their homes, view non-farm employment activities as an essential component to complement household income. They prefer non-farm activities because they think that such activities can be combined with their household duties" (1999:19).

I would also say that men are less attracted to non-farm activities especially to activities of the first type of non-farm activity that was identified earlier. I would argue that it is a result of the patriarchal ideology that men are breadwinners of the families and they need to receive a regular income either from agriculture or from other regular employment, which make non-farm activities of the first type not attractive for men. Women's economic contribution is seen as supplementing to the household income and receives a secondary status (although in reality this may not be so). This in fact has given women the opportunity to venture into non-farm activities, which men are not very much attracted to. However, as Amartya Sen (1999) says, the freedom that women have received in taking up new opportunities could be considered as the building blocks for their improvement of capabilities, which have helped in easing household poverty.

The rest of the chapter would discuss the involvement of rural women in two non-farm activities—Neem oil production and Cadju (cashew) processing, introduced by the University of Colombo, Participatory Rural Development Project. By involving in the two projects, women have obtained new skills, gained confidence and strength and financial achievements. Although it is true that women have gained many achievements and obtained some visibility and power within and outside the household, still woman's role lies in strengthening the family income so that she could perform her stereotyped gender role of caregiver more effectively. Therefore, I would argue that, woman having more capacity to contribute to strengthen the family income would not necessarily lead to a change in strategic gender needs and patriarchal attitudes. Before I discuss the situation of women engaged in two non-farm activities introduced by the University of Colombo Participatory Project, I would in the next section provide a brief description of the said project.

University of Colombo Participatory Rural Development Project

In July 1998 University of Colombo and Japan International Cooperation Agency (JICA) jointly initiated a participatory rural development project in the north-western province in Sri Lanka for three years. At the end of the third year the project was extended for further three years. The project operates in six villages in three Divisional Secretary Divisions.

Several development projects were implemented through the project. They are infrastructure, economic and social development. Several training programmes for skill enhancement and awareness creation for capacity development were conducted.

In the areas where the University project operates, Neem and Cadju are widely grown. The project having gained experience and knowledge on the local requirements and resources realized that both Neem and Cadju could be given a value-added advantage by developing them into profitable economic activities. The economic viability and the potentialities of the two projects were discussed at village meetings where both men and women participated. Villagers irrespective of gender felt that both projects could be important for income generation, but it is mainly women who came forward for both projects. While only women are involved in the Cadju project, a few men are in the Neem oil project. As I have said before it is mainly women who are attracted to such activities.

There are several reasons as given below:

First, although both these projects have the potentiality to be developed as a regular activity throughout the year, still it is seen more as a seasonal and a secondary economic activity. Therefore, men are less attracted as they think more in terms of a regular income.

Second, the activities related to both projects are seen more suitable for women rather than men. The peeling of Cadju is tedious and monotonous as the same activity is done over and over again and more than anything it is not pleasant as fingers can get affected by the juice (milk), which comes out, unless necessary precautions are taken. Similarly picking and collecting Neem seeds is too simple and not an activity for a man and it is more suited for a woman or child.

Third, women feel that this is an appropriate activity for them as they can do it without any interference to their socially accepted role of homemaker. Women need not go out of their homes and can attend to it while performing their day-to-day domestic activities. Women felt even when the Cadju processing would be done collectively at one place in the village (a building for this purpose is being constructed), they can attend to the activities without many disturbances to their traditional social roles. Therefore, women themselves have internalized that both these activities are more suited for them and not for men.

Fourth, women are more ready to take a risk and venture into a new activity. This may be because they know that even if they are not successful they have hardly anything to loose. Men's attitude is 'to wait and see', and let the women do first. If the business succeeds then men would join or take over from women.

Cadju Processing Project

Several activities are involved in the Cadju processing activity. First, the women collect raw Cadju nuts. Since individual women do not own Cadju lands they have to collect them from outsiders.

Women use different strategies to collect Cadju nuts, such as purchase from vendors who come to the village, purchase from traders close to the village who run small boutiques or purchase from places far from the villages. After collecting a sufficient number, women sit down and remove the shell and take out the kernel. They do this individually in their own homes. However, as said before women are planning to undertake this task collectively once the Cadju processing centre is opened in the village (a building is being constructed for this purpose and all other necessary matters are being sorted out).

Taking out the Cadju kernel is difficult, as it needs to be done without damaging. This is a skill, which everyone does not possess. Therefore, prior to commencing the activities women were provided with several trainings. The project linked the women to different agencies where such trainings were provided. Training was given in several areas, such as removing the shell and taking out the kernel, roasting the peeled cadju nuts, entrepreneurial skills and running small businesses. Some of these training programmes were held in the villages, while some took place outside the villages. When women had to go out they made necessary arrangements with their extended families to take care of household activities during their absence. In some cases the husbands also joined them.

While peeling the kernel, one needs to be skilful so that one would not hurt one's fingers by juice (milk), which comes out. The juice (milk) is harmful for the skin. While some women use gloves, some apply coal around their fingers. There is also a need to complete the task in a short time as otherwise it would not be a profitable venture. Therefore, one has to be skilful for the job. Once this task is completed the next task would be to roast the nuts. In the open market, roasted nuts fetch a better price. An oven is used for this purpose. At present, one woman is responsible for the activity as the oven is kept at her shop.

But once the building is constructed the oven would be kept at the centre. Once this happens, women have decided to employ someone for this purpose. Women feel that in time to come while they themselves are engaged in the activity they could also provide employment for several other women. After the nuts are roasted women sell them to outside traders. This task is also done on an individual basis. However, women go together to different places to find out the prices in the market and also share knowledge among themselves on the market prices. They also consult the facilitators and get their advice on marketing issues. Some men also assist women in marketing the products.

Although women are involved individually in the Cadju processing activity, they have formed into a group and registered as a formal village society with the Department of Cooperative Services. Women clearly understand the importance of working as a group and all efforts are taken to strengthen their society. The society has a president, secretary and a treasurer elected by the members. The society meets regularly and in addition whenever necessary, office bearers of the society meet separately to solve immediate problems.

The society maintains a bank account and each member pays initially Rs 500 for the accumulated fund and a monthly membership fee of Rs 5 to the society. Members are entitled to credit and majority has made use of this facility. As explained before, women have to collect a sufficient amount of Cadju nuts for which they need to have money in their hands to purchase raw Cadju nuts. Women have made use of credit facility for this purpose. Women have to pay back the loan in instalments and the repayment rate has been recorded as highly satisfactory.

Neem Oil Project

Neem is a tree, which is found widely grown in the villages where the university project operates. Prior to the implementation of the Neem project, villagers neither realized nor did they have the capability to use Neem for economic advantage. Neem seeds just fell under the trees and in a very small way some villagers sold the seeds to traders. The study team members of the project had several discussions with the villagers to educate them on the comparative advantage of Neem and the added value that could be generated. Villagers irrespective of gender realized the importance of the Neem and how it could be transformed into a viable economic venture around which several villagers could benefit. However, as in the Cadju project it was mainly women who came forward to the project.

At the commencement of the project the villagers collected Neem seeds from within and outside village and sold to a foreign exporter. In order to export the Neem seeds, it was necessary to wash, sterilize and dry the seeds under proper conditions. The required training was provided to the villagers who were willing to be involved in the project. After a number of occasions of exporting Neem seeds, the project realized that Neem could be also sold in the domestic market, as there was a good demand. The local demand is for both seeds and oil. Since Neem oil could fetch a better price in the market, it was decided to open a Neem oil-extracting mill in the village. Two such mills are operating in two villages. The required machinery and buildings were provided by the project. The necessary know-how was also provided to the villagers. Today, villagers are proud that they are able to make full use of a tree, which earlier did not have much importance.

The collecting of Neem seeds is done individually. Even children engage in this activity and collect seeds fallen in their home gardens. Although collecting Neem seeds is done on an individual basis, like in the Cadju processing, a few villagers, mostly women have formed themselves as a group. This group has also registered as a village society with the Department of Cooperative Services. Similar to Cadju society, here too members pay a monthly subscription fee and a payment of Rs 500 for the accumulated fund at the time of joining the society. The members are provided credit to purchase Neem seeds. Here too, repayment rate is quite satisfactory.

Women in the Cadju Processing and Neem Projects

In this section a few cases of women who are involved in the two projects and their narratives will be presented. The analysis that would follow would be based on the women's experiences.

Case 1: Wimalawathie[1]

Wimalawathie is 24 years old, born in Kohobagaswewa. She is the youngest of a family of nine children and unmarried. She has three sisters and five brothers. Both her parents are living. All her sisters and brothers are married. While two sisters and three brothers are living in the village the others have migrated to different places.

Wimalawathie stopped schooling after she failed her General Certificate of Education (O Level) Examination. After schooling her parents sent her to a sewing class, but she could not make use of the training, as she did not have a sewing machine at home. She then wanted to apply for a job at a garment factory, but her parents did not approve it. However, she did not want to depend on her family and wanted to earn a living.

Wimalawathie has a friend who is running a poultry farm. Seeing the friend's achievements, she was influenced to start poultry in a small scale. She received the necessary advice from her friend. Wimalawathie managed to influence one of her brothers to start poultry. Today, both sister and brother are engaged in poultry in a large scale. The University project has helped them in their poultry activities.

Wimalawathie says, that she was keen on university project activities from the commencement. She had participated in all meetings. She is engaged in the Cadju project and she is a member of the society. She is very happy that she is involved and she sees the potentiality for the Cadju project to develop. Wimalawathie collects Cadju from vendors who come to the village. She says, "I buy from vendors who pass through the village. We (others engaged in the activity) have knowledge about the prices outside the village and therefore the vendors cannot cheat us. We do not go together to find out prices as the Mudalalies (shopkeepers) then reduce the prices. But we all discuss with each other about the prices".

Earlier Wimalawathie sold her Cadju nuts to small shops at the urban centre near to her village. But today she sells her Cadju nuts to a large-scale Cadju centre in the town. She has developed contacts with some officers and as a result without much difficulty she sells her products. She applied for credit and she has made use of it to improve her economic activities. According to Wimalawathie the interest rate compared to other formal and informal sources, is low. However, the women want to get the interest rate further down as she says, "We first had to pay 15 per cent interest. But later we discussed with the officers and brought it down to 13 per cent. We want to discuss with the officers and bring the rate further down to 7 per cent. Today, we know how to bargain".

Wimalawathie, in addition to being a member of the Cadju society, is also a member of other societies. She is the treasurer of the Rural Development Society formed by a NGO operating in the village. She was also the treasurer of the Neem Society, but resigned from it, as she does not have time due to her involvement with poultry work. She says many times she has been asked to be the treasurer of the Funeral Aid Society (this is a society which is highly male dominant), but she has refused as she does not have time to spare. However, even with her busy schedule, she never fails to attend the monthly meeting of the Cadju society. She says that all members make it a point to attend the meetings as any person getting absent would have to pay Rs 100 as a fine. Due to some reason if a woman cannot attend the meeting her husband (if not, an adult member represents her family)

Wimalawathie is happy to talk about the achievements and the benefits of the project. She says, "Today, we (women in the society) help each other more. We have a good understanding among us and we are more friendly and cooperative. We now see the importance of helping each other. We do 'Shramadane' (giving voluntary labour) for village activities, such as cleaning the graveyard and the premises of the community hall, etc. We now want to help a poor woman whose husband is a drunkard. If we can at least give her some help to build her house, we feel that her husband will allow her to join our projects. We are also now trying our best to stop men from drinking. We once got together with few men and stopped brewing of illicit liquor. We have come to know that once again this menace has started in one household and also some men are bringing liquor and selling it in the village. We want to report to the Officer in Charge at the Police Station."

Speaking about her own achievements, Wimalawathie said, "My brother (employed in the Army) and I together acquired five acres of land and we have started to grow Cadju and Neem. I am keen to improve my poultry and whatever I earn I invest on that and I want to expand it to a big farm. I can then give employment to others. I also spend for household things. I bought a new sofa set (this was kept in the house but was covered with polythene to protect from dust). I will not start to renovate the house right now, as I want to first improve my economic activities. Once I am economically stable I am thinking of renovating the house".

When asked about her marriage, Wimalawathie started blushing. Her mother also joined in the conversation. It was apparent that Wimalawathie's parents and brothers and sisters were looking for a partner for her. They said men always look for dowry even though the woman has an income source. Wimalawathie smilingly said that a few days ago a man visited them and that was the tenth man that came to see her. She seemed to like him, but there was a problem as he was working in Nikaveratiya (a place away from the village) attached to the Department of Animal Husbandry. Wimalawathie's family members do not want to send her away as her mother said, "When daughter goes who is going to look after us" (although she is not the only family member staying in the village). When I asked her what she would do, her answer was, "my parents and brothers will decide".

Case 2: Sumana

Thirty-seven years old Sumana is married. She has four children, three sons and one daughter. Their children are seventeen, fifteen, eleven and nine years old. Sumana went to school up to Grade five. She got married at the age of eighteen to her first cousin. Her husband was twenty-two years when they got married. Both she and husband were born in Kohobagaswewa.

Initially after marriage they stayed with Sumana's mother. At that time they ran a small shop in the village. They had good business and lived without much economic difficulties. But, one day to their dismay an intruder shot at her husband while he was in the shop. He was sick for a long time and he lost one kidney. During this time Sumana and her family faced many economic difficulties. Due to the desperate situation, Sumana migrated to the Middle East as a domestic worker. She stayed there for two years, but did not want to continue, as her employer did not pay her properly. She then decided to stay at home and work as a labourer and help her husband in the shop.

When she returned home, she was sad to know that her eldest son had stopped schooling. During this time, the University of Colombo project was operating in the village and she decided to engage in project activities. She first became a member of the Action Committee formed for project activities. Later when the

Cadju project commenced she became a member of the Cadju society. Today, she is the Treasurer of the society.

Today she not only peels Cadju nuts, but she is also responsible for roasting the nuts as the oven is kept in their shop. All other women bring their Cadju nuts to her and she is paid for her labour. The oven was bought from the project. Like other women she has also taken a loan, which she has used to improve her economic activities. She is also involved in the animal husbandry project, which the project has also funded. She says, "If not for these projects I would have had no other option but to go again to Middle East. In that case other children's education will also get disrupted. Thanks to the project we are ok and I want to see my children educated. I would do any thing to get my children educated. Whenever I get money from selling Cadju nuts I buy things for my children's education and I also invest on the shop and on other economic activities. Recently, I started poultry in a small way where I sell eggs in our shop. I get up at 4.00 in the morning to make string hoppers and hoppers so that I could sell them in our shop. My husband also helps me. When I have to attend to society work, my husband helps me in cooking. All this happened only recently".

She goes further to say, "Before I joined the projects, I was really shy and afraid to speak in front of a gathering. Today, I have no fear to speak in front of any gathering. Earlier no officer talked to us, not even the Grama Seveka, but today he speaks and discusses with us about village activities. Today he addresses me as "Madam Treasurer" (giving respect). Earlier I was afraid to talk to officers, but now it is not so. Now I know how to operate a bank account. Every month I go to the bank to deposit the membership fees. I also keep all accounts of the society".

Sumana feels that they are role models for other women. She says that other women even from other nearby villages inquire about their success. According to Sumana, other women are surprised to see that women in the society are helping each other and the unity developed among them. Young women comment, "if old women can engage in Cadju project why is that we cannot engage". Sumana is certain that more women will come forward for village activities.

Case 3: Swarna

Swarna is thirty-eight years old, married and having two sons, aged twelve and eight. Swarna was born in Matara in the southern province (very far from her present village). Her husband is a native of the village. Swarna is the youngest in a family of five. She has three brothers and one sister. She went to school up to G.C.E. (O) level, but could not sit for the examination as at that time her father died and she had to leave school. Thereafter, she went to work at a garment factory.

While she was working at the factory, her brother brought a marriage proposal to which she agreed. The man was a friend of her brother. In 1991, she married. Her husband at present is an Army officer and he is working far away from the village. He comes home only when he is entitled for leave. Her mother-in-law also lives with her.

Swarna sews garments and sells them to a shop in the town. She also teaches a few girls sewing and charges a fee. Girls who have learnt sewing from her, assist her in the sewing. She pays them. There were three young girls sewing at the time I visited her.

Swarna is a very enterprising woman. In addition to her sewing she is also involved in cattle farming. Recently, they had bought a piece of paddy land and it is under her name. Her husband did not want to have the land in his name.

Swarna is a member of the Action Committee formed by the University Project and also the Treasurer of the Neem Society. There are eighteen members in the Neem Society, out of which thirteen are women. Sumana attends to all financial transactions related to the society. A bank account is maintained. She buys Neem seeds from village people and also from the outsiders. To collect Neem from outside the village, she uses her contacts. The members in the society meet once a month. The committee members meet more often, especially at the time when the building for the oil mill was constructed and when the machinery was installed. She is also the treasurer of another society maintained by a NGO that is operating in the village. She says she received a training of maintaining accounts and running a small business. Sumana says, "Today women come forward. They talk without fear. They are not shy and they have lot of confidence, which they did not have earlier. Projects have given lot of strength to women. The village is developing. If the village develops and people have more money more people will buy my clothes. I now want to open a shop in the village (a building for this purpose is being constructed). My family is business oriented. My father ran a bakery. If we have electricity I could have done many things".

Swarna's daily work schedule is very tight. From the time she gets up until she goes to sleep she attends to many things, as she alone has to do everything. Every day before she goes to sleep she speaks to her husband over the telephone. She says she does not mind spending for a telephone as she is also earning from it by providing call facilities to villagers for a payment. She also attends to emergencies at the village, as she was a mid-wife before she got married.

Case 4: Prema

Prema is thirty-two years old and she was born in Kurundewa. She received education only up to G.C.E. (O) level. She is married twice. At the age of nineteen she got married first. She has one son from her first marriage, who is twelve years old and he stays with his grand parents but comes often to his mother's house. Her first marriage ended up in divorce. Her husband was an alcoholic and had treated Prema very badly.

After the divorce, Prema went for employment in a garment factory. During this time her parents looked after her son. She met her present husband quite accidentally while travelling by train. Her son who was also travelling with her became friendly with this unknown man without knowing that he would become his stepfather. This encounter gradually developed into a friendship and later he visited Prema's house and proposed to her. Prema's second husband is working at a private firm outside the village. He comes home only during the weekends. She has one child from the present marriage. Prema is very happy that she is married for the second time as she says; the present husband is like a 'god'. Everytime the husband goes for work, Prema worships him.

Prema's first husband did not allow her to join any activity of the project. But her present husband has allowed and encouraged her to get involved in project activities. She is the President of the Neem Society. She is also a member of the Action Committee.

Today, Prema is actively involved with project activities. She says, "We women have benefited a lot. Today we can get credit, which we use for economic activities. To say the truth, at the beginning I was afraid to take a loan, but speaking to 'Mahattaya' (facilitator) I felt I should apply for a loan. Now I am not afraid. We are now trying to get the interest rates reduced. In fact, we have written a letter asking for a reduction. At the beginning I really did not know how to get our society registered. The first day when I went to get the society registered I had to meet the Commissioner of the Department of Cooperative Services. I was really afraid. She even scolded me. But now I am not scared, I have gained lot of confidence by working in the Neem project. Because of the project, we now know how to save money and to keep accounts. Today, I keep all daily accounts and show them to my husband when he comes for the weekend. More than anything, a lot of trust among villagers has developed. There is more unity among villagers".

Prema uses different strategies to collect Neem seeds. She buys seeds from both villagers and from outsiders. She maintains a good network to collect Neem seeds from outside the village. She gets the assistance of a relative living outside the village and also the regular vendors that come to the village to sell household items, such as spoons, utensils, etc. She gives them an advance so that they could purchase from different sources.

Prema wants to see her two sons well educated and she will do whatever she can to earn. She works in the fields. She also makes string hoppers and hoppers in the morning and sells them to the 'Mudalalie' (shopkeeper) in the village. For her, every cent is important. Her husband once met with an accident and he could not work for two months and during that period they survived with Prema's savings. Prema hopes to complete the house that they have started to build.

Transforming Women's Lives: Path to Empowerment?

As stated earlier, the University of Colombo Participatory Rural Development Project created new income sources for villagers by introducing non-farm activities in the rural areas. As noted before, it was mainly women who were attracted to the new economic initiatives. Through their involvement, several changes came about in their lives. Thus, in this section the attempt would be to understand the changes that have come in the lives of women and to analyse how far women have gained empowerment. The analysis will be based on the presented case studies, women's narratives, information gathered through focus group interviews and researcher's own experiences in involvement in the project since its inception as a member of the study team.

The project from the initial planning stage was careful neither to be gender biased nor to evolve a separate space for women differentiated from men. While understanding the specific women's needs it never tried to introduce women's projects (WID approach) but made it a point to involve women in the mainstream development initiatives of the project. The recruitment policy of the project in the appointments of facilitators was clear on the gender balance and as such, both women and men were recruited. At the village level too when forming Action Committees the project insisted on a gender balance as a requirement. Therefore, from the start, space was created for women to have an equal place with men to participate and decide on development activities.

The Cadju and Neem projects are two main economic projects introduced by the project. They have great potentiality to develop as viable economic activities. Both these projects are still in their initial stages but even though this is the case, several positive social and economic impacts could be seen. Since these economic activities were introduced as a secondary economic activity not many men were attracted. As noted before these activities were seen more as activities suited for women because of not deriving a regular income therefrom, and also because women could perform their traditional social roles while deriving an additional income to the family.

At this stage it is necessary to understand what we mean by empowerment. This is a term, which is widely used in academic writings and by NGOs, across the world. I would refer to Agarwal's definition of empowerment:

> a process that enhances the ability of disadvantaged ('powerless') individuals or groups to challenge and change (in favour) existing power relationships that place them in subordinate economic, social and political positions (1994: 39).

Thus, empowerment is related to power. Therefore, the power relations that operate between men and women within the family and outside the family is important to understand how far women have been empowered. It is socially accepted and legitimized that man has the overall power in the family. Man is the head of family as he is considered as the main income earner. However, today we see more and more women entering the labour market and deriving income. Stepping beyond the family and receiving income should provide women the required capacity to challenge existing power relations. Economic empowerment should strengthen women's ability to challenge gender inequalities. However, I wish to argue that as long as women perceive their economic role within the narrow boundary of family welfare, it does not help very much, even though with several achievements to change power relations that operate between men and women as shown from the women who are engaged in the non-farm activities mentioned above.

As mentioned before prior to the university project, both Neem and Cadju were not used as value added products. They were a wasted resource in the area. But today there is an organized effort to make use of both Cadju and Neem. In both projects during the season of Neem and Cadju women have been able to earn an income. However, in time to come the expectation is for these economic activities to bring a regular income to those involved. At this point it is important to see how women have used their income. Mainly, women have used the money for family welfare, especially for children. Sumana, Prema and Swarna were keen to educate their children and whatever extra money they earned was used for children's welfare. Sumana was relieved that today due to her involvement in the Cadju project she did not have to look for employment abroad as she knew that it would disrupt her children's education. Many said they were able to purchase school bags, water bottles, shoes and other requirements for their children going to school. A few women said they deposited the money in children's bank deposits as one woman said, "The money I received I divided among my three children and deposited them in their bank books. I did not use a cent for household expenses".

Women have also used the money to invest in other economic activities that they are engaged in, such as poultry and to keep new items in the shop.

There were only two women who said that they used the money for themselves. One woman said the money she received from Neem was used to purchase new clothes for herself and her daughter. An elderly woman in the Cadju project said she used the money to go on a pilgrimage.[2] Thus it is very clear that strengthening the family economy was the main concern of the women. Whatever the personal achievements, women still worked within the framework of family and their income was devoted to the family rather than to their personal welfare. Much has been written about women's acts of altruism (Agarwal, 1994; Sen, 1983, 1990). Economic changes, such as women's involvement in gainful employment can bring about changes in the perception of personal welfare.

I would rather argue that women still hold on to their perception of family welfare than personal welfare. However today, the family members, especially husbands, have started to recognize the economic contribution that these women make to the family as important. As such husbands support and cooperate with their wives in order for them to be successful in their activities. As in the case of Sumana her husband attended to household work when she had to be absent from home to attend to her economic activities. Whenever Sumana could not attend meetings, he represented her and this was the case with other women too. In the case of Prema and Swarna their husbands were employed outside the village, but they approved and encouraged their involvement in the project activities. As several women said since the involvement in these new economic activities there has been more unity and cooperation within the family. This is because husbands see the importance of the additional income that comes to the family. I would therefore argue that men would help in household activities when necessary due to pragmatic reasons, but would maintain the status quo within the family and women continue to perform their traditional social roles.

It is however, correct to say that women in the process of engaging in the Cadju and Neem projects have been able to challenge some of the old pre-conceived ideas about women's abilities and competences. Women have gained many intangible resources, which may provide them the opportunity to act as agents of development rather than mere beneficiaries and clients. Empirical data points towards this transformation in the villages covered in the study.

It is very clear that women involved in Cadju and Neem projects have gained much self-confidence and strength. Other than what the women have told, the researcher herself has observed this change in the lives of women. At the initial stages when the University project was introduced to the villagers, women hardly spoke in the meetings although they participated. They always sat behind men and kept silent. But today the situation is different where women speak and articulate their views. The fact that the women were able to get the interest rates reduced for credit shows their bargaining power. As stated before, women are proud to say that, today they are not afraid to talk to any officer and to address any gathering unlike in the past. This has entailed them to take ownership and responsibility on the economic activities. Women regularly meet to discuss their individual achievements and problems and share one another's experiences. They also reflect on their future strategies, which they later discuss with facilitators and the study team. This has helped them not to limit themselves as mere participants in the project but to take ownership in the development activities.

It is not only the economic gains that women obtained from the non-farm activities, but they also had access to knowledge and obtained many skills, which they were deprived of before, due to their disadvantaged position as poor rural women. While it may help to change women's perceptions about themselves, what is shown from the cases of Sumana, Swarna and Prema is how they have used the knowledge gained for better household financial management. Today they are able to organize their household activities better. This once again shows that women still operate within the family framework. Strengthening the family economy is the prime objective for women to engage in the economic activities.

The trust and unity developed among women is a great strength for women. Although income is derived on an individual basis, women help each other and they want to be in a group and see that no one drops out. Women whose houses are by the roadside help other women to collect Neem seeds and Cadju nuts as they have better chances of meeting vendors who come to the village. The group formation has given them a new collective identity and it has made them socially and economically accountable to one another (Kabeer, 1994).

All what was said before are definite achievements gained by women in the non-farm activities. However, I would argue that even though women have gained many achievements, still women's strategic gender needs are not met as patriarchal attitudes and norms still persist in the society. Women do not in any way challenge their inferior position within the family. They do not want to create any disharmony within the family by asserting themselves. Prema sees her husband as a 'god' and worships him. It may be partly because this is her second marriage. Swarna says that whenever her husband comes home on leave, she devotes her entire time for his welfare. Wimalawathie waits for her family members to decide on her marriage. Therefore, I argue that if women are to be empowered, then women getting merely material and non-material gains would not be sufficient unless men change their attitudes and values. It will then be possible for women to perceive their personal welfare as also important and think beyond family welfare.

Conclusion

Women throughout history have contributed to both household and rural economy. However, they have been marginalized and received a secondary and inferior status. Men have taken a dominant position in agriculture, having access to land and acting as performing the role of the decision maker. However, women dominate non-farm activities, especially that are carried out as part time and off seasonal by agricultural households to supplement income. Such activities are often visualized as not suitable for men. Therefore, women have entered into such non-farm activities. This has enabled women to gain economic benefits and develop their capabilities and to create more visibility and importance in the household and community. However, even with such achievements, women still operate within the family framework and work towards strengthening the family. By strengthening the family income alone would not necessarily empower women. It would in fact strengthen the existing gendered status quo within the household and in the community rather than challenge the inequalities that operate. Women need to address their strategic gender needs. However, it is also absolutely necessary that the transformation should occur not only among women but similar changes should occur in the patriarchal attitudes and values that men hold on to.

■ Notes

1. Pseudonyms are used to ensure anonymity.
2. Visiting religious places. There is a strong belief among Buddhists that worshipping religious places bring merit.

■ References

Agarwal, B., 1994. *A Field of One's Own Gender and Land Rights in South Asia*, Cambridge, Cambridge University Press.

Binswagner, H., 1983. *Agricultural Growth and Non-farm Activities, in Finance and Development*, June 1983.

Department of Census and Statistics. 1997. *Changing Role of Women in Sri Lanka*, Colombo, Department of Census and Statistics, Ministry of Finance and Planning.

de Zoysa, D.A., 1995. *The Great Sandy River: Class and Gender Transformation Among Pioneer Settlers in Sri Lanka's Frontier*, Amsterdam, Het Spinhuis publishers.

Dunham, D., 1992. *Rural Non-Farm Employment: Some Conceptual Issues*, Institute of Policy Studies, Colombo, June 1992.

Kabeer, N., 1994. *Reversed Realities: Gender Hierarchies in Development Thought*, London, Verso.

Knox, R., 1981. *An Historical Relations of Ceylon*, (Reprint), Colombo, M.D. Gunasena, originally published in 1681.

Leach, E.R., 1971, *Pul Eliya*, Cambridge, Cambridge University Press.

Munasinghe, I., 1998. *Women in Ancient Ceylon*, Dehiwala, Sridevi Printers, (published in Sinhala).

Pussepitiya, S., 2002. *Structural Adjustment in Agriculture in Asia & Pacific*, Tokyo, Asian Productivity Organization.

Risseeuw, C., 1988. *The Fish Don't Talk About the Water: Gender Transformation, Power and Resistance Among Women in Sri Lanka,* Leiden, E.J. Brill.

Robinson, M.G., 1975. *Political Structure in a Changing Sinhalese Village*, Cambridge, Cambridge University Press.

Schrijvers, J., 1985. *Mothers for Life*, Delft, Ultgerverij Eburon.

Sen, A., 1983. Economics and the Family, *Asian Development Review,* 1 (2), 1983.

Sen, A., 1990. 'Gender and Cooperative Conflicts', in I. Tinker, *Persistent Inequalities: Women and Development,* New York, Oxford University Press.

Senanayake, S.M.P. and Dissanayake, L., 1999. 'Development of Non-Farm Activities in the Monaragala District', MONDEP Working Paper, No.1, Colombo, University of Colombo.

Thambiah, S.J.,1958. 'The Structure of Kinship and Its Relationship to Land Possession and Residence in Pata Dumbura Central Ceylon', *JRAI*, 88, 1958.

Tennakoon, D., 2000, *Dimensions of Rural Poverty in Sri Lanka*, HARTI Thesis Series No. 1, Colombo, Hector Kobbekaduwa Agrarian Research and Training Institute.

Chapter 9

Single Women and Motherhood in Sri Lanka

The Consequences of War

Selvy Thiruchandran

One would imagine that due to changes that have taken place within the family where the headship has changed from male to female, the women, as mothers have also to play the roles of the fathers as well. The war that had affected Sri Lanka for more than two decades have left its scars in very many ways and one of which is the creation of female-headed households. Many men were killed as combatants, as onlookers, and as civilians who got caught in the cross firing and aerial bombings.

This chapter will deal with how the mothers have fared, have coped with the problems and faced the double role imposed on them. Has the boundary crossing come naturally to them or do they have to undergo suffering in transforming their roles?

How they dealt with their own deprivations and how they coped with the experiences of their children's deprivations, essentially form the material from which conclusions are drawn as to how motherhood as an ideology and a strategy has been operationalized. The violence at the political level has created a series of problems for the society, but the problems faced by the women are generally hidden and they remain invisible. More often the State apparatus is most insensitive to the women's sufferings. The sufferings of women as revealed by the narratives of the women, it is hoped will be included in the grand narration when the history of this disaster of political violence is written. Victims need to be identified and not blamed. It is an effort to translate individual women's experiences into a meaningful discourse.

Motherhood is generally seen within certain fixed qualities such as nurture, sacrifice, kindness, love and tolerance—as a package within an emotional and expressive framework. It is also spoken of as comprising supremely virtuous qualities, the violations of which are cast off as unwomanly and unfeminine. The feminist critique had seen the feminine ideology of motherhood as an exaggerated notion, which in practice has heaped the unshared burden of childcare needs on the mother—the difference between the ideology and practice of motherhood. The difference between the institution of motherhood and the personal experience of a mother's love has also to be differentiated. This is also a feminist claim. Motherhood is seen as a superimposed role on women by the male power, which has divorced itself from the care-giving role for the children. While the mother's roles are carefully defined within the family/household system, the duties and functions of childcare are also divided between the spouses. Those relating to food, dress and emotional needs are assigned to the feminine gender as feminine functions. Those relating to discipline and education are connected to masculinity and are assigned to the male members, usually the father, though the uncles and grandfathers may also have some authentic authority to exercise. Boundary-crossings where the women have combined the men's role, with their maternal role may become possible, when mothers have become professionals, and have got the education and training in various fields, but the feminine roles have rarely crossed the boundaries, they remained static thereby creating a double or treble burden on wives and mothers.

The mother-child relationship has basically an appearance of an emotional trap. The shock and the intense feeling of misery that followed the brutality of the deaths or disappearances of the spouses have deeply affected the wives. Their levels of trauma though are varied. Eighty-one women have contemplated suicide according to their confessions. Whether they were temporary and passing feelings of dejection and frustration or serious attempts at suicide, the fear that their children will be reduced to a state of orphans or that they will roam the streets as uncared-for beggars has prevented them from committing suicide.

The attempt at suicide was brought into the discussion to show the levels of their depression and helplessness and the reason for not committing suicide was explained as the deeply felt anxieties of the mothers towards the children. The women on their own brought the subject of suicide into the dialogue.

The children's emotional levels differed according to their ages. The small children, the mothers said, were openly expressive and outspoken about the missing fathers. But the older children above fourteen years were withdrawn, pensive and even reacted with hatred towards society. These children were also more supportive of their mothers, offering physical help, consoling them, talking words of wisdom not usually common among children of this age. Experiences have become the agents of tutoring the common-sense wisdom:

> Don't worry we will look after you. We will get a job soon. We have to be strong and face the future.

These are some of the mature words spoken by them. Some of the boy children, the mothers said, are angry with society (*samukatotai kopam*) have dropped out of school at the age of fourteen, sixteen, and thirteen with the idea of getting jobs. However, they did not succeed in getting jobs. These children were constantly arguing with the mothers for not providing pencils, exercise books, good food and clothing. One such boy said he would avenge his father's killer. Another said:

> Our father committed suicide, deserted you and us. Why should we worry? He did not care for us.

The way the mothers have to handle the small children and cope with the emotional duress raised by the children were the worst experience of the mothers as far as their narrations were concerned. These children are too small, three to twelve years of age, to understand the concept of disappearance or desertions or killings by the army or navy. In all such cases the missing father remained a mystery beyond their wordily comprehension. The mothers said they were too frightened to tell the truth of the disappearance or the killing, but simply hid the truth. They said they have to constantly repeat that he is abroad and that he will come soon.

Some of the intelligent questions asked by the young children have caused misery to the mothers:

> Why we have no father? Arul and Ravi have fathers. He carries them, plays with them, they go out with him. They are very proud because they have fathers.

Statements and queries such as these were repeated by the mothers with tears in their eyes and the mothers said they have no answers:

> If he has disappeared he will come back soon. Till then let us wait. We don't like to wear new clothes or celebrate festivals till he comes. Why is he taking so long to come? You can write to him to come back soon. If *(vappa)* father lives we too can have toys, good food and good clothes.
>
> You are scolding and beating me when my father returns I will complain about you to him.
>
> We are like orphans. No nice things in life. We are not like others in school. My mother is not like others. She does not dress well. She is always thoughtful and unhappy. She gets angry too often or for nothing.

The mother overheard her ten-year old daughter's conversation with her friends. This mother said that she tried to correct herself after this.

A ten-year old understood that his father was shot and killed. He constantly asked the mother:

> Why was he shot? Who shot him? What did my father do? Did he suffer pain at death?"

This child suffered from the shock and the sudden death of the father. He got high fever and shouted in his sleep. The doctor had advised the mother to tell the child that the father is keeping fine in the other world and not to worry. Another child immediately after the death imagined that the father was talking to him in his sleep. He wakes up and runs around in distress. The mother took the child to the temple and the priest gave holy ash to put on his body. They all believed that the father's soul is hovering around.

The child of the father who had disappeared came to know of what has happened to the father from his schoolmate. The mother's version was that he is abroad:

> What would have happened to *(vappa)* father? Where would he be? What would have they done to him? Will they give food when he is hungry? How happy will we be when he returns.

These are thoughts in vain.

There was a case of a woman whose daughter and son-in-law were killed by the soldiers. She was bringing up the orphan children. She said she doesn't talk to the children (aged 7, 9 and 11) anything about their parents' deaths.

One mother told me that when her son's playmate's father who lives next door brings toys and food and sweets to his child her son looks at the scene with eyes full of sadness. He speaks nothing and goes inside the house. Such scenes break her heart. The whole episode of misery is met with silence. She feels she just cannot talk to her son who knows that his father was killed.

> I told my son that your father is in India. Then one day he asked me "why are you keeping flowers for his picture. Only for the dead, people keep flowers". I admitted the truth. He was very thoughtful and moody for two days, refused food. I was very upset over his behaviour. I watched him constantly and took him to the shop and visited my friends. Then he improved.

Some children within the age group of eight and ten were subjected to the syndrome of fear psychosis. After the death of their fathers they became sick, the shock was too much. After that, any noise or noise of crackers upset them. They run inside the house and either cling to the mother or hide under the bed. Despite mothers' deep emotional ties toward the children they were quick to admit rather frankly that the children had become a burden—burden not of mere responsibility, but a burden of emotional turmoil on them.

However, there were mothers who said that there was harmonious relationship between them and the children, though this was not the general pattern. Children do take part in the house management. There is discussion and mutual consolation for each other; these mothers found the children a source of help. There are many categories of women, some were deserted by their husbands and two committed suicide and five were killed or disappeared and two died of natural causes. Though some of the children had bitter memories of their father whom they felt had betrayed them, they were good to their mothers and sympathized with them and understood their struggle in life.

There was another category of children who were neither good nor bad, whom the mothers accepted as too young, irresponsible, immature or going through the patterns of natural growing up. Motherhood intervened so as not to project images of bad children.

It is the third category that we are concerned about, the children who are a strain on the mothers. One need not overtly join the mothers to condemn them but to understand the levels of their behaviour should also be one of the objectives of this study. How the school and the neighbourhood behaved towards the children is also another contributory factor. Perhaps this needs to be investigated more in detail, but as far as single parenthood and how the mothers felt, managed and coped with the problems is a more significant aspect in our present study of the female-headed households.

The children had often reacted with a lot of hostility and bitterness towards the mothers, and the mothers had a lot of emotional outbursts—they cried, sobbed when they related the many episodes of the revolt of the children. Disobedience of the children they felt was the worst behaviour but the verbal attack of the children caused them even more pain.

> You should have died too. Our father will not beat us, scold us. You are ordering us, you tell us, don't go there and here. Come home before dark. We don't want you. We want our father.

> If *(vappa)* father were alive he would give rice (food). You are starving us. You have no job, no money. We have no education. What kind of a mother are you? To go to school we have no shoes. When we come home we have no food.
>
> Why did you give birth to us? Give us rice or squeeze our necks and kill us.
>
> When (*vappa*) father was living we had good food. Now our mother does not give us good food.

A few of them even beat the mothers.

> I will kill those who killed my father. How nice if *vappa* were alive.

With these words he goes to attack the mother.

Poverty though not the sole cause, has the greatest bearing on the children's behaviour. Some of the children who are equally poor did not behave in the same manner. The most stubborn child in the same family behaved violently whereas the others were less stubborn. Hence, one needs also to take note of these differential attitudes within the same poverty levels. Many mothers complained that the children behaved violently towards them. Apart from verbal abuse they also had attacked them or tried to attack them while the other children prevented them. Hence, the need to go beyond the economic variable and identify the other reasons. Our speculation and the tentative argument is that other social, psychological reasons too could have triggered or even caused the turmoil in the minds of the children.

Before going into such an analysis the fact that the mothers suffered needs to be emphasized. The mothers felt that they were inadequate for the ideal of motherhood. They felt guilty that they were not living up to expected social standards. They also feel disgraced when neighbours comment about the children's behaviour. Their transparency did bother us and inflicted subtle burdens on us. Having listened to the problems and not able to suggest solutions has indeed made us also guilty. The guilt of inactivity is a continuing problem for researchers of this kind when the research is not linked to some remedial action.

The causes for the behaviour of the children can be explained variously. But an easy way to identify and capture the whole process is to classify it as the fatherless syndrome. The fatherless syndrome as we see it is not based merely on the children's perception of themselves but on how society, the school, the neighbourhood and the peer groups perceived the children. It is a two-way process. How the deprivations affected the children and how they have constructed these experiences into attitudes and behaviour is one aspect. How the others viewed them, perceived them and how they talked and behaved towards them and how this talking and behaviour have contributed to specific constructions in their own minds is another process. This latter aspect has to be brought into the discourse of deprivations.

Like the widows who have been rendered inauspicious by the loss of the husbands, the children are also subjected to a kind of stigma. The level of the stigma of course varies according to the manner under which the loss of the father has been affected and according to the class position they belong.

At school, that the father has deserted the mother and the children is treated as a stigma.

> You are the son/daughter of the father who ran away.

This is how the fatherless syndrome is constructed. The father who can desert the wife and children can certainly be viewed with contempt but to hold the wife and children responsible for the father's default cannot be explained. Their social status is devalued and they stand condemned in the view of the public. The sympathy that they should get is transformed into a low status which is ridiculed.

You have no father, how do you manage? What do you eat? ask the neighbours.

Kaimpenn Valarta kalusarai, kavali, the rowdy the lowly son brought up by a widow is a term commonly used on children who have no fathers.

The peer group at the school and in the neighbourhood say:

> You don't sit in front (with) of the father and eat your meals *Vaapakku etiraha irunta soru tinnavilli.*

This statement puzzled me a bit for I have not heard this before nor did I realize that the fatherless syndrome was ever expressed through such a conception as eating along with the father. Inquiries revealed that it is a common expression among the

Muslim community which has a great deal of stigma attached to fatherless children.

It is also a social expression of the status of the father in the family and in society which automatically enhances the status of the children. Conversely this also conveys the relative insignificance of the mother and the greater insignificance of the widow.

The patriarchal subjection conveyed on the children was a common occurrence among the Muslims, while the patriarchal culture remains excessively present in all kinds of social interaction including speech and dialogue. What is visible is the social content of the economic deprivation related to poverty or lack of monetary resources. Even the mothers unconsciously subscribe to such overtones when they tell the children with good intentions:

> You have no father. Therefore you should not get into unnecessary arguments with your friends. No one will stand up for you in the event of quarrels and fights. Their fathers will come out and side them, stand for them and protect them. I can't do that.

They advise the children so that they would not get into humiliating situations but they do not realize that it is negative advice. Being a woman and a widow, she thinks she is helpless against other men who are fathers who protect and stand up for their children—fatherly instrumentalism as one may term this. But she is also passing that helplessness on to the children by her own subjection to patriarchal norms. The womanly, passive, inactivity entrenched in the consciousness of the mother is one thing, but that she is socializing the daughters and sons, the 'fatherless' children who should really stand up for their rights is another aspect. That the children are psychologically not prepared to stand up for their rights but made to succumb to social pressure and social inequalities is a third aspect. That their pent-up feelings and emotions have found expression inside the home against their own mothers is a plausible explanation for their behaviour.

The mothers perceiving themselves as powerless are committing the children and themselves to particular values and norms that finally lead to the children controlling the mothers. The class belonging of the mothers in these instances is a contributory factor. They lack both social and economic power. Hence their compliance.

Besides, the mother/women/widow combination still remains a code name for the domestic domain despite the fact that the public man is removed from the picture in their own existence. But the other man/father in the public domain is seen as instrumentally active, protecting and standing up for their own children. The asymmetrical power relations perhaps legitimizes the proverbial social expression of the *kaimpenn valarta kalusarai*, brought up by the widow/husbandless woman concept. Apart from the meaning of inauspiciousness which is present in the content of the statement, the lack of power is also embedded in it. In fact, power emanates both from the auspiciousness of the living husband, which offers social and personal power to the women in the society in which they are living, and from the economic power which is the class position of the woman. Widows lack both powers. Hence the status of the children who are in the custodial protection and care of the manless single women.

Having a dialogue/discussion with the children should be a logical requisite of any research on the family/household. What we are saying now of the children, are from what the mothers told us, the versions interpreted by us. One is not sure how the children perceived the relationship and its related aspects of living within the family and the household.

The law in Sri Lanka which is an expression of our aspiration says that children till the age of sixteen should be compulsorily in school, studying. The reality is sadly different. The gap between our objectives and aspirations and the socio-economic reality is indeed great and has not caught the attention of our legislators and lawmakers.

However, at the level of ideology one is struck again with divisive aspiration when the women were describing their aspirations. Around 90 per cent of them said that the boys should be educated or they should be given training in skills so that they can get jobs and the daughter should be married and get 'good husbands'.

The kind of responses one gets to the death and disappearances of the spouses are of utmost importance for they signify a whole process of how their world views have developed with regard to the life process. The women, it would seem have used various expressions to describe their feelings. Those whose spouses had committed suicide and those whose husbands had deserted the women were bitter about the process of desertion and felt cheated and rejected. However, they have over time developed new aspirations in life.

> He found me boring because I became ill, went behind other women and then finally married one of them. He cheated me. I feel deceived.
>
> He left me, while he was living with me. I did not think this would happen. He left me and married another woman. I felt deceived.

She then described the situation through a proverb, *Sirai valvai vita sirattai valve mel* which translates thus: Eating from a coconut shell (i.e., life of poverty) is better than a life of imprisonment. Imprisonment here simply means emotional imprisonment, i.e., lack of an outlet for sharing feelings and emotions with her husband. She feels that life is less problematic though she is poor now.

Another woman's story is slightly different. The husband was alcoholic and irresponsible, would not keep any job. There was no income. Hence he fought with me often. Between duty and the guilt of negligence he suffered and had it out on me. Often there were arguments between us. One day he left me and the children.

Kamala said her husband got into debt. Unable to pay the debts he disappeared never to return.

> It is six years since he left me. I had to pawn the jewels and sell the land to settle the debt. His irresponsibility and cowardly behaviour has shaken me. I could not get over the agony for many months. The women had mixed feelings. Feelings of dejection, of having been let down, of having been cheated and rejected.

Some of these women have also a sense of relief after the desertion of their husbands. But they were also aware of the social status and lack of the protection that the husband gave them. As the wives of men they had a status as a full member of the community and family. The economic variable of the loss of the breadwinner had no bearing in these cases as their husbands were not the providers anyway.

The children too had no inhibitions or pretence. They were openly hostile to the fathers for having abandoned their mothers. One Muslim child's reaction ran thus:

> Our *vappa* (father) is no good. He is wicked. He left us. But you don't get another *vappa* for us. I don't want another *vappa*, my own *vappa* is not good. Why another man?
>
> "Must beat our father" said another child.

The latter was in response when the two children went to visit the father and his second wife and her people closed the door on them.

Another mother related an incident, which was even more repulsive.

> When my youngest daughter saw the father on her way to school, she asked him money to buy food. He turned the other side and went away.

These incidents as related by the children have upset the mothers a lot. Even the children were affected. They were angry and depressed.

Another mother said if some others talk about their father, they say:

> Don't talk about him. When he decided to leave us, to destroy our lives, when he made us stop our education, he stopped being our father.

Though the mothers share the children's feelings and are able to understand them, they are particularly concerned about the tone and the hostility and the manner of violence in the children's tone. Both mothers and children are affected with deep scars in their minds. Much depends on the type of the social growing up of the children. There is a lot of speculation as to how they will behave when they are adults.

The reaction of the two wives whose husbands committed suicide were not of a hostile nature. Though they too felt let down and disapproved of the cowardly act, they had feelings of sympathy too. However, they were not willing to forgive them. The children of these mothers did not know yet that their fathers had committed suicide. They were made to believe that they died due to natural causes. Those whose husband and fathers died of natural causes have the least psychological affliction. Their problems other than those of their sexual vulnerability and loneliness fall within very clear patterns of an economic variable.

Human beings construct meanings from the social environment and from the political, social and economic conditions. They are influenced always by external factors which create, recreate, construct, reconstruct and deconstruct meanings. In dealing with the death or disappearance of the husbands one sees a subversion of the dominant patriarchal ideology where the loss of the husband now is treated with disgust and not with feelings of loyalty. It is socially inappropriate to talk of husbands in such a manner, but the women did speak against them. Women do not respond to social situations, uniformly and they do protest and condemn where they should. They are not passive but voice socially necessary protests. Protests which are subversive of the patriarchal order.

When one compares the state of these women who were subjected to various kinds of violence from various quarters, the women whose husbands had committed suicide or those whose husbands had deserted them felt better and were able to recover, soon and easily. The comparative levels of their sufferings offered easy explanation and the explanation was evident to one who listened to them and saw them. The children however, have personalized the loss of the father in terms of betrayal, deception and negligence. They have not compared themselves with the other children whose fathers were subjected to various types of violence. As young and looking up to a father's love and care they are severely affected by the manner in which they were rendered fatherless.

The social isolation of children at various levels has in fact led to a denial of peer group belonging to many children. At school some of the children had traumatic experiences and they refused to go to school. The colleagues at school ask them "where is your father. Is he a tiger (LTTE)? How did he die?" They are also ridiculed while many such other unkind remarks were made at them. Fifteen mothers had similar experiences of peer group problems and the children refused to go to school. Where there are days that they were pulled up by the teachers at school for not having paid the facilities fees, other children look down upon them. This humiliates the children who take complaints home and refuse to go to school.

The children are subjected to another kind of ridicule. Like how the widows are blamed for their widowhood and referred to as someone who has eaten your husband. The fatherless little children are also referred to as *tahapanai tintani*—you have eaten your father. These terms signify another process and is meant to call a person unlucky. It is because of past bad deeds, bad *karma*, that you are suffering without a father; the children do not understand the signification, but simply know that it is a derogatory reference to them.

There are indeed other reasons for which the children suffered. Though not common in our sample, four mothers told us that their children were ridiculed as refugees, as strangers, as not belonging to the village. They were isolated and secluded as a result. Their children were not accepted into sports, games and other extra-curricular activities. Two such children dropped out of school. Just as a child wanted to avenge his father's killers, there was another with the same feelings of revenge. This is a case not of death but desertion. The child sees the mother's suffering, had seen her in tears or crying and sobbing. The youngest child (12 years old) one day had told her "I want to kill my father, tell me where he is. Is he alive?"

The mother had to deal with him.

> After this incident I stopped crying in his presence and pretend I am happy. I do not discuss the financial problems. The children will be affected, they will stop schooling and may want to earn something. Even at school he is a lone ranger and children avoid his company.

Generally the mother-child relationship was emotionally satisfying. The children sympathized with their mothers, appreciated their services and there was a great deal of physical help from the children. Older children were found to be a source of consolation for mothers and there was consultation between the mothers and children on the financial management and to cope with crisis situations. This is a redeeming factor and has kept the mothers good and in sturdy conditions with the result, having moved away from the traumatic conditions of the aftermath of the tragedies, the women have become strong and willing to face the future. It is the economic deprivations that bother them most.

But the situation of the young widows with young children is pathetic and needs to be brought into the arena of counselling and more discussions with them are needed.

Socially, education is considered as a power base and males have become the agents of power. The mothers' primary concern was the children's education. They are worried that the children may go astray. In their view education makes people complete human beings. It brings honour, self-respect, power and money. *Aalahaventum*—they must attain complete membership to the community is a wish put forward by all the women. In their attitude there are no differences between the girl child and a boy child. We were often told that girls should be married well to good husbands as their life depends on finding good husbands; no woman said that their sons should get good wives and that their lives depend on good wives. It appears that they are aware and are willing to concede that power lies with the man and it is up to him to make life happy or unhappy for their daughters. The deciding factor of the lives of their daughter is not education, economic assets but a good husband. This fear of the future of their girl children loomed large in their consciousness and they expressed in various ways, their hope and prayers towards finding a 'good man' for a husband. However, education is equally important, more important for boys. The need to educate the girls was stressed by seventy-two women. This factor cannot collapse into a consciousness of gender equality but more towards a practical wisdom line. The mothers do not want their daughters to suffer as they are suffering now. In the event of them becoming widows, education would find them gainful employment. In the event of their husbands deserting, divorcing or committing suicide, their daughters will not be reduced to this shameful existence. *Mariyatai ketta valkai*—of having to beg and being dependent on others. This has to be explained as a piece of wisdom that has emerged out of their experiences of suffering. Two intersecting views are evident here, good husbands for peaceful lives and education for gainful employment and social power.

It has to be emphasized that the school system identified as the ideological state apparatus in Althusserian praxis has taken on the role of an active agent, not of the state but that of a civil society. Where the bureaucracy has failed, the school has intervened to meet, to a very large extent, the needs of the civil society as far as the children were concerned. The teacher and the school principals seen within the idiom of a *guru* as someone who satisfies the needs of an education have also acted as redeeming agents of nursing the sufferings of both the children and the mothers. The mothers except in two cases have spoken favourably of the teachers. Their care and extra school vision that they have taken in the personal and psychological development of the children have been attested to by the mothers. The absence of the male father/husband was fulfilled by the teachers who are mostly males in satisfying some needs of the children. The women testified to innumerable instances where the teachers and principals went out of their bureaucratic rules to waive/reduce the facilities fees of the children, bought them pencils and exercise books, sent notes for the parents to come and meet them when the children needed special care and attention, when the children neglected their studies sent notes to the mother and met them, where children were trauma affected, they informed the parents. Non-speech pensive moods and non-concentration in the classrooms were identified as symptoms of trauma. Not only did they take special care of them but also advised the mothers of their children's mental state, mental illness, *manaviyati* as they referred to the situation in lay terms. Though the children were not treated by any psychiatrist, there was social interaction in the community with the school with the neighbourhood and the children were treated with sympathy by the adults. Though there was no medical healing process, there was the social healing process where the victims were treated with sympathy. The fatherless child syndrome was received sympathetically and with a lot of warmth by the teachers.

The refugee camp syndrome is even worse for the children. If we identified the different kinds of deprivations experienced by the children who live in the normal habitat as traumatic then the situation of the children in the refugee camp is even worse. The same type of the fatherless children's problems are also found in the refugee camps. No purpose is served in giving a descriptive analysis of the same syndrome but to speak of different problems will in effect add to the gravity of the situation of the children as a whole. The children in the refugee camp have lost their childhood.

They have become adults in their psychological make-up. There is such a congregation of people and collective consciousness of idleness among the children in the refugee camps while the mothers are at work inside or outside their make-shift homes. Their homes are really the little areas apportioned with dividing lines made up with saris and sheets. The children socialize with the neighbouring adults who play cards, drink, gossip or indulge in "vulgar sexual jokes". The children are party to all these adult games, where they pick up truths and half-truths. They are also exposed to habits of idleness where people sit and chat. Besides hearing they also see adults behaviour of intimacy as the adults themselves have no privacy. Their sheets and saris divided them from the others who are in another living space. Mothers or parents could not prevent them as they occur daily. There are no private moments between the children and mothers as they preferred the 'interesting' adult company of the males.

There were many school drop-outs in the refugee camp. The atmosphere was not conducive to serious studies. Dim lights, noisy people and radios and TV at full volume—they disturb everyone, with no one trying to organize any order. Children at the age of fourteen to sixteen with adult psyche dropped out from schools with the pretext of finding jobs, but they got no jobs.

The small children were subjected to a type of alienation in school. Branded as refugee children they were also looked down upon as backward. When they found themselves in refugee camps and found a school which enrolled them they have lost six or eight months of school hence they were 'backward' with low marks. Because of the time lost in the process of displacement they lost education too. This sense of alienation too is also one of the reasons for dropping out of school. These indeed are problems of the school-going children, but as single mothers the women have to bear the burden of responsibility. The children have gained the epithet of deviancy. The mothers suffered to see the children in such stages of deviancy. They get angry with them. They said they shout at them, but later feel sorry and a lot of tension results from the mother/son relationship.

A grown-up young girl was subjected to sexual harassment and the mothers have to constantly guard the girls. What they could not do with the boys, they were able to do with the daughters. Both in the refugee camp and outside, the mothers expressed feelings of great responsibility towards the bringing up of children. The absence of the fathers or the syndrome of fatherless children has heaped a tremendous burden of responsibility on the single mothers. This was expressed in various forms.

> The fatherless child should not be ruined. The fatherless child should be directed in the proper lines, *valikatta venum*—must show the path—is a phrase used constantly by the women.

They feel they are morally responsible for the future of their children. This responsibility has exhausted them both physically and psychologically. Women whose children have dropped out from school or turned deviant, disobedient and ill disciplined had a sense of guilt, which found its way in their conversation and in their manner of speech.

> I do not know what to do. How can I handle this huge responsibility, I break down and cry a number of times—the neighbours console me. His father would be very unhappy to see him like this, I have failed in my duty and the duty I owe him said a mother.

She felt she has failed in her duty to bring up a 'fatherless child'. Neither the child nor the extraordinary type of deprivation and the circumstances in which she is placed are taken into account. She blamed herself and herself alone. She was willing to own up to the blame and accept the guilt squarely. That motherhood has failed is her conviction.

Women's existence, both social and personal are affected in many ways leaving behind adverse, repercussions. They made no attempt to hide their feelings. There was a deep sense of alienation. Former friends, associates, relatives, society as a whole had isolated them. The cultural and socio-economic deprivations suffered by them had led to a process of self-alienation. A life negating principle to which they have subscribed would have totally traumatized them. The discordant relation between them and the rest of society was well pronounced in the way they conducted themselves, both in appearance speech and actions. The presence of the children was/is the only redeeming factor. The children's physical presence and the tremendous responsibilities they felt towards them and their future have made their lives purposeful.

Often they mentioned that they live for the sake of the children and that they are the only source of happiness.

> They console me. They need our love, for their sake I have to live, I have to laugh, if not for them I would have gone mad. I would have committed suicide. I forget my worries when I look at the children. I depend on my children for mental peace. They make me function. They are my agents. *Iyakkukirarkal,* and I act.

When discussing their sense of alienation and the role of the children as agents for de-alienation we are not certainly subscribing to a functional analysis, arguing the need of one or the other and for society to continue its peaceful existence. It is not to exalt motherhood, but to make one realize the fact that both the alienation process and de-alienation process are both taxing and have become burdensome to the women and to argue for a case for a change, a change for the better. For, when the children are out of the nests and sought out their careers and their lives the mothers the single women will be left alone again, subjected to sense of total alienation.

This section of the study has in fact raised a few conceptual issues regarding the family and the household. The family is no longer a private domestic sphere as the domain of personal relations limited to functions and roles of emotionality, such as love, nurturance, caring which are beyond reasons of rationalism or beyond the rationale of socio-economic or socio-political praxis. It moves in and out of a public sphere when it handles and deals with education, the market economy and the socio-cultural factors that go to the extent of constraining single women's mode of dress and behaviour within the idiom of a widow. Affective ties and issues of emotionality are not free floating. Women's domestic labour and public labour are conflated into a common fund. The single women are not in the private realm any more. However, their relationship to the children, which is anyhow characterized as emotionally intimate and private, have now reached new and fresh dimensions, when they have to deal with psycho-socio problems as well.

When the children compare themselves with other children from normal home situations and who are economically and socially better placed, it is the mothers who are dealing with their complaints. When the children got disturbed emotionally—shouting in their sleep, running around in distress, running away from the noise of crackers, the mothers dealt with the problem, often single-handed. This is not to say that this falls into the gender division of labour where the mother is dealing with an emotional problem of the child. This is rather, dealing with a problem of the emotionally disturbed children leading to imbalance and is rightly the vocation of a specialized professionally qualified person. This is not what Parson argued as women as wives and mothers provide the necessary emotional stability to satisfy the needs of men and children. This is beyond that function. This contests the argument which sociologists make on the private/public division. Women are not merely central to the private realm, is one argument but what is private and domestic and what is public and external to domestic is yet another question that arises when one compartmentalizes social processes. The question where do you place women and why do you have to separate and isolate the category of women is another question that arises here. The exclusive feminization of the role of mothering has to be questioned again and again. That the domestic need not remain fixedly gendered comes out of the female-headed household. That the women need not necessarily be identified with the domestic and the familial, comes up again and again in the complex manner in which society changes or introduces changes in its formation. Constructions which are gendered within the domestic sphere are increasingly contested. 'Natural' and 'familial' are ideas that are constructed within the domestic sphere but they are essentially social. The language 'natural' needs to be shifted into the social sphere which is perhaps what feminisms project basically is. However, terminologies such as feminist anthropology and feminist sociology should be abandoned and the process of a naturalization of the disciplines should take place which should automatically include a feminist vision into its discipline, thereby doing away with terms such as mainstream sociology and mainstream anthropology.

However, child labour was not a major problem in this society. They do not get jobs due to socio-political dislocations and hence not all of them who dropped out from school are working. However, children of all ages and both genders, both at home and in the refugee camps are seen doing a lot of domestic work, which is socially necessary. Looking after the little sisters and brothers, feeding them, bathing them when the mothers are at work, washing cooking utensils, collecting water, helping the mothers with the cooking are done at regular hours when they are not in school. Even a five-year old girl or boy is doing something constructive and useful as a help to the mother. While it has become necessary and the mothers want them to help, this has effectively reduced the children to playing adult roles. Childhood play and leisure are lost to these children. This is perhaps a class problem common to all the people in Sri Lanka who are in a particular class location and not peculiar to female-headed households. Perhaps a majority of them would not be doing this if they had the father to earn.

Households in the Refugee Camps, the New Habitat

Life in a refugee camp is a replica of life in an ordinary household. Men, women and children live together as a family in a household situation in smaller spaces of habitat. They cook and eat, share their resources and sleep under the same roof. Makeshift kitchens, living and bedrooms are the structural framework of their homes. The refugee camp resembles a commune in its structure taken together. Families have divided its whole space into individual homes but communal activities do take place not in cooking and sharing meals but in some activities. Spending leisure time together, playing games, enjoying each other's company, sitting around in groups, they share some part of this living. But they live another part in the private sphere within their little homes as family members in the limited space without doors or walls that separate the individual structures of their houses.

Two refugee camps are included in the study to identify the gender dimension of the problems. The structure and ideology of the household are analysed with its gender implications, within the matrix of change and experiences. Another interesting phenomenon that has become the focus of our study is the ethnic mix of the Sinhala and Tamil women living in close proximity to each other. This focus, we thought, would have political connotations. In fact this is an aspect that was discovered in the process of our research and did not form a part of the research design at the beginning. Women's own common sense politics and their understanding is an interesting intervention within the so-called private space of the household that we are studying.

When children wanted to avenge their fathers' killers, the response of the mothers was that there is no point in harbouring feelings of hatred towards anyone and destroying themselves in the process and becoming killers themselves. That the Trincomalee Tamils have not interacted with the Sinhala civil society or enjoyed the Sinhala neighbours' company or hospitality is a major factor in this process of constructing consciousness of friendship or hostility.

Dislocation and displacement have taken families to the refugee camps. The fear of attacks by the security forces and the LTTE have also forced families and single women to move into refugee camps, seeking safety. A few families felt that they would be provided with food if they moved into the refugee camps. The question may well be asked when dislocations and displacements are problems and equally traumatic for all who have undergone such miserable experiences why pick up on women's problems alone? Is this attitude not being women-centric or an attitude which is biased towards the female? That caste, class and gender inequalities persist and even get accentuated in times of crisis is a reality. The gender specific trauma has very special dimensions, especially when the women are single and with children. This data tends to be glossed over or taken for granted under the problems of refugees, dislocation and displacement.

This is also reflected in women's rehabilitation process initiated by the NGOs and the State. Women's organizations or NGOs with gender sensitivity realize this while on the field, more often belatedly. Hence, alternative strategies should take note of the gender dimensions. Our study becomes another eye-opener to planners and to the social scientists who refuse to take note of the gender perspective.

The gender specific burdens and responsibilities in the reproductive sphere are often carried out under very desperate conditions in the refugee camps. The single women live in fear of sexual harassment. The women who have males in the family are given protection. The men protect 'their' women, the girl children, wives and mothers, but look upon the other single women as sexual objects to be targeted. The single woman becomes sexually vulnerable, not being 'possessed' and therefore not protected. The women complained that there was no protection for them. The women were very careful not to name the offenders for fear of reprisals. There is some kind of solidarity amongst women, they look after the other women and grown-up girls when the elders have to go out of the refugee camps on various missions.

The human suffering of having to be displaced from their own habitat to which they were used and which has become part of their lives can only be understood when one experiences it. It was often told by the women—"You must undergo this pain to realize the depth of it, the agony". Of course we conceded the point to them without reservation.

They have little spaces partitioned into bedrooms, cooking area and perhaps a corridor. The partitions are done, rarely with a cardboard and often with saris and sheets donated by others. The women have to change clothes and sleep without an iota of privacy. They often ask another woman or a girl to stand on watch so that peeping toms can be avoided. The so-called rooms and kitchens have no doors.

It is the same scenario with the toilet and when bathing. Both men and women have to bathe from the same containers where the water is collected from the lorries on a daily basis. If the women wait too long so that the site is clear of men, there is no water left for them. They are not used to bathing in public, they were very shy at the beginning. But they said it still continues to be an uncomfortable experience as men do not usually behave well. They used a lot of euphemisms by way of explanation in their talk. They ended up saying "You must only experience to know". The single unprotected women indeed are more vulnerable to these experiences. The major problems in their own words was bringing up the children. The fatherless child syndrome becomes more pronounced in the life situation in the refugee camps. The children are exposed at a very young age to adult behaviour. Speech mannerisms, games and behaviour are copied without any checks and balances. The older men use these unprotected children to serve on them, send them on errands and the mothers are helpless by their gender and by their single status. Being older in age, these men have the power to order the children around. The mothers confessed that both the daughters and sons are exposed to the facts of life at a very young age. Lovemaking takes place in the open or behind the sari partition. Teenage marriages have become common as a result of these. One mother told us that children become bad, *Kettupokirarkal.* They grow up fast they are ripe when they are young, *Pinchila muthtuthukal.*

Male protections being absent, women on the one hand are vulnerable to sexual abuse. Being eve-teased, commented upon on their walk and mode of dress, they are sometimes openly invited but more often suggestively given signs. On the other hand they are scared to talk about these experiences, while being silent they are harassed, if they become vocal and identify the culprit to strangers and to those outsiders who appear powerful, the bureaucrats, the NGO personnel and the researchers came under this category, the situation can become dangerous and more overtly violent. It was a shameful experience for us to feel helpless and ineffective in offering any kind of remedial action, as we could not simply find out who is who. Their "this one" and "that one" remained unidentified throughout their conversations. We could only bring it to the notice of the NGOs that work in the camp and to the Assistant Government Agent (AGA) of Trincomalee. The women felt and rightly so, that the outsiders who come and go are not there to morally support them or protect them when retaliation takes place.

The general pattern in the women's consciousness was that they hated violence and war mongering and longed to have peace and tranquillity amidst them. There were many women who were yearning for peace and wanted the State and the LTTE to put a stop to the war brutality forthwith. There were instances where they politicized the personal, the whole familial household related experiences to the ongoing war. They were quick to identify the problem.

> The nation as a whole is under siege—siege of hatred, suspicion and "mutual murders". Our children are affected. What do we hope for them? Insecurity, worries, tension poverty and starvation. The war must stop.

Though many women shared this kind of helplessness, the women in the refugee camps were more articulate in their expressions.

With the father absent and the mother often depressed and sick and poor, the children are exposed to various problems at various levels. In most homes the children are found to be unhappy, malnourished, under-educated and often rebellious as remarked by the mother. That they are rejected from society for various reasons is one aspect of this story. That they are subjected to a series of negative attitudes is a far more tragic story. State terrorism, inter-ethnic tensions and rivalry have constructed a series of anti-feelings. What they experience in school both from peer group and from the school as an institution has another dimension. Poverty that has deprived them of all childhood desires has left deep scars in their minds. A mother's story of how she coped with the problem of a childhood longing has even subverted her own religion.

> My son asked me to buy him a bicycle. I cannot afford it. I told the teacher to tell him that it is against our Muslim culture. He didn't ask for it later.

That the teacher, under the circumstances has complied, is not strange.

The child as a refugee has constructed his/her own marginalization as an outcaste. Both in the village and in the school the refugees are treated as outcaste vagabonds. Among the communities that are affected by war, poverty and insecurity, there is a hierarchy created as refugees and those who belong to the land, their own habitat. The refugees are cast in an idiom of otherness and referred to derogatorily as refugee children as *ahatipillaikal* with social and economic meanings of marginalization. This construction is not a caste or class variation of hierarchy but something beyond that and is based on a belonging and non-belonging to the habitat and the land of one's birth.

The discussion with those living outside the refugee camps has brought out the same kinds of structural deprivations and basic needs such as water, privacy in shelters. But how they felt and how the others treated them within the construction of refugees have hurt them badly. They expressed their feelings at great length.

Household as Alienating and the Levels of Poverty

The household is not a personal dominion or a hide-out from the political world. It is always situated in the political spectrum, though with an image of being personal and private with in-built mechanisms to shield away the market-oriented competition woven around it. It is also constructed as a haven, as the domain of expressive love and care and religiosity. In reality however, this image is always contested in general and particularly for many women it is a site of unshared labour, a site of violence, a site of sacrifice and suffering. The single woman in the present household though is rid of the patriarchal structural dominance, the ideology of patriarchy which is pervasive crosses the boundaries of the door-step and the fences and is very much present in the form of gossip, sexual harassment and other exploitations and oppressive intrusions from the public domain.

Apart from these that are connected to the absent scenario of the husband, the other major problem faced by the women is poverty. Poverty which has made the child stop going to school, poverty which has created child labour of having to work outside the house and inside the house, poverty that has helped create disobedient rebellious children, poverty which has made the children attack the mothers, asking for food has also various other dimensions. It has converged with other social inequalities to create oppressive situations—the fatherless and husbandless syndrome by themselves would have been less traumatic, but the fact that it has economic repercussions which has led to lack of power, socially as well, had indeed created traumatic conditions for all those who live in poverty.

Women complained rather helplessly of the one or two meals a day, about the hungry children and the labouring children who earn a supplementary income to their mothers' wages. The bread-winners who have died have not saved enough. Not by design but by accident, the entire sample of hundred households of the Muslims and the Tamils are from a low class. Hence, this study is of a class that was earning a hand to mouth living even when the breadwinners were alive. Now without them the supplementary income the women earned has become the main income.

The women go to the field to weed and clear the soil for daily wages. They make food at home and sell them from house to house through the children who do this in the mornings before they go to school. This means the women get up at four in the morning. They did speak about the conditions of their labour and how tiring it is and how worn out they are by these daily chores and having to sit in front of the fire for long hours. Some of the women weave mats and rugs and sell *cadjans* which are taken to the market by themselves or the children. Thirty-six women said that they have no means of subsistence. Five are working as seamstresses, two are pounding paddy. Three are engaged in poultry, selling eggs and birds. Six are working from home, weaving mats, containers and cadjans. Three work for daily wages as weavers in a weaving centre. Twenty-six women are in some kind of petty trade-making and selling hoppers, string-hoppers, running small boutiques, rearing goats and cows and twenty women are working as agricultural labourers in the fields.

Poverty has affected the children in various ways. But the women are affected physically as well. They did not have to speak about their physical conditions much, though they did so. The women looked weak and pale, worn out by the physical labour on the one hand and lack of nutritious food on the other. They complained of various illnesses of which anaemic condition was the most frequent complaint. Aches and pains and arthritis were also talked of often. The women complained of black-outs and weakness. The complaints expressed by the women are symptomatic of both their mental and physical condition. One can easily come to this conclusion though not with medical precision. Whenever the women spoke of illness, they always linked it with the kind of labour they do for their living. Rice pounding, paddy pounding, sitting in front of the kitchen fire, in bending positions for long hours in the field and standing in the wet fields for long hours are related to chest pain, losing eye sight, body aches and arthritis. That they cannot continue like this, this miserable existence, this life of poverty, life of insufficiency, this life of hunger, and this life of starvation was repeatedly mentioned to us. They have a low esteem of themselves as living below standards. They are bitter and frustrated.

In a situation where there is shifting of positions within an interplay of socio-economic conditions, there is a general destabilization but the gender axis has also played its role and women get pushed into marginalized positions of poverty and ill-health. Whereas in the shared households women and men were equally poor, in the present situation the women have become poorer. These women are either unemployed or survive on depressed wage labour. Their physical labour is critical for their survival—often it is overwork under harsh conditions. Apart from this women who are used to restrictive social behaviour, subscribe to a practice of self-denial of comforts, food and other luxuries. They accommodate a lot of inconveniences and limitations for the sake of the survival of the family. We saw sick women underfed and under-nourished.

The other point to be emphasized is their ignorance of their right to health care. Their accessibility to national health care services is practically nil. The war situation has destabilized the state machinery to some extent but here again as women they are less cared for. The outreach of these services to the poor in general is insufficient, but for women it is worse.

How the women coped with the situation is an interesting story. Despite the very oppressive and frightening conditions of death and disappearances and this is more predominant, the women carry on. They do complain, weep and wail, curse and argue though an element of passivity and forbearance is sometimes projected as feminine values. Often when it comes to their personal needs, desires and handling of their own sexuality they succumb to various types of self-denials and impositions. Though restrained, their protests are loud. They experience patriarchal domination which manifests itself variously through sexual harassment and the like, are also against the war, against the killing and against the ethnic/communal violence perpetuated mutually and they give expression to these rather eloquently.

They are still hoping for a future, a future of peace and tranquillity. A return to normalcy is their first desire in terms of their priorities. Often this is expressed through sentiments regarding their children, the children's future, their education, their jobs, and daughters' marriages. Children are their assets, the nearest kith and the only hope in their lives.

Chapter 10

Bodies Without Rights

Violence in the Age of Globalization

Subhadra Mitra Channa

Assaults on women's bodies are not a new phenomenon. From times immemorial, women have been raped, kidnapped and humiliated at times of war and of conflict. In most of history we find that women's bodies have been fodder for the fight between men, for masculine honour and for the so-called welfare of society. But what is most alarming for us today is that in spite of overt ideals of society being otherwise, in an age when everyone is talking of human rights, women's rights and liberty and universal humanism, things are not getting any better; rather they are getting worse. In traditional times most of the attacks on women were from the outside but today with increasing modernization, the vulnerability of women is increasing even within the home.

The village community, the notion of visibility and primary group values had been traditionally viewed as insulating women from violence, at least to some degree. It was the urban jungle that was viewed as dangerous because of anonymity and lack of strong primary group sentiments. But with increasing opening up of the rural areas to global and national networks, the women in the rural areas are being subjected to newer forms of violence, precipitated by the intrusion of values and aspirations of the urban middle classes. With the opening of society, even of the rural interiors by mass media and migration, none is insulated from the effects of global consumerism. Thus female foeticide, dowry deaths and murder of women are today as much a part of the rural countryside as they are of the urban areas. The additional burden that rural women carry are those of poverty, ignorance, lack of education, lack of medical facilities, absence of basic resources, lack of information and insulation from aid providing agencies. Thus, a mismatch of traditional values with modern consumerism and individual aspirations have created a worse situation for women than was present even under traditional patriarchy, where the community played some positive role in providing rights to rural women. Women are now left defenseless and alienated in the face of impact of a globalization and modernity that they little understand or are equipped to cope.

What is 'violence'?

Before we embark on any discussion on violence we must agree on what is meant by violence, How do we put a name to the act? Indeed much of violence occurs because it is passed off as 'normal', it is not recognized as violence. In this category come all those acts that Bourdieu had called as symbolic violence, that are violent in psychological and emotional terms, without being physically so. Thus, in her study of a village in rural Uttar Pradesh, Wadley (1994: 56) writes, "In addition to the cultural norms that deny women the opportunity to speak, married women in rural North India are depersonalized or de-individualized through 'non-naming'. In her husband's village, a woman's given name is never used. Rather, she is called *bahu* by all senior to her in age (out weighing even *jati* considerations), while those junior to her address her by the appropriate kin term, *amma* or *mata*, 'mother'; *bhabi* 'brother's wife'; *dadi*, 'grandmother' and so on. Through such non-naming, a woman's individual personality is denied".

Thus a woman is not only relegated to a nameless existence, she is also faceless in her demands on the household.

Physical violence too is not always regarded as violence but may be an act justified by the moral order. In this category come all such acts where the interest of the collectivity is prioritized over the interest of the individual. The bodies of women are often regarded as the repositories of honour of their groups. In the middle period in Bengal, Inden (1976:1) observes that the moral code of the *kula*, or clan or *kula dharma* depended upon the actions pertaining to the rules governing the *dan* or the gift of daughters in marriage. Any inappropriate action in this regard; like the failure to marry off the girl in a pre-puberty age, failure to give the right amount of *bor pon* or dowry, failure to marry the girl into an appropriate family of right *jati* and standing, would pollute and bring *ninda* (criticism) or *apayasa* (ill reputation) to the kula for posterity. The entire bodily substance of the kula would be defiled forever. It was concern for the honour of the kula that led to marriage of child brides to elderly men and polygamy among the high caste *kulins.* There were also predominance of dowry among the high castes and some instances of torture of a bride by her in-laws, but murder was rare, abetment to suicide more common.

In Bengal, in the eighteenth century, there were many instances of parents killing their teen-age daughters when they could not find suitable husband for them beyond a respectable age of marriage. The reason was, as pointed out by Inden, kula dharma. The reasons for killing of daughters was firstly the parents felt it was their duty to preserve the honour of the kula that included a proper disposal of the daughter in marriage following caste norms. Secondly, the personhood of unmarried daughters was still unformed. A woman became a full person only when she was married. In her father's house, a girl was still an incomplete social person and her father had full rights over her *in rem*, that is, over her life as well. It was well within morality for a father to kill his daughter for honour.

Such was the case in other parts of India, such as in the north-western parts from where female infanticide had been reported from the nineteenth century. Although the British blamed this practice on the custom of giving dowries, researchers found that "even all who practiced bride-price, as well as Muslims practiced 'female infanticide'" (Oldenberg 2002: 5). The 1881 Northwest Provinces Special Census Report named seven caste groups as the ones most likely to engage in this act—the Jats, Gujars, Tagas, Ahirs, Rajputs, Minas and Ahirs. The reason for the latter for doing away with daughters could be multiple but the danger of daughters being abducted and also the high enrolment of men in the army and going away from home could be another. Also since men were seen as the main breadwinners, the role of women was marginalized in the household. But most importantly it was not merely dowry but the ignominy of being the father of a daughter that led families of high status to kill their daughters. Moreover, by the rules of hypergamy, it would be difficult to find grooms for girls of high status families. Since having an unmarried daughter was unthinkable, many preferred to do away with daughters altogether.

Personhood and Rights

Thus, violence is also related significantly to the concept of personhood. Who or who is not regarded as a complete social person? When are they viewed as dispensable? To what extent society views a person as being important and who are seen only as important in a secondary sense, as means to support the claims to importance of central persons of society. Thus daughters and wives are the means for a man's claim to high social status and which might be actualized even in their elimination.

The concept of human rights attaches itself to the concept of personhood. Society has always distributed rights according to its definition of personhood, and sentient beings considered having less complete personhood have been accorded less rights. Thus, societies vary to the extent that full social rights are given to categories such as male, female, child, married, unmarried, animal, etc. In the modern age it was recognized that at least all humans irrespective of their sex, class, ethnic affiliation and race were deserving of full human rights as humans. But ironically the very process of modernization incorporating in itself the processes of colonization, industrialization and capitalism failed to accord such rights to various categories of people like indigenous, black, children and women. In the contemporary post-modern world, that is shouting itself hoarse on the issues of human rights, we still find that the very processes of globalization and liberalism, set to usher in a world homogenous in its achieved and aspired development, is setting in motion forces that continue to degrade and devalue certain bodies; depriving them of full personhood and thereby basic human rights, such as right to life, safety and livelihood.

In an incisive study of gender relations Rao (1998) has described the concept of *sakshiyat* among the Muslim Bakkarwals of the North-Western region. The term sakshiyat is a term meaning 'personhood' and Rao has shown how personhood is a character that varies among men according to their power and prestige, but women are denied full *sakshiyat* as a category. Thus, while men in society can compete for power, women as a category are disqualified. This is the situation in most of rural India, women as a category, are muted, whether they belong to high castes or rich families or to low castes and poor families, they remain socially powerless. The construction of subjectivity is such that it is largely men who are deemed to have agency, because they are seen as social persons, the women are seen as mere objects. When it comes to negotiation of power, it is between men, women being only the means of that negotiation.

A most insidious aspect of the devaluation of women's personhood is their own implication in their subjugation. Thus, women are socialized from childhood to believe in their own inferiority and the unquestioning acceptance of patriarchal values. Thus a housewife considers it absolutely justified that she sacrifices her own share of the food for her husband and son. A sister thinks it is only right that her brother gets many more privileges than her and this is all achieved through women. It is the mother who as the primary socializer is instrumental in instilling these values in her own children. Women as upholders of the morality of the family and the society become a party to their own subjugation and that too willingly. This is what makes the hegemonic imposition of patriarchal values so difficult to break.

Concept of Honour and Hierarchy of Female Bodies

In certain parts of rural India, and my own field experience in the North-West such as in Haryana leads me to state that political games of male honour are often played out on women's bodies.

Traditional patriarchy, boosted perhaps by the 'masculanization' of the economy as in colonial times (Oldenberg, 2002; Chawdhry, 1994), prioritizes men as against women. But women, as pointed out by Unnithan-Kumar (1997), are important boundary markers between groups. The attack on a woman's body is symbolic of an attack on the honour of the men of her group. Thus, in Haryana there is a tradition of forceful penetration of a woman's vagina by a '*lathi*', a symbol of masculinity in Haryana culture (Channa, 1997). In situations of conflict between two groups, families, clans or castes; men of one group may waylay a woman of the rival group and subject her to such a shameful act of violence. The target is not overtly sexual, but the humiliation of the men of her group, although covert sexual fantasies and desires may be served by such an act. The rape or abduction of a woman may thus be a means of humiliation, not of women, but of men.

Women's honour is only an appendage to that of the men of her group. She is the means and not the end of the game of power, played by the men in society. It is towards playing their own games of power that men use the bodies of women as their pawns. When men attack the bodies of the women of rival or enemy groups, it is a form of emasculation, of de-masculanization of the men of that group.

In the same way and for same reasons, women of low castes have always been targets of sexual attention and violence from men of higher castes. In Haryana, women of Dalit castes said that they are always open to sexual assault by men of high and dominant castes. The low caste families never send their young women for work outside the house, like collection of fodder from the jungles or to get water from a distance. Only older women dare to go out of the house for such tasks. The reason was put forward by one old woman from a low caste: "The men of high caste will protect the honour of their women. Moreover because of the high status of their men, no one dares lay as much as an eye on the faces of women of high dominant castes. But who will save us? We are always easy prey". The message is clear, the high caste men always make it clear to the low caste men, that their masculinity is worth much less. It is the social power of men that decides the fate of their women. Women by themselves have little social personhood. They are what their men are.

It is through a woman's womb that the purity of the 'group'—whether race, caste or ethnic community is maintained. Thus, violation of this body is also a symbolic invasion of the community. Thus in the English language the words 'rape' and 'conquest' are linguistically, metaphorically and actually synonymous.

Violence and Patriarchal Values

Violence often becomes also a result of the contestation for space. It is here that the term 'empowerment' as applied to women becomes problematical. Mahajan and Madhurima (1995:44) have listed among the causes of violence in rural Punjab, the fact that a wife may be abused if the husband is threatened by her independence. In fact, in many cases of violence against women, it is found that the woman bears the brunt of the man's anger against society. Whenever a man is humiliated outside the house, he often releases his anger on his dependents, that is his wife and minor children. For example, out of the 115 cases studied in the work by Mahajan and Madhurima, 87 wives confided that their husbands have been violent and 58 admitted to violence being a routine matter in the household.

Even dowry is more about male worth than about just material greed. Although the material dimension cannot be discounted, what dowry symbolizes most of all is the superior status of the bride-receivers. Even in modern times this sentiment prevails and the more women are getting empowered and are able to be earning and decision-making members of the family, the more male anger is turned on them. Thus, many cases of so called 'dowry violence' is often reassessed as feelings of male inadequacy and jealousy. Dowry thus reflects not the status of the bride-givers but the status of the bride-receivers. The inordinate demands that men's families make for luxury goods are more as status symbols that should reflect their status rather than items that they need to consume.

This is reflected in the fact that as communities and groups rise in social hierarchy, they choose the suppression of women as the first step towards enhanced social status. Kapadia (1995:46) writes in her work in Tamil Nadu on the untouchable caste of Pallars, "A central irony characterizes changes in non-Brahmin marriages today. Those upwardly mobile salaried groups—that marry in a 'modern' manner, for money and status rather than 'for love of kin' are precisely the social groups in which Non-Brahmin women are losing their traditionally high status. In rural Tamil Nadu today, consequently, 'modernization' and urbanization are not leading to the emancipation of women from patriarchal norms—but to precisely just the opposite". A more disturbing trend is that as the men rise in social hierarchy the corresponding status of women falls. Kapadia (ibid:250) discusses how as low caste men get education and jobs, they start demanding dowry for they then feel that they have achieved high status like men of higher castes, "in rural areas such as Aruloor, it will be many years-if ever-before the majority of young women have the option of higher education and salaried jobs. Meanwhile the paradoxical situation of the devaluation of women in precisely those upwardly mobile groups that are 'modernizing' continues". However, as my field experience has shown me, even in rural areas where women have started getting education, the situation is becoming even worse. In rural Haryana, men boasted that almost every boy getting married is demanding 'at least a Maruti car'. The reason was that with the rise in education of girls, the parents were forced to look for boys of at least equivalent, if not higher education than their daughters. But the higher the education of the boy, the more dowry he demands and nothing is mentioned about the education of the girl as a positive attribute.

The Girl-Child: A Passive Victim

In rural India, it has been seen that women are the victims of violence for several reasons. Broadly one can distinguish between violence of the social type from the sexual type. The social type is what we have been discussing, where the woman and in most cases it is the girl-child who becomes a victim, most often of her own family and parents, because of her devaluation as a social person. Such a devaluation is also most often incumbent on the newly married daughter-in-law, and finds expression in her person being seen as of less value than the goods she brings as dowry. In case of illness her expectations are the least. She remains dispensable in her role as a sexual partner, as a wife. She gains some respectability in society only as a mother and that too of sons.

Data from a report prepared by the V.V. Giri National Labour Institute (Verma, et al., 1996) indicates that every year out of 12 million girls born in India, 3 million or 25 per cent do not survive to see their 15th birthday. A third of the deaths take place in the first year of life. In the period of 1979-83, 78,000 foeticides took place. In the poor and backward region of Salem in Tamil Nadu, 316 out of the 501 women interviewed admitted to having killed at least one of their new-born daughters. A study conducted by UNICEF has confirmed that most girls under five die of malnutrition. A report published by Venkataraman in *India Today* of June 1986, shows that among the Kallars of Madurai district, female infanticide has become increasingly accepted as the only way out of the dowry problem. Out of the 600 female live births recorded in the local hospital, every year, as many as 570 babies vanish with their mothers soon after birth and few of the babies return. Only the mother returns minus baby to get herself treated for coagulated breast milk. Thus girls are killed in India, not by rapists, not by criminals but by their own mothers who breast feed them after smearing their nipples with poison or stuff their little noses with flour or wheat chaff. What leads a mother who has carried a child in her womb for nine months, has given birth enduring all the pangs of childbirth to so cruelly dispose off the little life, without a second thought?

Dreze and Sen (1995: 141) have reported 37 million missing women in India and interestingly they observe that the force of excess female mortality, lie in the age groups beyond that of infanticide. This indicates only one thing, that deliberate and culturally conditioned neglect is responsible for the deaths of female children in very large numbers. Moreover, even in the older age groups, men outnumber women, thereby indicating that men have benefited disproportionately from the gains of technological advances. A peek into family budgets or daily routines or priority spending of households, always indicates that weightage is given to boys over girls, to men over women in all dimensions of life.

Thus violence comes in many ways. It may come as direct assault on a woman's body in form of rape, battering and murder; it may be a symbolic assault on her self-respect as human being, it may be an assault on her emotions and sanity, when a mother is forced to kill her own baby.

As social scientists, our greater concern should not be only for the heinous crime but for the deep-rooted causes of the crimes. What kind of social pressures are brought on to the parents that makes them party to the killing of their own children. In Salem, most women interviewed mentioned the high costs of dowry. But dowry itself has to be contextualized against the manner in which society views women. It is because women are seen as socially non-existent, that their lives can be snuffed out so easily.

Violence and the Process of 'Othering'

Let us now examine the second kind of violence against women, more popularly discussed in western works, namely that of sexual violence. Sarkar (2003:5335) writes about a new kind of violence raising its head in Indian society, the "'chillingly unique' nature of the violence-especially sexual violence against women and even children, presumably 'as a means of proving masculinity' of Hindu men". The sexual violence directed towards women can be of a pathological kind, like one finds among some rapists but quite often it is displaced frustration or an attack on the masculinity of 'other' men. Such 'othering' was latently present in traditional rural society as well, and raised its head in inter-caste and inter-community conflicts but the likes of the carnage seen in Gujarat is perhaps in Sarkar's words 'chilling'.

Another kind of 'othering' is the commodification of woman's bodies, by the forces of global capitalism that is penetrating deep into the hinterlands. Also the migration of poor rural men to the urban areas in search for jobs leads to a vulnerable situation for the women who are left behind as well as for the urban situation into which the men are forced. The men, exposed to a battering of confusing images through the mass media, where they see a kind of woman they have never experienced, get confused messages (Channa, 2004). None of whom they see on the big and small screen look to them anything like the real life women, their mothers, sisters and daughters. To them these women are like aliens and they cannot fall back on any existing moral codes to deal with them. Sometimes such situations may even lead to rape of western clad girls and certainly leads to rampant eve-teasing as on the streets of Delhi. It is reported that in the last five years, Delhi has seen a 40 per cent rise in its floating population and most of it comes from rural and backward areas. This is also the period when crimes against women have been on the rise at alarming rates in the metropolis. But what concerns us here is what psychological changes occur in the men as they migrate from the rural to urban areas and then again go back. The poison of glamour and corruption is got back from the cities to the villages and results in many acts of violence that may not have occurred in traditional times.

Another form of violence is the kind that we have seen in Gujarat, where the rural folk are drawn into the machinations of politicians to commit acts of violence. Such violence is rampant in the rural areas almost all over India, inciting caste and communal divisions to commit atrocities on innocent bodies, often on that of women and children.

Victims and Perpetrators: Marginalization and its Consequences

The increase of violence under conditions of social pressure and marginalization also leads us to rethink our attitude towards the perpetrators of violence who may often be victims themselves. Thus the drunken husband, weighed down by unemployment, the slum boy blinded by city glamour and the grind of poverty that leads people to seek out any means for survival. Every day we read about girl-children being sold deliberately to touts and of unsuspecting girls lured to the cities for prostitution. There are also forced marriages of young girls to old men and the willing adoption of prostitution by young women. The erosion of traditional means of income for many groups, the marginalization of the small farmers by globalization and displacements of rural people by mega-projects of the government, have all led to worsening economic situation for those, already at the fringes of society. In her study of rural Tamil Nadu, Kapadia has shown how the rising unemployment of men, because of introduction of modern technology has led to increased drunkenness and consequent violence against the wives. The men feel redundant and have their masculinity challenged, when they become dependent on their wives for sustenance. This frustration leads to violent behaviour towards family members especially the wives. Displacement also leads to erosion of traditional values and meanings of life, often built up around the places of residence. Once people cease to 'belong', they lose all attachment to tradition and moral values attached to tradition. This is the reason for increased psychological problems, including tendency to violence seen among the uprooted people.

A crucial basis of identity is 'belongingness' and a loss of identity may lead to destructive behaviour often directed towards ones sexual partner, or family members. Thus the modern world creates many situations of potential victimization of the vulnerable members of society. It is unequal distribution of power that leads to some categories based on gender, race, caste and class to be seen as less of persons than others. Women, as a category are sufferers though categories of women differ only to the extent that they may be subjected to varying forms of violence. Thus the affluent housewife may suffer from loss of self-esteem and humiliation, the upper caste woman may suffer from loss of personhood and suppression of expression while her low caste counterpart suffers from rape and hunger.

Conclusion

Thus, we have to use whatever voice we have at our disposal to bring to light all the forms of violence as also more importantly the social roots of this violence. It is only then that our grievances can be converted to action. In colonial times the colonial rulers blamed the Indian traditions, the lack of civilization and the barbarism of the 'natives' for atrocities such as female infanticide, vulnerability of widows, child marriage and 'sati'. Increasingly even Indians adapted the same attitude looking towards westernization and western education to remove the ills of the so-called 'tradition'. In post-colonial India, the spate of developments were all directed towards urbanization and industrialization, the leaders believing that modern technology and economic growth would remove most ills from society. They too blamed their traditions as superstition and indigenous systems as ignorant. I am not in defense of what happened to women in pre-colonial and colonial times; even though several authors such as Moore (1998), Unnithan-Kumar (1997), Chawdhry (1994) and O'Hanlon (1997), have clearly shown how it was colonial rule and not Indian 'tradition' which created conditions for Brahmanical rule and hardening of patriarchy. But one must concede that if there were ills to which women were subjected then, there are equal if not more atrocities done on women now.

Every tool that was devised to help women or society in general has been turned into a tool of oppression. Modernity and urbanization instead of raising the status of women has made them even more vulnerable to assault. In fact, the term 'sexual harassment' was coined in the mid-seventies in North America (Thomas and Kitzinger, 1977:2) a society probably considered to be most progressive at that time and region.

In pre-and colonial periods India was primarily a rural economy and society. Fledgling cities were also mostly rural in content although the British influence was marked among the middle classes. Most of the ills that plagued women were even then found more among the urban and high castes than among the rural masses, peasants and low castes. Sati was a practice only of aristocratic and high caste women and so was the practice of child marriage. In rural areas among the peasantry remarriage of widows was quite common and so was divorce. But violence against women did occur and even within the family. But unlike that what is found in modern times and in Western societies, this violence was rarely a sexual violence, it was almost always directed towards the daughters by the parents and only in some cases against the daughter-in-law. More than a century later the practice is still rampant and if anything it has spread much wider and into those communities where it was unknown earlier.

Western scholars have largely connected violence against women to sexuality, and the desire of the man to establish his sexual power over the woman. But it is necessary while discussing the atrocities committed against women's bodies in a society such as India, to keep in mind the multiple sites of violence and also the multiple forms that this violence takes and its diverse roots. When female foetuses are killed in the womb and when female children are neglected or starved to death, it need not be a form of sexual violence, but a culture where women are viewed as 'dispensable'. It can be a society where women can also be viewed as a threat to male sense of honour or pride.

■ References

Channa, S. M. 1997. 'Gender and Social Space in a Haryana Village', *Indian Journal of Gender Studies*, Vol. No. 1, pp. 21-34.

— 2004. 'Globalization and Modernity in India: A Gendered Critique', *Urban Anthropology and Studies of Cultural Systems*, Vol. 33, No. 1, pp. 37-71.

Chawdhry, Prem 1994. *The Veiled Women: Shifting Gender Equations in Rural Haryana: 1880-1990.* Delhi: Oxford University Press.

Dreze, J. and Sen, A. 1995. *India: Economic Development and Social Opportunity.* Delhi: Oxford University Press.

Inden, Ronald, B. 1976. *Marriage and Rank in Bengali Culture: A History of Caste and Clan in Middle Period Bengal.* Berkeley: University of California Press.

Kapadia, Karin 1995. *Siva and Her Sisters: Gender, Caste, and Class in Rural South India.* Boulder: Westview Press.

Mahajan, A. and Madhurima.1995. *Family, Violence and Abuse in India.* New Delhi: Deep and Deep Publications.

Moore, Erin P. 1998. *Gender, Law and Resistance in India.* Tuscan: The University of Arizona Press.

O' Hanlon, Rosalind 1997. 'Cultures of Rule, Communities of Resistance: Gender, Discourse and Tradition in recent South Asian Historiographies', In H.L. Seneviratne (ed.) *Identity, Consciousness and the Past: Forging of Caste and Community in India and Sri Lanka*. Delhi: Oxford University Press, pp. 147-176.

Oldenberg, Veena Talwar 2002. *Dowry Murder: The Imperial Origins of a Cultural Crime.* New York: Oxford University Press.

Rao, Aparna 1998. *Autonomy.* Oxford: Berghahn Books.

Sarkar, Mahua 2003. " 'Community' and 'Nation': Groping for Alternative Narratives", *Economic and Political Weekly*, Vol. 39, Nos. 51 & 52, pp. 5335-5337.

Thomas, Alison M. and Kitzinger,C. 1977. *Sexual Harassment: Contemporary Feminist Perspectives.* Buckingham: Open University Press.

Unnithan-Kumar, Maya 1997. *Identity, Gender and Poverty: New Perspectives on Caste and Tribe in Rajasthan,* Oxford, Berghahn Books.

Venkataraman, S.H. 1986. 'Female Infanticide: Born to Die', *India Today*, 5 June, 1986, pp. 26-33.

Verma, A.P. et al., 1996. *Women Labour in India.* New Delhi: V.V. Giri National Labour Institute.

Wadley, Susan 1994. *Struggling with Destiny in Karimpur, 1925-1984.* New Delhi: Vistaar Publications.

Chapter 11

Emerging Women Leadership in Panchayati Raj Institutions

The Punjab Experience

Prabhjot Kaur Kahlon

The 73rd Amendment in the Indian Constitution was a culmination of the process, which began with Article 40 of the Indian Constitution expecting the states to organize village panchayats and to endow them with such powers and authority as may be necessary to function as units of self-government. This amendment mandated the minimum one-third reservation for women in Panchayati Raj bodies, which is one of the most important aspects of this constitutional initiative. This amendment brought unlimited opportunities for the women to participate in the grassroots level politics to ensure that the voice of the rural women is heard. In this way the role of women at the grassroots level is not limited only to their involvement in the decision-making but also in the rural development process. This involvement is envisaged mainly for the welfare and development of rural masses including children and aged. Besides these traditional activities, their capacity for constructive decision-making and managerial roles is recognized and strengthened to empower them to have more access to developmental resources and services.

This empowerment process led to the emergence of new rural leadership among the women. Their newly acquired role as a leader provides them an opportunity to lead the rural masses. After the 73rd Amendment, the nature and pace of development have become complex, which calls for a dynamic and result oriented leadership (Mishra and Dhaka, 2004). The leadership must be democratic and enjoy the confidence of the people of the village. Democratization of rural leadership has been one of the major contributions of Panchayati Raj Institutions (PRIs). This leadership deals with rural power structure, which is an integral part of any system—social, economic or political. In this process the rural leadership emerged at village, block and district levels. These leaders have constant interaction and face-to-face contact with rural masses (Vidya, 1997). It is through these leaders that the wishes and aspirations of the rural masses are met. In this sense, they are the 'eyes' and 'ears' of the rural people.

The very functioning of PRIs depends mainly on the quality of leadership, which plays a significant role in promoting political development and democratic growth. The success of PRIs itself depends largely upon the quality and competence of leadership available at the local level. Therefore, it is important to study these grassroots leaders who have acquired power through democratically elected bodies and who are going to be actively involved in eliciting people's cooperation in the implementation of programmes and plans relating to socio-economic development of rural areas. Moreover, the success and future of PRIs will to a large extent depend upon the quality and competence of leadership available at local level. Therefore, it is imperative to know the pattern of emerging women leadership to understand the potential thrust of these bodies.

Women in Panchayats

The Panchayati Raj system which was initiated mainly for people's participation in the politico-economic process remained incomplete because of various reasons but more specifically, lack of desired women's participation in it. The advocates of the Panchayati Raj system wanted that rural women should not only become the beneficiaries of development, but more importantly the contributors to it. Balwant Rai Mehta Committee also emphasized that women should find representation in the rural political institutions. It recommended that beside the 20 members of the Panchayat Samiti, there should be two women "who are interested to work among women and children" as co-opted members. Similar provision was suggested with regard to the village panchayats (Balwant Rai Mehta Committee, 1958) As a result of this recommendation some states[1] took steps in this direction to ensure women's representation but the state of Punjab did not adopt it in a straight way and opted for co-option where women could not be members through elections (Mishra, 1998). Despite the provision of nomination or co-option, women could not play an effective role in the PRIs. The system of nomination or co-option meant sheer patronage of the dominant political or social groups and the women who were nominated had practically neither any role in panchayats nor any experience in working for the women and children. Their representation in these bodies came to be symbolized by 'tokenism' and not by a meaningful association (Manikyamba, 1989).

On the other hand, some states[2] gave up nomination or co-option and resorted to reservation as the only way of ensuring women's representation in the PRIs. The demand for reservation of women in adequate proportion in the various representative bodies had thus been persistent. In the recent years, special efforts were being made to ensure women's representation in the PRIs in the wake of the 73rd Constitutional Amendment Act which reserves one-third of the seats for women in the PRIs.

73rd Amendment and Women

This amendment made one-third representation of women at different levels of Panchayati Raj Institutions a reality. It is a historical and landmark event in the political history of independent India. This amendment made a provision of "not less than one-third including the seats reserved for women belonging to Scheduled Castes and Scheduled Tribes of the total number of seats to be filled by direct election in every panchayat shall be reserved for women and such seats may be allotted by rotation to different constituencies in a panchayat" (Mishra, 1998).

This Act relates to the leadership of women in PRIs, i.e., Village Panchayats, Block Samitis and Zila Parishads. According to it, the participation of women in PRIs involves:

(1) women as voters;
(2) women as members of political parties;
(3) women as candidates;
(4) women as elected members of the PRIs taking part in decision-making, planning, implementation and evaluation; and
(5) women as members of *Mahila Mandals* and their association with voluntary organizations. (Bhargava and Vidya, 1992).

The enactment of the 73rd Amendment Act, with a view to involve women in decision-making, provided psychological empowerment and a sense of political efficacy, to those who had been left out earlier, to influence public decisions which also affect them.

It may be mentioned here that more than one million women were elected to the three-tier Panchayati Raj system all over the country after this amendment. This development has made a significant beginning as this process of empowerment of women in PRIs enabled them to re-examine their lives, recognize the sources and structures of power and initiate action to challenge the existing ideologies as well as structures and institutions of power. It is also expected that this transformation would enhance their mobility and provide them an opportunity to decide about the various core issues and ultimately make them independent in their judgment. It would also transform them from politically passive persons to active agents of political and social change (Buch, 2000).

Punjab Experience

Punjab is one of the most advanced states in the country, with a high per-capita income, high productivity in agriculture, a well-developed physical infrastructure and a relatively high human development index. This development in the state is the outcome of the interplay of a variety of factors, such as political, economic, demographic and geographic. In the Indian context, rural development assumes greater significance as three-fourths of its population still lives in rural area. Strategically, the focus of planning was to improve the socio-economic conditions of rural society, especially its underprivileged sections. In this way, the economic growth with social justice became the proclaimed objective of the planning process under rural development programme. Punjab is one of the economically developed states of India. Not only is its average per capita income much higher than

Table 11.1

Trends in Number of Gram Panchayats in Punjab (1968-1998)

Region/District	*1968*	*1973*	*1978*	*1983*	*1992*	*1998*
Majha						
Gurdaspur	870	1056	1246	1335	1451	1589
Amritsar	1009	1045	1080	1088	1164	1268
Doaba						
Kapurthala	236	340	427	449	490	533
Jalandhar	833	878	1055	1084	1113	886
Hoshiarpur	835	1035	1294	1350	1432	1314
Nawan Shahr	—	—	—	—	—	440
Malwa						
Rupnagar	611	629	716	757	805	856
Ludhiana	805	824	877	884	840	871
Firozepur	658	756	907	931	1036	1202
Faridkot	536	542	552	552	581	180
Bathinda	481	510	516	516	278	303
Sangrur	574	657	683	685	703	727
Patiala	970	1059	1258	1318	1035	1063
Mansa	—	—	—	—	241	243
Fatehgarh Sahib	—	—	—	—	428	438
Moga	—	—	—	—	—	191
Muktsar	—	—	—	—	—	265
Total	8418	9331	10611	10949	11597	12369

Source: Department of Panchayats and Rural Development, Punjab.

many other states of Indian union, but the number of people living in an absolute state of poverty in this state is also much lesser. The introduction of green revolution technology in 1960s completely transformed the rural economy of Punjab. An increase in the agricultural income gave a spurt to other sectors of economy (Jodhka, 2003).

Table 11.2

Total Members of Elected Representatives (Panches and Sarpanches) of Gram Panchayats During 1968-1998

Region/District	*1968*	*1973*	*1978*	*1983*	*1992*	*1998*
Majha						
Gurdaspur	4942	5963	7746	7683	10748	10677
Amritsar	6638	6985	8234	7176	8951	9328
Doaba						
Kapurthala	1431	2092	2918	3440	3032	3554
Jalandhar	5159	5988	7602	7049	8211	6229
Hoshiarpur	5106	5576	7191	7224	10696	8705
Nawan Shahr	—	—	—	—	—	3103
Malwa						
Rupnagar	3195	3415	4948	5978	6380	5676
Ludhiana	4676	4780	6327	5167	6428	6540
Firozepur	4371	5082	5848	6250	6342	8341
Faridkot	3581	3748	4417	4339	4806	1418
Bathinda	3055	3380	3893	4392	2407	2589
Sangrur	3807	3833	5226	5239	4932	6067
Patiala	5728	6424	9060	9078	7366	7001
Mansa	—	—	—	—	2005	2013
Fatehgarh Sahib	—	—	—	—	2807	2754
Moga	—	—	—	—	—	1690
Muktsar	—	—	—	—	—	2157
Total	51689	57266	73410	73015	85111	87842

Source: Department of Panchayats and Rural Development, Punjab.

The process of change was further accentuated by the strengthening of PRIs. Under this, the power and the decision-making have shifted to the panchayats at the village level. In the village panchayat, the elected members were entrusted with the decision-making powers. Earlier, the village panchayats consisted of village elders and the headship was either hereditary or was elected by consensus. The decentralized planning under this set-up brought with it the decentralization and delegation of powers (ibid.).

Table 11.3

Total Number of Scheduled Caste and Women Sarpanches During 1978-1998

Region/District	*Scheduled Castes*				*Women*					
	1978	*1983*	*1992*	*1998*	*1978*	*1983*	*1992*	*1998*		
								GEN	*SC*	*Total*
Majha										
Gurdaspur	124	100	92	266	27	19	30	396	130	526
Amritsar	44	32	32	278	26	—	1	278	139	417
Doaba										
Kapurthala	59	49	67	111	11	6	7	122	61	183
Jalandhar	257	217	45	252	25	4	3	163	136	299
Hoshiarpur	186	202	201	313	17	13	21	286	151	437
Nawan Shahr	—	—	—	112	—	—	—	92	55	147
Malwa										
Rupnagar	65	51	20	143	18	4	4	206	68	274
Ludhiana	46	41	49	206	12	6	3	186	103	289
Firozepur	21	16	25	166	12	6	11	320	86	406
Faridkot	8	9	14	45	13	4	12	36	23	59
Bathinda	16	7	7	62	9	7	4	67	36	103
Sangrur	31	13	29	140	1	2	8	170	72	242
Patiala	104	37	58	153	16	8	11	281	76	357
Mansa	—	—	8	51	—	—	1	5	25	79
Fatehgarh Sahib	—	—	24	90	—	—	5	103	42	145
Moga	—	—	—	42	—	—	—	41	22	63
Muktsar	—	—	—	69	—	—	—	53	35	88
Total	961	774	671	2499	197	79	121	2854	1260	4114

Source: Department of Rural Development and Panchayats, Punjab.

Under 73rd Amendment, the new PR Act 1994, came into force in place of the Gram Panchayat Act 1952. On 21 April, 1994 (Punjab's Panchayati Raj Act 1994) was formulated. New rules were framed under the provision of this Act and the first elections to 138 Panchayat Samitis and 14 Zila Parishads were held in 1994. In June 1998, first Gram Panchayat elections were held under this Act. In these elections, a total of 31,053 women representative were elected out of a total 87,842 members. The total number of women sarpanches was 4,114 (33.23%) out of this 2,854 belonged to general category, 1,260 belonged to the Scheduled Castes and seven to the backward castes (Punjab Development Report, 2002).

This level of participation of women became possible only with the 73rd Amendment through which these women came into public area for the first time to usher in a new era. These changes in panchayat legislation have made it essential to provide space to these women in village panchayat as they were elected on the basis of reservation.

Methodology

The focus of this study is on rural women leaders who became sarpanches of the village panchayats under the 73rd Amendment. Major emphasis is on the type of leadership that has emerged in rural area as a result of the panchayat elections held in 1998, which was the first panchayat elections held in the state after the implementation of the 73rd Amendment Act. The focus is to throw light on the socio-economic and political profile of rural women leaders in Amritsar and Gurdaspur districts of Punjab. The study is based on empirical information and the data has been collected from 60 villages headed by women sarpanches.

Bases of Leadership

An analysis of the socio-economic and political background of women leaders is important in shaping the nature and level of participation of the women sarpanches in village panchayats. It is not possible to have broader understanding without knowing the profile of the elected leaders that includes education, caste, occupation, political background, awareness and participation. It is believed that an adequate explanation of leadership pattern can only be offered by making a close study of the background and environment from which they have come up.

Socio-Economic Profile of Women Leaders

The variables reflecting the socio-economic and political profile of the respondents that have a bearing on their role perception, performance and behavioural patterns as grassroots leaders can be analysed as follows:

Education

Education is the key that opens the door to life, which is essentially social in character. Illiteracy restricts one's capacity to give thoughtful judgment on issues of importance. Rural development is a very complex task, which needs to be understood in proper perspective. Education facilitates the development of a progressive attitude in individuals to understand such complexities and resolve socio-economic and political problems. One cannot deny the fact that an educated and aware leadership is the need of the day. It will not only help in understanding the programmes and schemes of the rural development but in its effective implementation as well.

Table 11.4

Educational Level

Education	*No. of Sarpanches*	*Percentage*
Illiterate (used thumb expression)	15	25.00
Can only write their names	10	16.67
Primary	11	18.33
Middle	4	6.67
Matric	11	18.33
10+2	1	1.67
Graduate	5	8.33
Others	3	5.00
Total	60	100.00

In Punjab, the literacy rate has been rising. It was 58.51 per cent in 1991 and increased to 69.95 per cent in 2001, an increase of 11.44 per cent during the last 10 years. Punjab has fared well in reducing the gap between male and female literacy—male literacy rate increased from 65.66 per cent in 1991 to 75.63 per cent in 2001 and female literacy rate from 50.4 per cent to 63.55 per cent. Female literacy rate in Punjab is considerably higher than all-India where 54.16 per cent of the female are literate. Inspite of these positive trends, there are still 94.35 lakh (including those in 0-6 age group) illiterates in the state (Census of India, 2001) and it is also a matter of great concern that the rank of Punjab went down from the 12th position in 1971 to the 16th position in 2001 (Census of India, Punjab, 2001) at the all India level.

Table 11.4 shows the level of education of women sarpanches in which 25 per cent were illiterate and used their thumb expression, 16.67 per cent could just sign whereas 18.33 per cent had primary and same number were matriculate and only 8.33 per cent were graduates. The remaining 5 per cent were those who had done Elementary Teacher's Training (ETT), diploma in pharmacy, etc. Majority of them felt that they are not capable to participate, the reason they cited was that as, they were not much educated so they felt very shy and inferior. It is important that educational facilities are made more accessible in rural areas so that women can play a meaningful role in the society.

Caste and Religion

Caste has been one of the basic features of Indian social structure since ancient times. Though the principle of democratic government presupposes equal opportunities to all, irrespective of race, caste, religion and so forth, but the problem with earlier panchayats was that the members of the higher dominant castes comprising of landlords generally dominated them (Buch, 1993).

Even today, caste plays a major role in rural areas. It is a factor that cannot be ignored and still plays a significant role. In 1998 Punjab Panchayat Elections, the total number of elected women sarpanches was 33.23 per cent out of this 2,854 (60.37%) were from general castes, 1,260 (30.62%) from scheduled castes and 7 (9.01%) from backward castes. Punjab has lesser percentage of backward castes. With the reservation policy, people from lower castes have an opportunity to become village head.

Table 11.5
Caste

Caste	*Category*	*Religion*	*No. of Sarpanches*	*Percentage*
Jat	GC	Sikh	24	40
Mazbhi	SC	Sikh	18	30
Rajput	GC	Hindu	2	3.34
Mahajan	GC	Hindu	4	6.67
Ramdasia	SC	Sikh	3	5.00
Sansi	SC	Sikh	5	8.33
Kabir Panthi	SC	Hindu	1	1.66
Megh	SC	Hindu	1	1.66
Mahasay	SC	Sikh	2	3.34
Total			60	100

Table 11.5 shows that majority of women leaders had come from Jat caste followed by Mazbhi's and others. Around 40 per cent belonged to Jat caste and 30 per cent belonged to Mazbhi's whereas 6.67 per cent belonged to Mahajan caste and a few belonged to the other scheduled caste categories. We also find that a good percentage of the elected representatives belong to the deprived sections of the society. This representation enables them to have a greater role in PRIs.

Occupation

Occupation is also one of the important ingredients of leadership as it determines familial social status and acceptability in the society. The occupation of the elected sarpanches had been an important factor to determine their leadership pattern.

Table 11.6 clearly explains that majority of women sarpanches 71.67 per cent were performing their usual household activities and were totally dependent on their families, whereas 3.33 per cent were teaching in village private schools, 10 per cent each were running small grocery shops and rearing cattle for selling milk, etc., and 5 per cent were doing agriculture labour in the village.

Table 11.6
Occupation

Occupation	*No. of Women Sapranches*	*Percentage*
Domestic household	43	71.67
Private Job	2	3.33
Shopkeeping	6	10.00
Selling milk	6	10.00
Labour	3	5.00
Total	60	100.00

Income

Income is also an important indicator of social and economic status. Traditionally, people with better economic status used to wield good influence in the rural politics. In other words a person having good economic status in the village was supposed to become member or sarpanch of the panchayats. However, because of the 73rd amendment, the people belonging to the lower income/ economic status got the opportunity to be the village head.

Table 11.7
Approximate Monthly Income from all Sources
(as stated by women sarpanches)

Income per month	*No. of Women Sarpanches*	*Percentage*
Upto - 500	5	8.33
501-1000	11	18.34
1001-1500	8	13.33
1501-2000	8	13.33
2001-5000	6	10.00
5001-8000	11	18.34
8001-15000	6	10.00
Above 15000	5	8.33
Total	60	100.00

Table 11.7 shows that the majority of respondents belonged to the lower income group, i.e., Rs 2,000 per month. These figures are tentative and based on the answers of the respondents and

general idea of the economic status of the family reflected through their ways of life, as few of them particularly SCs were still living in one- or two-room houses. Many respondents took a lot of time to respond to this point, as they themselves were not sure of it.

Political Profile

Participation in public life introduces political orientations in the personality of an individual and it is here that the socialization process of the potential entrants into politics begins systematically (Sirskar, 1970). The recruitment of political leaders is concerned with the role of various agents of socialization, which occur on top of general political socialization. There are many studies on Indian political elites which have established that the political background of the respondents family influence the political aspirations and career of women leaders. Hazel D'Lima's study of Maharashtra women in local government affirms these findings. She writes, "The engagement of family members in socio-political activity reflects a certain atmosphere in the home environment which inevitably affects the members of the family" (D'Lima, 1973).

Family is the first school of socialization, which initiates a child to belief, opinions, attitudes, norms, values, value orientations and behaviour expectations in a society. An individual acquires political values, develops political attitudes, and increases his/her political knowledge through various socializing agents like family, peer groups, schools, mass-media, political parties etc. The level of political participation is generally higher in families where politically active members are present than in those where no one is active in politics. To ascertain the political experiences in family, the respondents were asked whether any member (parents, husbands, relatives and friends) of their family (parental or maternal) was attached with any public organizations, i.e., PRIs, political parties and any other socio-political organization.

Table 11.8 reveals the political background of the respondents and a majority of them have come from politically active families. These women had willingly plunged into the fray as most of them who had exposures to political activity within their own families or were a part of the panchayat set-up. These were directly supported or backed by their family members and their entry into the village panchayat became quite easy. The others got the benefit of resolution, but the resourceful persons in the village also backed them but all of them had the first entry into the village politics.

Table 11.8

Membership of Respondent's Family Members in Socio-Political Organizations

Type of Organization	*No. of Sarpanches*	*Percentage*
Panchayats	24	40.00
Panchayat Samities	5	8.33
Zila Parishads	1	1.66
Chairman of Cooperative Society	7	11.67
Chairman of Marketing Committee	1	1.67
Political Parties	9	15.00
None	13	21.67
Total	60	100.00

Motivational Factors

Motivation has been defined as energy mobilization within each individual to satisfy certain basic physical, social and egoistic needs. Patterson and Boynton (1969), offer five categories of motivational factors, i.e., personal gain, civic duty, sociability, political mobility and policy orientation. Motivation can come from any of the sources like, to hold a better position in political life, inspiration to do something for the betterment of women or the development of village or both may have been inspired by family, friends, caste associations and political parties.

Table 11.9

Motivational Factor

Factors for Contesting Elections	*No. of Sarpanches*				*Total*
	Yes	*%*	*No*	*%*	
Personal interest	7	11.67	53	88.33	60
Family background	36	60	24	40	60
Supported by villagers	45	75	15	25	60
Persuaded by political parties	10	16.67	50	80.37	60
Asked by caste/community leaders	24	40	36	60	60

The study indicates that only 11.67 per cent women contested elections on their own personal interest whereas majority of them, i.e., 60 per cent were inspired by their family members as they were involved in political activity. About 16.67 per cent families had affiliation with different political parties. The 40 per cent women sarpanches were approached by their caste/community people.

View of Women Sarpanches on Reservation Policy and their Opinion on the Role of Women in Gram Panchayat

The 33 per cent reservation through 73rd Amendment Act for women at all tiers had made a significant beginning as it provided a legal foundation from which women's involvement in grassroot democracy is ensured. Hence, it was equally necessary to probe the views of women sarpanches on the reservation policy and the role of women in gram panchayats.

Table 11.10

Views of Women Sarpanches on Reservation Policy

Views	*No. of Sarpanches*	*Percentage*
33% reservation is good	27	45.00
Percentage of reservation should be increased	12	20.00
Reservation is of no use	17	28.33
Can't say	4	6.67
Total	60	100.00

Table 11.10 indicates that out of 60 women sarpanches, 27 (45%) supported the reservation in its present form while 12 (20%) advocated that it should be increased. A large number of them, i.e., 17 (28.33%) expressed their views that it had no use while 4 (6.67%) could not say anything about it.

Political Awareness

Awareness indicates the extent of knowledge or information about the surrounding social reality. Political awareness is related to one's knowledge about the political system, structures, functions, etc. In order to examine the level of awareness of women sarpanches, questions as mentioned in Table 11.11 were asked.

Table 11.11

Level of Political Awareness

Questions	*Yes*	*%*	*No*	*%*	*Total*
Do you know about three-tier system?	29	43.33	31	47.67	60
Heard about it	31	51.67	29	43.33	60
Knew that the seat in their village was reserved for women	60	100	-	-	60
Do you know that 33% reservation of seats for women at all three-tiers?	21	35	39	65	60
What is your tenure?	60	100	-	-	60
What is the composition of Gram Panchayats?	43	71.67	17	28.33	60
What is the minimum age of voting?	39	65	21	35	60
What are the objectives of PRIs?	31	51.67	29	43.33	60

This table reveals the awareness and knowledge about the PRIs of women leaders. All leaders were aware about their tenure and knew that the seat in her village was reserved for them. Only 43.33 per cent knew about the three-tier system and 35 per cent knew about the 33 per cent reservation of seats for women in all tiers.

Political Participation

Political participation is the hallmark of a democratic set-up. Success and effectiveness of a democratic system largely depend upon the extent to which equal, effective and actual participation is provided by the system to all its citizens. The present study also focuses on the level of participation of women sarpanches in political activities.

Attending Meeting

One of the important variables of participation of elected leaders is to participate in the discussion and attendance in meeting. According to the Punjab Panchayati Act 1994 the meeting of Gram Panchayats is to be held at least twice a month at a public place within the 'sabha' area whenever called by the sapranch.

Table 11.12 shows that 41.66 per cent of women sarpanches who were supported to preside over the meeting did not attend these at all, during five-year tenure 1998-2003. Only 36.67 per cent attended regularly while 21.67 per cent attended rarely.

Table 11.12

Attendance at Panchayat Meeting

Frequency	*No. of Sarpanches*	*Percentage*
Regularly	22	36.67
Rarely	13	21.67
Never	25	41.66
Total	60	100.00

Generally, in rural society, women were not allowed to take keen interest in attending meetings. Surprisingly enough, it was the male members of their family who attended meetings on their behalf, i.e., husbands, father-in-laws, brother-in-laws or sons. These women hardly got a chance of participating in the decision-making process, which ultimately deprived them from working effectively at grassroots level. During field study, it was quite interesting to note that the husbands and sons of the respondents were taken into confidence to get information rather than the respondents themselves. These women sarpanches were de-jure village heads while the panchayats were managed by de-facto heads, i.e., husbands, father-in-laws, sons, etc. Majority of them were of the view that they did not attend because of socio-cultural norms of the rural set-up. Women themselves, male members of the family and society do not like that women should sit among male members of their village and participate in discussions. They just signed the papers without questioning.

Role Performance and Perception

Leadership is one of the main ingredients in a democratic system and the survival of leadership depends upon the role and performance. The efficacy of a leader lies in articulating and protecting the interests of the community they represent.

The role performance of these women leaders attribute their existence as a sarpanch in the village to 73rd Amendment Act, which empowered them and ensured their participation in political process. They became the village heads and first citizens of their respective villages. However, the existing socio-cultural complexities are a serious blockade in their way of smooth functioning as a village leader. These factors are acting as a deterrent in many cases. For example, at night, if any emergency arises, women sarpanches obviously are not allowed to move out of their houses. Even in some cases, they are not free to move out in daytime to settle any dispute among the villagers. Again, their husbands and sons usually do the job. Even for official meetings at the panchayat or block level, parents/in-laws/husband's permission is necessary. Some of the Scheduled Caste women sarpanches had frankly confessed to a sense of inferiority complex because of their low, social, economic and family status. They also expressed inability to play the role of sarpanch assigned to them. Practically, a large number of them could not participate effectively and independently in meetings and development work because of their being Dalits. It was also found that the majority of village sarpanches particularly Dalits was elected with direct/indirect support of the dominant caste/class in the village. Ironically, none of the women respondent was aware of the various aspects of 73rd Amendment related to the reservations. However, they all know that the village from which they had contested was reserved for them. This shows that inspite of all provisions for women empowerment the real power still lies somewhere else.

It has always been the contention that equality in all spheres is inseparable from active political participation. Women after all, have been subjected to exploitation for ages and thus cannot break the shackles of illiteracy, poverty and traditions overnight. Only reservation cannot be a way of the true empowerment of women because it continues to be the role of patriarchy proxies of female relatives, i.e., male persons will get entry into the politics under the cover of women's reservation. No doubt, that political participation can give a new direction to the empowerment of women by highlighting their problems and finding solutions but to make it successful, it needs sincere efforts from different quarters. Women agencies and movements should frame their own agenda for women's empowerment in all spheres of life and make it a mass-movement. It should challenge political parties and groups to fulfil their commitment regarding gender equality.

In the present scenario, fast changes are taking place in the world in general and India in particular. Women might have played merely a dummy role in comparison to their male counterparts until today, but it is believed that this situation may not continue for a long period. It is hoped that by the turn of few years they will be much better placed educationally, politically and socially, as they are today and consequently will play an effective role in decision-making. The need of the day is to have a change in the right direction. Empowerment is not a process, which is horizontal or vertical. It is a process, which goes round in a circle. Here the beginning ends in a change and the change leads to another beginning (Chandra, 1997).

■ Notes

1. The Maharashtra Zila Parishad & Panchayat Samiti Act of 1961, provided for the nomination of one or two women to each of the three bodies, in case no women was elected. The Andhra Pradesh Panchayat Samiti and Zila Parishad Act provided for the co-option of two women for each samiti, in addition to the possibility of women members finding membership of PS through the electoral process. In Haryana there was a provision for the co-option of one woman member to the Gram Panchayat, one or two women members to the panchayat samiti and two members to the Zila Parishad .
2. Andhra Pradesh, Karnataka and Bihar amended their Acts and provided for 15 to 30 per cent reservation of seats for women.

■ References

Bhargava, B.S. and Vidya, K.C. 1992, "Position of Women in Political Institutions", *Journal of Rural Development,* Vol. II, No.5, September, p. 603.

Buch, M. N. 1993. "Review of Rajni Kothari's State Against Democracy", in C.F. Siddiqui, *Inter-Caste and Inter-Community Relationship,* New Delhi: Commonwealth Publishers.

Buch, Nirmala 2000. "Women's Experience in New Panchayat: The Emerging Leadership in Rural Women", *Occasional Paper* No. 35, Centre for Women's Development Studies, New Delhi.

Chandra, Shanta Kohli 1997. "Women and Empowerment", *Indian Journal of Public Administration*, Vol. XLIII, No.3, July-September, p. 398.

CRRID, 2002. *Punjab Development Report*, Chandigarh.

D'Lima, Hazel. 1983, *Women in Local Government: A Study of Maharashtra*, New Delhi: Concept Publishers, p.47.

Government of India, 1958. *The Balwant Rai Mehta Committee Report*, New Delhi.

Government of India, 1959. *Report of the National Committee on Women's Education*, New Delhi.

Government of India, *Census of India (Punjab) 1991-2001.*

Govt. of Punjab, 1994. *The Punjab's Panchayat Raj Act 1994,* Department of Legal and Legislature Affair, Chandigarh.

Jodhka, S.S., 2003. "Contemporary Punjab: A Brief Introduction", cited in M.S. Gill (ed.) *Punjab Society: Perspectives and Challenges*, New Delhi: Concept Publishing House.

Manikyamba, P. 1989. *Women in Panchayat Raj Structures,* New Delhi: Gian Publishing House.

Mishra, Suresh and Dhaka, Rajvir S. 2004. *Grassroots Democracy in Action: A Study of Working of Panchayati Raj Institutions in Haryana*, New Delhi: Concept Publishing Company.

Mishra, Sweta 1998. "Women and the 73rd Constitutional Amendment Act: A Critical Appraisal", cited in Sebasti J. Raj and Edward Mathias (ed.), *People's Power and Panchayat Raj: Theory and Practice,* New Delhi: Indian Social Institute.

Patterson, Samuel C. and Boynton, G.R. 1969. "Legislative Recruitment in a Civic Culture", *Social Sciences Quarterly,* Vol. 50, p.252.

Sirskar, V.M. 1970. *The Rural Elite in a Developing Society: A Study in the Political Sociology*, New Delhi: Orient Longman's Ltd.

Vidya, K.C. 1997. *Political Empowerment of Women at the Grassroots,* New Delhi: Kanishka Publishers.

Chapter 12

Towards an Engendered Poverty Paradigm in SAARC

Nandini Azad

For over five decades since South Asian countries became Independent, they have been absorbed in cluster after cluster of policies based on apriori theorizing and eclecticism. These have often precluded responding to the reality of the success achieved by the poor and women (who represent a major indispensable resource) of generating growth through a new accumulation process. Reformists of conventional capitalist or socialist paradigms and transitions have also failed to transcend this eclecticism.

To recall, in the seventies, strategies for poverty eradication were part of a large belief in the concept of 'growth-with redistribution' and of meeting basic minimum needs through focused government policies. The 1980s was an era of fiscal belt-tightening in both South and North countries and saw a shift in approach of major multilateral and bilateral development agencies, away from redistribution/basic needs towards structural adjustment and market-oriented economic reforms. Poverty, as such, was relatively low on the priority list during the 1980. By the 1990s, a 'new poverty agenda' had surfaced as a counterpart of the so-called 'Washington Consensus' on structural reforms. In the beginning of 21st century, all actors in the development process have converged their agenda on poverty reduction. The renewed attention to issues of poverty and distribution constitute a welcome departure from the theme that dominated much of the development discourse during the last quarter century, when concern with macro-economic stabilization and adjustment was at the centre of the policy agenda. Poverty reduction has thus re-emerged as an important item on the agenda of global development.

After a more than a decade of preoccupation with 'stabilization and growth' by the early 1990s, mainstream policy institutions pronounced a renewed interest in attending to the problems of global poverty. These concerns are given greater voice and urgency through the series of global summits. In South Asia, despite decades of endeavours, various efforts to eradicate the worst forms of poverty and to encourage equitable and sustainable growth have as yet made only a dent. Of late, there has also been increasing emphasis on two other agendas in the wider development framework—namely, good governance and decentralization. A 'new poverty agenda' was the outcome with multilateral development agencies identifying 'labour-intensive growth' as a central tenet. More recently, there has been serious apprehension in the way women and their needs are being addressed in anti-poverty analysis and policies. The relationship between gender and poverty has also gained empirical validity in varying degrees in different contexts. The gender analysis of poverty also requires unravelling the manner in which gender differentiates the social process leading to poverty in its multifarious dimensions.

As far as gender and poverty are concerned women's participation in development paradigm is an important factor and the initiatives of the informal sector in this direction, i.e., formation of civil societies and community-based organizations for addressing pro-poor issues is an important endeavour. The Working

Women's Forum (WWF) paradigm is about women's empowerment, sustainability and accumulation, a model for replication.

The Challenges

After three decades of research focused on gender and development, it is clearer than ever before that there is a critical need for a gender-specific development paradigm of analysis. The essential issue is how best to incorporate awareness of the implications of gender into all areas of policy-making and planning so that women's needs can be met, their capabilities enhanced, and their opportunities enlarged. The critical questions are: by what means can women's capabilities—as individuals, as citizens, and as members of families—be enhanced? Through which institutional mechanisms can the wide gaps between current situations and potential improvements be bridged? How can pervasive inequities be corrected? And how can the women of South Asia achieve greater degrees of autonomy in their personal, economic and political lives?

Reducing poverty is no doubt a major political challenge. It involves overcoming class-based interests in inequality and it requires effective public institutions to deliver resources to create opportunities for the poor, frequently in the face of local opposition when poor women are the target of these kinds of interventions, resistance can be even more intense than opposition to pro-poor measures. If one of the objectives of promoting social and economic improvements in women's lives is greater gender equality, such interventions challenge the social prerogatives of men, even poor men. Considerable institutional capacity to resist local patriarchal interests is required to persist with these measures. Institutional capacity to deliver development resource effectively, and institutional autonomy from vested interests, have been perennial pre-occupations of development planners the world over. But discussions within institutional capacity-building in development rarely consider what this would mean from the point of view of women, except sometimes to assume that whatever is good for the poor will automatically benefit poor women too (i.e., for example, the household approach vs. the rights based approach in programme planning). But gender equity programmes can arouse gender-based resistance as well as class-based resistance, even within the institution promoting these measures. It is time to ask what kinds of changes are needed to enhance the capacity of development institutions to respond to women's needs, and to represent their interests in development planning.

Gender, Development and Poverty

In South Asia, it often seems that the interaction between religious, cultural beliefs and practices on the one hand and contemporary globalized social economic forces on the other hand occur in such a way that structure of patriarchy are reinforced. Indeed as Jean Dreze and Amartya Sen have demonstrated, "on their own" the forces of development and modernization do not necessarily lead to a rapid reduction in gender inequalities. As a result in comparison to men and women around the world (except Sub-Saharan Africa) South Asian women are least likely to be literate, to have access to primary and reproductive health services, to enjoy civil, political and legal equality with men, and to enjoy economic and social security on the basis of their own work.

The culture of patriarchy is deeply entrenched in the SAARC region, and gender biases are held not only by men but also by women. Women are often convinced that the work they do for their family is their duty and as such women do not expect any recognition, monetary or otherwise, while the work that men do is truly valuable, both socially and economically. Similarly, women do not participate in decision-making, believing it to be the realm of men. Patriarchy remains unassailable in South Asia, under the cover of gender-blind policies that take existing gender relations for granted while women's particular concerns are relegated to 'women' issues. Attitude shift in society as a whole is required for breaking out of this culture of patriarchy, and this is why the gender question is not just one about women, but about both women and men and how they interact.

The overall picture for gender related development is poor in SAARC region, even in comparison to the region's human development level. In every South Asian country, the Gender-related Development Index (GDI) is lower than the Human Development Index (HDI). All the South Asian countries except Sri Lanka and Maldives have GDIs of less than 0.500, subjecting women not only to low overall achievement in human development but also to lower achievement than men. Even worse is the Gender Empowerment Measures (GEM) which highlights the extent to which women are involved in economic activities and active in the political realm. The inequalities faced by women in SAARC region is invisible—activities such as family care, household maintenance and the informal sector market are often excluded from the system of national accounts. The work they do remain invisible, unappreciated and inadequately compensated.

Gender Inequality in South Asia

The Beijing Conference was a milestone in the progress towards women's advancement. A far-reaching 'Platform for Action', based on the Nairobi 'Forward-looking Strategies', provided global commitments and action points in a wide range of areas to achieve the three objectives of the Conference—equality, development and peace. All the UN conferences in the 1990s—the World Summit for Social Development in Copenhagen, the Vienna Conference on Human Rights, the Cairo Conference on Population and Development, the Rio Conference on Environment and Development, the Children's Summit in New York, and the Education for All Conference in Jomtien not only underlined the essential links between women's empowerment and social and economic development but provided frameworks for action and follow-up mechanisms.

The Beijing Platform urged each government to draw up its own national plan of action and formulate specific strategies for eliminating existing gender gaps in access to education and health care, opening up economic and political opportunities for women and ensuring their human rights. In South Asia, as well as in other regions, progress has been made in raising consciousness and undertaking research to identify bottlenecks and actions to improve women's position and conditions. Yet gender equality has remained an elusive goal in most societies. South Asia has to go a long way still to realize the ideal of complete gender equality, which is a sine qua non for both development and peace in the region.

Large-scale, grassroots women's movements have arisen in response to the economic discrimination faced by the millions of

South Asian women and men who have been disadvantaged by post-colonial development processes, and whose means of livelihood have been threatened by globalizing economies. Contemporary women's movements have also joined forces with environmental movements to voice alarm about environmental degradation that threatens lives and livelihoods

Through decades of research and activism, South Asian women's movements have struggled to put the issues, e.g., women's lack of political power, gender-based economic disparities, reproductive health issues, the need for economic justice, human rights issues, the need for peaceful development—at the centre of NGO and government development agendas. The struggle is a difficult one, often given the lack of commitment by governments, the power of feudal and patriarchal social structures and the demands of globalizing economies for cheap labour and high profits.

Despite the very rich history of South Asian women's efforts, today women in South Asia suffer greater poverty of education, health and nutrition, and greater lack of access to economic, political and legal opportunities, relative to their male counterparts as well as to women around the world. Although the degree of discrimination varies from one country to another, the overall picture is that of a region where pervasive inequality in one form or another has perpetuated the prevailing unequal structure. What is needed is not only to raise the collective consciousness of the region for speedy implementation of the global and national commitments that governments have made, but also to put structures and finances in place for proper implementation.

Equality of Economic Opportunity

South Asian women are almost invisible in national economic accounting systems. Even when women are counted as workers, they constitute only 33 per cent of the total official labour force. Women earn only half as much as men, are concentrated in the informal and agricultural sectors, and have almost no bargaining power as regards the conditions of work. Efforts to ensure economic equality must take into account women's economic circumstances, economic capabilities and the current state of a country's economic activity. Meaningful efforts to enhance women's economic activity and remuneration require a combination of enlightened legislation, comprehensive research, and thorough data collection. Political commitment to improving women's economic status is a necessary starting point, but that commitment must be supported by proper implementation machinery.

At the national level in South Asia, women's ministries, departments, commissions and bureaus remain under-funded and lack in the authority required to plan and implement policies and programmes for women's advancement and equality. While women remain severely under-represented in political office, the civil service and other public bodies, the application of the principle of affirmative action is not only rare, on many occasions it is used on behalf of men and against women.

To implement the agenda we have outlined, it is useful that there be a stronger women's ministry with authority; human and financial resources as for example, the ministry of finance or foreign affairs. Legislation has often codified male privilege; women remain unable to gain equal access to inheritance or property. The ingrained preference for boys ensure that girls do not have the same access to education, that they do not receive same level of nutrition; same consideration in decision-making; a gendered division of labour reinforces unequal and discriminatory practices. Although women perform some of the heaviest, dirtiest and most labour intensive work, much of that labour remains invisible as it occurs either within the household or in the unregulated informal sector. One Indian study estimates the amount of work outside home by married women to be between 6.15 and 7.53 hour each day. In Bangladesh some studies estimate that women spent between 70 and 88 per cent of their time in non-market work. The vast majority of South Asian women work in the informal sector or in unpaid family assistance which account 96 per cent in India, 75 per cent in Nepal and Bangladesh and nearly 65 per cent in Pakistan.

Gender inequalities are rarely mentioned in the policy debate on poverty in this region. There is need for thinking about institutional capacity building from a gender perspective and how can institutions be reoriented to respond to the interests not just of the poor but poor women. Women's right to equality with men is accepted and promoted in international development organizations, development organizations and in development plans and policies of many developing countries. Yet actually achieving equal rights has proven difficult. Notions of gender equality are profoundly counter-cultural in many societies. Efforts to promote women's equal entitlement to resources and equal opportunities to flourish in their productive and private lives, encounter considerable social resistance.

Fourth World Conference on Women, built upon the anti-poverty momentum of the World Summit for Social Development. High on the United Nations agenda is combating against poverty, based not only on economic growth but also on the achievement of social goals including gender equity to translate such commitments into effective policies, indicators capable of reliably identifying gender differences in well-being is necessary tools.

Civil Society for Women's Equality

Achieving meaningful and sustainable gender equality requires the creation of a new relationship between governments, civil society and international governmental and non-governmental agencies. Although governments must act in those spheres, which are their responsibility, the best hope for engendering the kind of change that is necessary lies with the institutions of civil society. In most South Asian countries, it is these institutions—grassroots, community-based and non-governmental organizations, professional groups and the media—which have gender-specific agendas, have identified the problems faced by women, and have specific programmes of action.

Most of these NGOs have established networks of members and affiliated bodies. They are able to react more quickly than governments to acute situations, having more flexible organizational structures. They also have valuable experience of successes and failures in implementing programmes. Some of these groups work to alleviate poverty and to enable economically marginal women to earn a living. Some provide informal education and vocational training to working women. Others pressure governments to meet national and international commitments on women's rights and to enact gender-sensitive labour legislation.

Some publicize human rights issues, such as dowry deaths, domestic violence and so-called honour killings, which threaten many women. Some groups function as women's health-care advocates. For some, workers' rights are the focus; there are organizations of domestic workers, agricultural workers and home-based labourers. There are also organizations whose purpose is to influence public and governmental discourse on the host of issues reaching to poverty. The role of civil society in increasing women's participation in public life is one of the few positive factors. Civil society initiatives have helped to organize women and to create awareness on a range of issues from health to poverty eradication to basic rights. A significant number of women work for civil society organizations, either on a voluntary basis or as paid employee. The development-oriented initiatives reach more women in both urban and rural areas.

Women's Participation in Development Paradigm

Advocating a pro-poor and pro-gender growth strategy where poor women also participate directly as subjects in development seems the most relevant development strategy in South Asia where the feminization of poverty is most evident. The pivotal element in this process is social mobilization where organizations of poor women work in partnership with a restructured state and a socially responsible private sector. To illustrate these possibilities, new social movements and organizations of poor women such as the Working Women's Forum (WWF) are converging with efforts to decentralize and to share power at the local level. New ground by investigating in depth the three important agendas of governance, decentralization/devolution and poverty eradication in their complementarities are thus essential. The key issue, therefore, with respect to economic initiatives by these poor women in the participatory development paradigm has been to enable the poor to break out of this local nexus of power, keep their surpluses in their own hands and assert the right to resources included for them.

In the participatory development paradigm, empowerment involves shifting the 'location' of poor women from the margins of the existing structures of power into the mainstream through building of countervailing power. Poverty eradication implies small improvements in the economic and social conditions of the poor women through greater self-reliant activities.

The conventional paradigm conceives of decentralization as a set of formal administrative measures without changing the 'balance of power' at the local level. Participatory development implies decentralization or a provision of 'space' for empowerment. Therefore, in this paradigm an institutional link is required between local government structures and autonomous organizations of the poor.

Demonstrating these, the WWF case highlights how poor women and their organizations have been socially mobilized to take centre stage in household, community and state level decision-making by support/intermediary organizations. The manner of mobilization and animation (individual/group/community) through economic and political issues is the focus of analysis in this case—indicating the need for recognition of the new gender and equity model of development.

The Gender and Equity Model

Women workers in the informal sector (89% in India and 94% worldwide) and their survival amidst conditions of starvation, squalor and social oppression raises fundamental issues on the questions of gender relations, structural poverty and social integration. It also demonstrates the socialized resilience of the women worker in South Asian countries where they operate within the threefold inequality of caste, class and gender, surviving by indigenous methods and ingenious mechanisms, despite discriminatory conditions and severe drudgery.

Poor Women in the Informal Sector

Workers in the informal sector are dubbed 'unemployed' and 'underemployed' due to the perception that it is a residual sector. Its invisibility also causes the commonly held misconception that it is a 'no growth' or 'low growth' sector, which has to be subsidized. Women in this sector work either in service provision, trading, petty production or manufacture. They provide goods and services to this sector as well as subsidize the organized sector workers. These goods and services can be classified as service provision (food shops, that is, from the pavement or house front, washing, traditional birth attendance, tailoring, etc.), trading (hawking/vending of fruit, vegetables, fish, flowers, etc., retail trading of clothes on instalment, utensils, plastic vital goods, groceries, etc.), petty production/manufacture (cigarettes, incense stick production, milk production, lace-weaving, screen-printing, silk-weaving, soap manufacture, pickle-bottling, wire bag-making, leaf-plate production, mat-weaving, detergent manufactures, etc.). It is therefore indisputable that the informal sector not only produces goods necessary for its marginalized population, but also sustains a large number of economically productive activities, and provides diverse services to a large segment of the working population.

The informal sector is mainly unorganized and invisible as it combines low capital investment, underreporting of work roles, class composition, unskilled non-technicality and labour intensiveness. The nature of the sector has aggravated its viability, visibility and powerlessness. Despite adverse conditions, the existence of a self-sustaining, non-protected growing sector such as this, is contrary to the notion that capital intensive industrialization is the only mode of growth. Amongst traditional trade unions, an effort to organize women workers in the informal sector at the grassroots level is viewed with suspicion. People in any sector have a right to organize in order to demand rights. Women as a group of workers handling many single occupations in the informal sector certainly have the right to unionize themselves. Factual evidence proves that many of the above-mentioned occupations pursued by women, have very oppressive structures and despite their hard work, their contribution is underestimated and undervalued. Their status as workers is continuously being challenged in the work environment. The informal sector in South Asia is akin to those of other countries in terms of conditions of work, but it is entirely different in its cultural setting for poor women, as powerlessness for women is enhanced by the barriers of caste, class and gender. To achieve any results in terms of development, organizations like the Working Women's Forum (WWF) were required to create a counter-culture which challenged the pillars of Indian tradition in its manifestation as related to gender. Five interwoven threads of oppression can be discerned: class exploitation, caste inferiority, male dominance, isolation in a closed world and physical weakness. These are explained briefly below:

(1) Class exploitation is visible in the supplier-buyer relationships undergone by WWF's members such as lace-makers, agarbatti-makers, bidi workers; it is also discernible in the low wages paid to wage-earners, wherein women's earned surplus accrues elsewhere; their access to credit is mostly mediated by the money-lender whose exploitation in South Asia is well documented elsewhere.

(2) Caste inferiority restricts women's mobility and formulates cultural norms for their social behaviour. Lower caste women (the bulk of WWF's membership, i.e., about 85%) have often been subject to 'pollution norms' whereby upper caste women would not sit, touch, dance or eat with them. These barriers deny access to development resources and information, as low caste women are unworthy of development.

(3) Patriarchy in the South Asian context is embedded in the values of tradition, customary practices or law and based on culturally determined subservient roles for women. Roles for women have been restricted to those in and around the household with a view to restricting mobility. Intra-household distribution of less food to women and girl children leads to physical weakness and is compounded by traditional values and superiority of male children. Women are subjected to continuous childbirth and poor women are confronted from birth to death by superstition, dowry problems, wife-beating and general lack of access to decision-making.

(4) Women are viewed as housewives, marginal or supplementary income providers but not as home managers, economic producers, community leaders or cultural catalysts.

(5) Ill health, numerous children, chronic debilitation, inability to use health services (too distant, too expensive, no time, inaccessible) also make it hard for poor women to break out of their trap. The position is more acute when they are widows left with children. Many are caught in the sequence of pregnancy and childrearing. On top of all this, many poor working women suffer occupational ailments such as back and joint pains, chronic hand sores, headaches, damage to eyes

and so on due to long hours of sitting, hard work of rubbing and rolling and concentration on intricate lacework continued into the night by poor light. ("We have lost our eyes by doing this", said many.)

(6) Trapped in closed walls created by tradition, culture and poverty, poor women are apathetic, fearful and ignorant of "everything to do with the written word", and this combines to immobilize them in the house, the compound, the street or the village. Children are often pawns in this syndrome, which limits their access to schooling or to earning to augment the family income. It is in this environment of powerlessness that WWF intervened to help poor women to create the foundations of a development model based on altered gender relations, by challenging structural poverty, spearheading social integration, and by transforming labour into capital with the surplus retained for poor women's needs.

An Intervention: The Case of Working Women's Forum

The Holistic Approach

Economic exploitation and social oppression called for a new model of development and intervention based on women's innate wisdom and response, modelled on existing indigenous collectivities utilizing local modes of communication. The Working Women's Forum (India) facilitated this holistic and equitable intervention model based on 'women-centred' development. It also rejected a piecemeal approach to the development and based its services on a holistic perception of gender roles (i.e., women's roles as economic producers, home managers and community leaders).

Today, the WWF operates in fourteen different cultural contexts with a membership of 7,00,000 members. In Tamil Nadu it works in Chennai, Kancheepuram (silk weavers), Vellore (cigar rollers), Dindigul (inland labourers), Adiramapattainam (fisherwomen), Dharmapuri (weavers). In Andhra Pradesh it works in East and West Godavari districts, in Karnataka it works in Bellary, Bidar and Bangalore city (agarbathi workers). WWF also promotes replication through training partner organizations in Orissa, Uttar Pradesh; and its sister concern, The Independent Commission for People's Rights and Development, working in

Jharkhand, Bihar, Orissa, Madhya Pradesh, West Bengal, etc., enhances pro-poor/ pro-gender capacities of 861 small rural NGOs in advocacy/social mobilization capacities.

In 1978, the WWF was formed with 800 members to help women workers in the informal sector, but has grown today into a union of over 7,00,000 workers in the three southern states of India. The union has a positive effect on the lives of over one million family members. Apart from the President of WWF, early initiators themselves were poor women from the city slums of Madras (Chennai).

Group Security System

In groups of five to ten members, WWF catered in its early days only for poor and destitute women with no financial or social standing. They mostly lived in conditions of extreme poverty and dehumanization. Such insecure living and working conditions made both young and older women join WWF groups in large numbers to achieve economic and social independence. This gave them a new status in life. Illiterate and unaware of their rights, cheated by money-lenders, middlemen and exporters, these women found some economic and social security in the solidarity provided in the WWF group.

Women experienced solidarity with other oppressed women and began to break out of a closed world to organize themselves. Simple methods of communication and consciousness-raising based on individual stories, skits, folk songs/puppetry with a local flavour made WWF groups acceptable. Women identified easily with the other women and this led to the building of their own organizations. This new experiment of leadership in the WWF initiated with the creative potential of poor women had far reaching effects on other poor women in the neighbourhoods. Trained in communication skills, women reached other poor women quickly and in large numbers.

The WWF's group security system soon brought out traditional caring mechanisms. From this they moved to crisis management, business counselling, bulk-buying, childcare, health care, and sports units, as well as providing information, initiating social action against wife-beating, dowry, alcoholism, drugs or economic action against wholesalers, exporters, middlemen, landlords, or civic action against police, municipal authorities, public distribution system, village panchayats, local bureaucracies and so forth. WWF groups became locked into a continuous chain of grassroot women's groups rapidly becoming a movement due to their simple and culturally acceptable design.

Growth of Working Women's Cooperative Credit Societies

In 1981, the WWF established it own WWCS, a maiden effort of its own credit system under the Tamil Nadu Cooperative Act, with a token financial capital of Rs 2,08,000 in Chennai. While the nationalized commercial banks had been unable to identify and reach the poor on a large scale, WWCS not only reached the grassroots but also expanded its operation quickly among poor women in other areas. As for credit recovery, WWCS had been able to achieve a recovery rate between 90 and 95 per cent, while the national average of recovery in commercial banks was only 30 to 40 per cent.

WWF's programme strategy of credit became an effective instrument of social change resulting in the economic independence of poor women. Through their collective wisdom, women realized that the most critical need for survival was access to low-interest working capital. The economic roles of women were strengthened without being dependent on local money-lenders. Many a dependent home-based producer, working under sub-contractors, now became an independent producer. Women helped each other and persuaded other poor women engaged in unproductive efforts to change to productive ventures through credit assistance from the WWF. Credit facilities reduced pawning of household articles to the money-lenders as well as indebtedness generally. Women experienced a better quality of life in the matter of household food, security, basic needs, children's education, better housing facilities, etc. Women have learned to keep custody of their hard earned income. Such a change in social attitudes among poor but illiterate women resulted in promoting alternative leadership within the household. Women learned the use of financial institutions and how to operate through group process and group dynamics. The WWF adopted the cooperative and collective structure so that poor women had a stake in the financial institution. The repayment rate on loans has been high.

By 1995, the WWCS operation of cooperatives under three different state cooperative laws, merged under a central government framework to become the first Indian cooperative network for women with flexibility to federate with similar cooperatives on a national basis. Today, it has a turnover of about 100 crore Indian Rupees having transformed itself as the Indian cooperative network of women.

The Accumulation Process: The Poor are Efficient

The Sequence

The accumulation process by poor women has taken place at WWF in a particular sequence and the process has been replicated in various other socio-economic contexts. It is therefore a viable strategy that has led to a sustained process of development and has cost effectively reached large numbers of poor women within a minimum time. The change from indebtedness and oppression to productive employment and growth, as well as empowerment, has taken place in WWF in about a decade. The process can be categorized in three phases.

Phase I

Where all other institutional systems had failed to give poor women access to credit, WWF's credit intervention helped them to gradually pay off old debts before they could start to make capital investments.

Phase II

With a lessening of the debt burden and with diversification and growth in enterprises, household food security and quality of physical living were made possible.

Phase III

At the height of this change, once stabilization of businesses occurred, asset creation in the form of education, sanitation, housing and jewellery has taken place, with simultaneous increase in awareness, enhancement of social status, dignity and empowerment. Emerging from the organizational power and collective action is a social platform of 70,000 groups who are making inroads into the panchayat local government system (WWF's members have been elected to some panchayats), generating demand for government services including the public distribution system, hospitals, schools, or dealing with and challenging civic, municipal and police authorities for solutions and redressing social oppression through creating alternative structures based on women as new leaders in the household and the community. In terms of growth this process has effectively demonstrated that poor women contribute to the macro socio-economic growth process.

Some Quantifiable Economic Results

The process has shown significant results based on empirical evidence suggesting that the strategies of poverty eradication adopted by WWF have been institutionalized for sustained development and are ideal for multiplication.

Poor Women are Bankable

WWF has sufficiently proved that poor women in the informal sector are eminently creditworthy. They save, they invest, they borrow and they pay back loans. If they have been appropriately sensitized the repayment rate is as high as 95 per cent. The fact that the original capital of less than Rs 1 crore has been rotated over (over Rs 80 crores) and the rate of repayment is often over 95 per cent amply testify to this. When WWF played the role of intermediary, guaranteeing loans for poor women, this helped to move the overall process. However, as WWF's orientation was not towards social banking, this led to hardship for their members in the beginning. Processing was slow because of the rapid expansion of membership and the cost of processing (economic and social cost) was high considering the obstacles. Attitudes of banking staff were discriminatory towards poor women and humiliating for them. Flexibility in assessing needs or loan sizes and geographic limitations led the WWF to initiate an alternative structure with poor women as shareholders and creators of a new banking accumulation process, whereby they kept the surplus in their own hands.

Poor Women's Enterprise System Can Grow

This belies the popular contention that micro-enterprises in the informal sector have little potential for growth or capital accumulation. WWF's experiment has shown that poor women achieve appreciable growth in terms of increased income and profits, expansion of markets, capital formation, improved technology and decreased indebtedness.

Poor Women Can Save and Create Assets

Women in WWF have demonstrated that through cooperative efforts and training they can be motivated to save at levels much higher than the informal sector average with 10 to 15 per cent of the income going into savings, 5 to 10 per cent being utilized for investment and a further 5 to 8 per cent for asset creation.

Poor Women Can Provide Household Food Security

It has become very clear that WWF's first three loans helped households achieve household food security. As well as credit, training is provided on value-added nutrition and equitable intra-household food distribution that is not prejudicial to females. As a social action, the public distribution system is pressurized by WWF's groups to provide better quality products without hoarding, black marketing, etc., and to improve access to food resource. In this way, organized poor women assert their right to resources to which they are entitled.

Poor Women Can Effect Social Change

With more economic stability, women have moved from mere economic activity to the social sphere through consciousness-raising and training. Appropriate capacity building schemes such as education, vocational or skill training, child labour rehabilitation, community health programmes and social action have been initiated.

Technological Choices

WWF's members have been able to move from simple to appropriate technology in most cases, and to more complex technology, depending on the size and number of loans and type of trade, in other cases. For example, in Madras (Chennai), where lending has been in operation for seventeen years, a wage-earner who initiated a leather goods workshop with a Rs 1,500 loan has now been able to shift to a bigger unit with several machines. Vendors who started with head-loading have moved to a hand cart and now use mopeds for business operations. Burmese repatriate women who used tailoring machines for hand embroidery with successive loans have moved to enterprises producing synthetic rain-coats and gloves. Many of these enterprises are run on a cooperative basis. Simple weighing machines have given way to sophisticated scales; rice-cake sellers compared to the old stone grinding machines now use electric grinders. This has also pushed up the minimum wages for women who were either agricultural labourers or construction workers earlier.

Sustainable Human Development

One of the manifestations of human development is an improvement in the physical quality of life. This has emerged as a clear trend in WWF's experiments involving several socio-economic backgrounds. It has been made possible by following a particular development strategy which takes into account women's roles and needs and is based on poor women's participation and one consequence is the emergence of a social and economic advocacy platform. Credit was the base to which other social development targets like health, literacy and training could later be attached in order to achieve greater growth and equity. The most visible indicators have been in the following areas:

Health

After three years of economic activity and still unable to perceive the benefits of increased income, women started to realize the incompatibility of large families and small incomes. This led to the initiation of a comprehensive health, nutrition and family-planning programmes. It was initiated in a modest way: leaders were selected from the target communities, trained and sent back as health workers to infuse into the community the much needed health, hygiene and environmental education. It has reached a population of half a million through 1,000 health care cooperatives managed by an equal number of health leaders from slums and villages. The programme has been acclaimed for its holistic community-based approach to mother and child care, with nutrition and birth spacing being emphasized as the surest way to achieve all round improvements in the reproductive health of women, thereby strengthening their productive role and restricting the reproductive one. The impact on environmental health was already visible when health leaders began clearing access roads and providing sanitation with the help of the group. The holistic concept of development is therefore, overriding in the practice of all WWF's strategies.

Skills Training

When poor women's critical needs are more or less satisfied they move on to assert their rights to better services to which they are entitled, from the state or other organizations. This could be seen in many instances. For example, members who were vendors and petty shopkeepers desired social mobility for their daughters. They felt this could be achieved not just by formal education but by skill or craft training to prepare them for gainful employment. This led to initiation of vocational centre for adolescent girls in the urban areas and other types of skill training such as lace and rope-making in rural areas. (ILO supported a diversified skill-training centre in Narsapur a decade ago). Today, several of WWF's members are skilled master trainers for government programmes in lace-making.

Services

Poor women's commitment to equitable growth is reflected in their new protest movements. They are taking up issues of human rights, environmental concerns, demand for accessible and affordable services from the bureaucracies, and fighting for social change from stereotyped systems of caste, dowry and widow remarriage as well as health and training programmes. Women of the WWF were also responsible for setting up the first childcare centres in the urban slums to cater for the needs of infants of working mothers. The members themselves took turns in the centre's day-to-day functioning. This set a precedent for the *Balwadi* centres that were later set up by the government. The entire process has thus become humanized and is aimed primarily at providing services for women. At the same time needs have been translated into lasting values, utilizing the innate wisdom of the poor.

Self-confidence

As most WWF members like to explain, their life in the 'Sangam' (as the members call their cooperatives) is about 'boldness'—the boldness to face their daily existence, their community and to confront the fear of injustice and oppression. This is made possible through their participation in meetings and workshops that help to build up solidarity and boldness. These qualities greatly enhance their self-respect. This, along with the collective consciousness born out of the group system, gives the strength for collective action, improves articulation, generates power to overcome obstacles and achieve their objectives, hence reflecting their empowerment. The success of struggles on local issues brings forth a resolve to participate in issues such as environment struggles that are in the wider national interest.

Conclusion

The lessons from the shifting paradigm is that since poor women are the central actors on our stage, both poverty and gender subordination must be transformed by vision. We want a world where inequality based on class, gender and race is absent from every country and from the relationships among countries—we want a world where basic needs become basic rights and where poverty and all forms of violence are eliminated. Each person will have the opportunity to develop her or his full potential and creativity, and women values of nurturance and solidarity will characterize human relationships. In such a world, reproductive relations will be redefined: childcare will be shared by men, women, and society as a whole. We want a world where the massive resources now used in the production of the means of destruction will be diverted to areas where they will help to relieve oppression, both inside and outside the home. We want a world where all institutions are open to participatory democratic process, where women share in determining priorities and making decisions. Only by sharpening the links between equality, development and peace, that one can show that the 'basic rights' of the poor and the transformation of the institutions that subordinate women are inextricably linked. These can be achieved together through the assertion of women' rights and a gendered model of development emerging from the SAARC region where poverty is aplenty but growth with dignity is not far off.

Notes on Editors and Contributors

Nazneen Ahmed is a Fellow at the Bangladesh Institute of Development Studies, Dhaka. A Masters from the University of Sussex, she also holds a doctoral degree from Netherlands and has published on gender issues.

Jaya Arunachalam is Founder and President of Working Women's Forum (India). A leading activist and development professional, she has been a vital spokesperson of poor women and her grassroots mobilization efforts has spearheaded a movement of poor women using micro-credit intervention. She is the recipient of numerous awards nationally and internationally. She is the author of *Women's Equality: A Struggle for Survival* (2005).

Nandini Azad holds a doctoral degree in development planning and anthropology from Syracuse University (USA). She has wide experience as consultant in the Human Resources Development Ministry, Government of India. She is currently Chairperson, Independent Commission for People's

Rights and Development, New Delhi. In 2005, she was advisor of Monitoring and Evaluation with the Planning Commission, Government of India.

Subhadra Mitra Channa is professor of anthropology in the Department of Anthropology, University of Delhi. Her current areas of research interests are gender, globalization and urban anthropology. She is an office bearer of the Committee on Women of the International Union of Anthropological and Ethnological Sciences.

Ramanie Jayatilaka is professor of Sociology at the University of Colombo, Sri Lanka. She holds a doctoral degree from Jawaharlal Nehru University (New Delhi) and has participated in numerous international seminars. She has a number of publications to her credit both in Sociology and Gender studies.

Seema Joshi is an Associate Professor in Economics at the Indian Institute of Public Administration New Delhi. She combines teaching and research and has participated in numerous seminars and publishes on Gender, Labour Market and Human Capital issues. This paper was written when she was at Kirorimal College, Delhi University.

Prabhjot Kaur Kahlon is an advanced doctoral candidate in the Department of Political Science, Guru Nanak Dev University, Amritsar.

U. Kalpagam is a professor at the G. B. Pant Social Science Institute, Allahabad. She has published extensively on Gender and Development issues, including *Labour and Gender: Survival in Urban India*, Sage (1994). She is both an economist and an anthropologist.

Fazila Banu Lily has been a long time activist of the women's movement in Bangladesh. Currently based in Canada, she was earlier a development activist in the Sunamganj Development Project in North-Eastern Bangladesh. She has participated in numerous international and national seminars and conferences.

Hina Nazli is an economist with Innovative Development Consultants, Islamabad. She was formerly with the Pakistan Institute of Development Economics at Islamabad. She has published widely on gender issues in Pakistan.

Puspa Ghimire Niraula is a lecturer in Women Studies at the Padma Kanya Campus of Tribhuvan University, Kathmandu. She has participated in numerous training programmes abroad and is active in research and teaching on gender and development issues.

Preet Rustagi is a Senior Fellow at the Institute of Human Development, New Delhi. A doctorate from JNU (New Delhi), her interests are in the areas of Gender and Development Studies, Labour Market Studies, Village Studies, Studies on Human Development and Crimes against women. She has participated in many national and international seminars and conferences. This paper was written when she was at the Centre for Women's Development Studies, New Delhi.

Selvy Thiruchandran is a well-known activist in the women's movement in Sri Lanka. She is the Director of Women's Education and Resource Centre (WERC, Colombo) and the editor of the *Sri Lankan Journal of Women's Studies*. Her work on post-trauma counselling to women has been widely appreciated. She has numerous important publications to her credit.

Index

Abdullah, T.A., 1
Acharya, M., 123, 137
Acharya, Meena, 58
Adams, R.H. Jr., 21
adult literacy
  among Pakistani women, 18
  among rural women, in Bhutan, 10
  in India, 28
  in Nepal, 14
  in South Asia, 76
  in Sri Lanka, 23
Afsar, R., 146, 153
Aganon, Marie E., 81
Agarwal, B., 29, 54, 181, 182, 198
Agarwal, Beena, 72
Ahmad, Munir, 104
Albee, A., 26
Alderman, H., 104
Amin, S., 148
Anand, Sudhir, 9
Antony, Piusch, 42, 66
Arif, G.M.F., 98
Arnold, Fred, 53
Artur, Luis, 107
Arun, Shobha V., 73
Asghar, C., 104
Ashe, Jefferey, 109
Aturupane, Harsha, 52

Banerjee, Narayan, 42
Bangladesh, 3, 141
  female labour in, 169-72
  rural women in, 3-10, 141-56
  women in, 143-44
Banu, D., 7
Basnyat, B.B., 15
Beteille, Andre, 44
Bhadra, C., 123
Bhargava, B.S., 248
Bhatt, N., 16

Bhutan, 10
ethnic groups in, 11
rural women in, 10-14
states of women in, 11-12
Bilquees, F., 117
Binswagner, H., 182
Bittman, Michael, 73
Boyce, 10
Boynton, G.R., 258
Braga, Carla, 107
Buch, Nirmala, 248

Carr, M., 49
Chandra, Shanta Kohli, 263
Channa, Subhadra Mitra, 236, 240
Cheston, S., 95, 109
Chishti, S., 104
Chowdhry, Prem, 236, 242
Crossette, B., 8
cultural pluralism
in South Asia, 44
Cunningham, G., 174

de Zoysa, D.A., 181, 182
DeGraff, Deborah S., 52
Delamonica, Enrique, 74
Deshpande, Sudha, 78, 84
Dex, Shirley, 73
Dhaka Rejvir S., 246
D'Lima, Hazel, 257
Dissanayake, L., 183
Dreze, Jean, 72, 161, 168, 173, 239
Dunham, D., 182

economic empowerment
of rural women, 41-42
employment
in Pakistan, 99-100, in the informal sector, 101-2
empowerment, 49, 94-95
dimensions of, 95
escalator hierarchies, 59

Faruqee, Rashid, 21
female infanticide, 234

Gamage, N., 26
Ganesh, Kamala, 42
gender
and poverty, in South Asia, 268-69
Gender Development Index (GDI)
in Pakistan, 94
gender discrimination, 72
in South Asia, 72, in labour market, 78-85
gender equality
efforts towards, 45-49, in South Asia, 49-56
gender gap
in wages, 85
gender violence
in Bangladesh, 9
globalization, 107
effect of, on rural women in Pakistan, 107
Goetz, Anne Marie, 8
Gothoskar, Sujata, 84
growth-with redistribution
concept of, 265
Gunathileke, R.M., 27
Gurung, J., 11, 12

Halim, S., 6
Hariss, B., 72
Hartmann, 10
Hashemi, Syed M., 7
Hashmi, S.M., 109
HDI
  in India, 28
  in Pakistan, 18
He, Jane J., 21
health services
  in Nepal, 17
  in rural Pakistan, 21
Heyzer, Noeleen, 73
Hirway, Indira, 48
Hoddinott, J., 63
honour
  concept of, and hierarchy of female bodies, 235-37
Hotchkiss, D., 15, 16
human capital discrimination
  in South Asia at the pre-entry level, 74-75, against women, 75-76
human development
  gender-bias nature of, 76-78
Huq, L., 148
Hussein, Ameena, 27

Inden, Ronald B., 233
India, 28
  rural women in, 28-34
Indian Constitution, 245
73rd amendment in the, 245, and women, 247-48
informal sector, 83, 275
  in South Asia, growth of, 83, and conditions of women workers in, 83-85
  poor women, in, 274-77

Iqbal, J., 23

Jahan, I., 6
Jain, Pankaj S., 7
Jhabvala, R., 87
Jodhka, S.S., 250
Jordans, E., 4
Joshi, Heather, 73
Joshi, Seema, 74, 75

Kabeer, Naila, 9, 46, 49, 63, 94, 109, 154, 155, 156, 200
Kalpagam, U., 31, 42
Kanbur, Ravi, 48
Kanji, Nazneen, 118
Kapadia, Karin, 237, 238
Karlekar, Malavika, 44
Kelkar, Govind, 65, 66
Khalily, Baqui, 7
Khan, N.A., 104
Khan, S.A., 117
Khandker, Shahidur R., 7, 8, 9, 108
Khundker, N., 149
Kitzinger, C., 243
Knox, Rebert, 179
Krishnaji, N., 48
Kuhn, L., 95, 109
Kumar, S.K., 15, 16
Kumar, V., 26
Kazi, Shahnaj, 70, 118

Latif, Abdul M., 9
Leach, E.R., 182

Leonhauser, I.U., 10
Levy, C., 73

Mahadevia, Darshini, 48
Maharjan, K., 15
Mahmud, S., 148, 149
Majumdar, P.P., 151, 153
Malhotra, Anju, 52
Malik, S.J., 103
Manikyamba, P., 247
Mathema, Madhuri, 41, 54
Mathie, Alison, 174
Mehrotra, Santosh, 74
micro-credit, 108
  and women empowerment, 108-10
  in Nepal, 123-24
  in Pakistan, 110-14
Millennium Development Goals, 2, 48
  progress towards, in South Asian countries, 2
Mishra, Suresh, 246
Mishra, Sweta, 247, 248
Moore, Erin P., 242
Morduch, Jonathan, 9
Moser, C.O.N., 73
mother-child relationship, 205
motherhood, 204
Mujeri, M.K., 152
Mukhopadhyay, S., 41, 48, 49, 50, 51, 60, 66
Mumtaz, Khawar, 103
Munasinghe, Indrani, 179

Nabi, Ijaz, 38
Nazli, H., 103
Nepal, 14, 121
  rural women in, 14-18
  women-oriented micro-credit programmes in, 123-27: impact of, 127-31; weaknesses of, 132-34
new poverty agenda, 266
non-farm activities, 182
  in Sri Lanka, 183, women in, 183-84
  types of, 182-83

O' Hanlon, Rosalind, 242
Oldenberg, Veena Talwar, 234, 236

Pakistan, 18
  GDI in, 94
  HDI in, 18
  rural labour market in, 98-106
  rural women in, 18-23, 93-94: empowerment of, 95-98; impact of globalization on, 107
  women's participation in agriculture in, 19
Papanek, Hanna, 58
Parrott, L., 109
Parveen Kumar, 7
Parveen, S., 10
Patterson, Samuel C., 258
Paul, D.C., 4, 7
personhood
  and rights, 234-35
  concept of, 234
Pitt, Mark M., 8

poverty, 161, 266
  and exclusion, 163
  and inequality, 162
  and underdevelopment, 163
  and vulnerability, 163
  in Nepal, 17
  in Pakistan, 21
  in rural Bangladesh, 8, 164-66, women and, 166-69
  people's perception of, 163-64
  types of, 161-62
PRIs, 246
  women in, 246-47, in Punjab, 248-52
Punjab, 248
PRIs in, 249-52, emerging women leadership in, 252-63
Pussepitiya, S., 177

Qureshi, Saeed, 21

Rahman, Zillur H., 164, 166, 175
Rao, Aparna, 235
Regmi, Shree Kant, 16
Riley, Ann P., 7
Risseeuw, C., 42
Robinson, M.G., 182
Rosenegger, P., 10, 12
Rozario, S., 146, 147, 154, 155
rural economy
  in Bangladesh, changes in, 144-49
  in Pakistan, impact of globalization on, 106-7
rural labour market
  in Pakistan, structures of, 98-106
rural life
  in Bangladesh, 6
  in Bhutan, 12
rural women
  in South Asia, 1: Bangladesh, 3-10, 141-56; Bhutan, 10-14; India, 28-34; Nepal, 14-18; Pakistan, 18-23; Sri Lanka, 23-28
rural women's work
  in India, 63-65
  in South Asia, 56-65
Rustagi, Preet, 53

Saadullah, M., 4, 7
SAARC, 49, 268
Samath, Feizal, 28
Sangari, Kumkum, 42
Sarkar, Mahua, 240
Sathar, Zeba, 70
Sather, Z., 118
Schrijvers, J., 182
Schuler, Sidney Ruth, 7
Sen, A., 158, 198
Sen, A.K., 61, 72
Sen, Amartya, 72, 161, 168, 173, 183, 239
Senanyake, S.M.P., 183
Seneviratne, Kalinga, 27
SenGupta, Rina, 8
Sheikh, K.H., 98
Siddiqui, R., 107
Sirskar, V.M., 257
Sonpar, Shobna, 48
Sontheimer, S., 15

South Asia, 43, 49, 270
gender inequality in, 269-70
HDI in, trends in, 2
rural women in, 1
women in, 270-71
Sri Lanka, 23, 177
rural women in, 23-28
women in agriculture in, 178-82
women in non-farm activities in, 182-84
Sultana, N., 103
Sundarshan, Ratna M., 41, 48, 49, 66

Taylor, Lance, 74
Tennakoon, D., 179
Terzieff, J., 22
Thambiah, S.J., 182
Thomas, Alison, M., 243
Tinker, Irene, 73
Toufique, K.A., 144, 145
Turton, C., 144, 145

Unemployment
in Pakistan, 99
Unni, J., 31
Unnithan-Kumar, Maya, 236, 242

Verma, A.P., 239
Vidya, K.C., 248
Vijfhuizen, Carin, 107
violence, 232
and patriarchal values, 237-38
and the process of 'othering', 240-41

Wadley, Susan, 232
Wennubst, Piuss, 160, 168
White, 10
Wickramasinghe, A., 24, 25
women's empowerment, 94
efforts towards, 45-49, in South Asia, 49-56
in Bangladesh, 152-55
in Sri Lanka, 195-200
role of micro-credit in, 108-110
women's equality
role of civil society in, 272-73
women's movements, 96, 270
work burden
females vs males, 85-86

Yusuf, Shahid, 7

Zeidenstein, S.A., 1
Zohir, S.C., 149, 153
Zwarteveen, M., 4